ECONOMIC TRANSFORMATION IN CHINA

ECONOMIC TRANSFORMATION IN CHINA

Ajaz Ahmad Rather,
Imtiyaz-ul-Haq

KALPAZ

ISBN : 978-93-5128-005-7
Price : ₹ 999

First Published, 2015

Published by

Kalpaz Publications
C-30, Satyawati Nagar,
Delhi-110052
Ph. : 9212142040
E-mail: kalpaz@hotmail.com

Laser Typesetting : Rudra Computer Graphics, Delhi
Printed at : G. Print Process, Delhi

Cataloging in Publication Data—DK

Courtesy: D.K. Agencies (P) Ltd. <docinfo@dkagencies.com>

Rather, Ajaz Ahmad, author.

Economic transformation in China / Ajaz Ahmad Rather, Imtiyaz-ul-Haq.

pages cm

Includes bibliographical references (pages) and index.

ISBN 9789351280057

1. China—Economic conditions—1949- 2. China—Economic policy—1949- 3. Rural development—China. 4. Rural development—Government policy—China. I. Imtiyaz-ul-Haq, author. II. Title.

DDC 330.951 23

Contents

Preface 7
List of Figures 9
List of Tables 11

1. Introduction **13**
Rural Transformation • Importance of Rural Sector • Statement of the Study • Literature Review • Methodology and Data • Limitations of the Study.

2. Pre-Reform Period **28**
China in 1949: A Profile • General Economic History of the Period • The Rehabilitation Phase: 1949-52 • The First Five Year Plan, 1953-57: Soviet Model • The Second Five Year Plan: Great Leap Forward, 1958-62 • The Readjustment Period: 1963-65 • The Third Five Year Plan, 1966-70: Cultural Revolution-1 • The Fourth Five Year Plan, 1971-75: Cultural Revolution-2 • Post Revolution Period: 1976-77 • Comments.

3. Post-Reform Period **84**
Introduction • Nature of Reforms • Institutional/Historical Change in the Post-reform Period • Macroeconomic Variables (unit: per cent) • Primary Sector • Secondary Sector • Services • Poverty Reduction in the Post-Reform Period • Health • Education.

4. Rural Transformation **136**
Introduction • Institutional Change in the Historical Perspective • Agricultural Sector • Income • Household Expenditure • Consumption • Assets • Rural Poverty • Decline in Poverty • Rural Employment • Education and Literacy • Infrastructure • Challenges to Rural China • Rural-Urban Inequality • Intra-Rural Inequality.

5. **Relevance of China's Reform Experience to India** **217**
Relevance of Comparison between India and China • Country Profiles: India Versus China • Development Policies from 1980s: A Comparison • Policy Effectiveness: A Comparison • Relevance of Rural Policies of China to India • Agriculture/Rural Centric • Decentralisation • Human Resource Development • Conclusion.

6. **Summary and Conclusion** **231**

Appendices 237
Bibliography 289
Index 307

Preface

Ever since world war second, after which a large number of developing countries achieved independence, economic development has been the much cherished goal of these countries. Nonetheless, it has been equally elusive for many of these despite their substantial mental and physical efforts through huge resource mobilisation in the planning processes. For most of the developing countries overall results, after experimenting with the planning and market strategies, have been dismal. Thus much of the developing world still awaits a chance of being well provided in terms of economic privileges. A major chunk of the population in these countries still lack good health, education, roads, and gainful employment. These people have an extraordinary urge for but pragmatically doubt the prospects of a bright future. The scenario not only portrays a gloomy picture of the developing world but even of the science of economic development itself.

In contrast to the other developing countries, China's approach to the process of economic development in the aftermath of the reforms in late 1970s has been a success story and a phenomenon of great significance. It, on one hand, helped millions to move out of poverty and achieve an acceptable standard of life and, on the other hand, it made deep impact on the issue of planning and policy in the rest of the world. In contrast to the experience of other developing countries and conventional wisdom of the science of economic development, China's singularity of development strategy as well as the ensuing results have put the science of economic development introspect its core concerns in terms of policy.

Among many peculiarities of the development strategy of China, perhaps the most obvious has been its focus on rural sector of the economy. While as major policy thrust in other developing economies was placed on heavy industrialisation, China gave priority to rural industrialisation. Due to deliberate focus of economic policy on the rural sector, the impact weighed heavily on the overall performance of the economy. Once the transformation entitled the rural population with economic resources, much of the secondary objectives like heavy and sophisticated industrialisation started moving the market and planning channels. Rural transformation proved itself to be the fulcrum of economic development. Despite the fact that India seemingly has experienced some good economic growth phases, comparison with China reveals a vast difference in the performance and achievements of the two countries, although India and China share many commonalities in terms of population, geographic size, state of development, etc. Ever since China's phenomenal economic progress-in the late 1970s when China initiated economic reforms-in comparison to India's moderate, the possibility of comparison between the two has progressively decreased and brought more contrasts to the fore. The focus of the policy in the two economies has been markedly different. While India's reforms aimed at external balance and industrial growth directly, China did the opposite by focusing on internal balance and agriculture. This corrected the basics of the Chinese economy that made it fit for a strong take-off.

The central purpose of writing this book is to understand the nature of transformation of Chinese economy in general and the transformation of the rural economy in particular using diverse though simple measures and parameters. An utmost care has been taken to keep the economic analysis closely related to theoretical dimensions to make analysis rigorous and meaningful. Broadly, this book seeks to provide some insight into the following areas:

(i) The status of a wide range of macroeconomic parameters in the pre-reform phase.
(ii) Impact of the reforms on overall macroeconomic indicators.
(iii) Nature of reforms initiated in the rural sector of China.
(iv) Process of structural change in rural economy of China.
(v) Impact of reforms on social indicators in rural China.
(vi) Relevance of China's rural economic reforms to India.

We hope that this book will prove helpful to the students, research scholars, academicians and especially to the planners and policy-makers in devising the policies focused on the strategic transformation of rural India. Although, in this endeavour we have tried our best to gather relevant information from the concerned quarters and reliable sources, yet there is always a scope for further improvement.

Imtiyaz-ul-Haq,
Ajaz Ahmad Rather

List of Figures

3.1	Growth of GDP, 1978-2003	94
3.2	Growth: GDP, Primary, Secondary and Tertiary Sectors, 1978-2003	95
3.3	Structural Change in Composition of GDP, 1978-2003	97
3.4	Total Employment Growth Rate	98
3.5	Employment Growth: Total, Primary, Secondary and Tertiary	99
3.6	Structural Change in Employment	102
3.7	Growth: GDP verses Total Employment	103
3.8	Growth: Primary Sector Output, 1978-2003	105
3.9	Growth: Primary Sector GDP versus Total GDP	107
3.10	Primary Employment Growth	109
3.11	Total and Primary Employment Growth	110
3.12	Growth: Primary Output and Employment Growth	111
3.13	Secondary Sector Output Growth, 1978-2003	113
3.14	Secondary Sector Output and Total Output Growth, 1978-2003	114
3.15	Secondary Sector Employment Growth, 1978-2003	116
3.16	Total and Secondary Sector Employment Growth, 1978-2003	117
3.17	Growth of Secondary Sector Output and Employment, 1978-2003	119
3.18	Tertiary Output and GDP Growth, 1978-2003	120
3.19	Growth: Tertiary Sector and Total Employment 1978-2003	121
4.1	Employment and Output Shares of Primary Sector	141
4.2	Structure of Gross Output Value of Agriculture	147

List of Tables

3.1 Investment and Savings 104
3.2 Total Fixed Investment Rate 104
3.3 Poverty Reduction in China: 1981-2004 123
3.4 Expenditures on health services by source 125
3.5 Health Indicators 126
3.6 Longevity in the Post-Reform Period 126
3.7 Types of Health Agencies 127
3.8 Number of Health Workers 128
3.9 Literacy 129
3.10 Structure of Student Enrollment 130
3.11 Full Time Teachers by Type 131
3.12 Energy Balance in China, 1980-2003 132
4.1 Gross Output Value of Farming, Forestry, Animal Husbandry and Fishery and Related Indices 144
4.2 Yield of Major Farm Crops Per Hectare (kg/hectare) 150
4.3 Output of Major Farm Crops Per Capita 152
4.4 Output of Major Farm Crops Per Agriculture Labourer 155
4.5 Sales of Main Agricultural Products of Rural Households—1 156
4.6 Sales of Main Agricultural Products of Rural Households—2 159
4.7 Development of the Rural Nonfarm Sector, 1978-1997 161
4.8 Fertiliser use, Irrigation and Mechanisation Indices 163
4.9 Government Expenditure for Agriculture 164
4.10 Net Per Capita Income of Rural Residents 166
4.11 Percentage of Rural Households Grouped by Per Capita Annual Net Income 167
4.12 Changing Economic Status of Rural China 170
4.13 Composition of Net Income of Rural Households by Source, 171
4.14 Composition of Net Income of Rural Households by Income Type 172
4.15 Household Business Income of Rural Households by Source (Sector) 173

4.16 Total Expenditure of Rural Households 176
4.17 Composition of Total Expenditure of Rural Households 177
4.18 Composition of Living Expenditure of Rural Households 178
4.19 Consumption of Major Food Items of Rural Households—1 180
4.20 Consumption of Major Food Items of Rural Households—2 182
4.21 Number of Major Productive Assets Owned 185
4.22 Main Durable Goods Owned 187
4.23 Absolute Poverty of Rural Households, 1978—2007 190
4.24 Employment: Total, Urban and Rural 193
4.25 Rural Labourers at the Year-end 196
4.26 Structure of Rural Employment 198
4.27 Education Level of Labourers of Rural Households 200
4.28 Public Spending in Rural China, 1978-97 203
4.29 Irrigated Area, Consumption of Chemical Fertilizers 205
4.30 Hydropower Stations and Electricity Consumption in Rural Areas 207
4.31 Per Capita Annual Income of Urban and Rural Households 211
4.32 Net Income and Gini Coefficient 213
4.33 Rural-Urban Differentials in Infant Mortality 213
5.1 Profile of China and India 220
5.2 Key Development Indicators for China and India 221
5.3 Poverty in China and India 223
5.4 Correlation: Income Growth and Poverty Reduction 225
5.5 Impact of Growth of GDP Per Capita on Poverty 226
5.6 Agricultural Output and Trade 228

1
Introduction

1.1. Introduction

Perhaps no other subject is theoretically as challenging and indispensable as the subject of development economics. Every society has an innate urge to provide itself with varieties of facilities that entitle it to higher standards of life. Living longer, having better education and wealth to spend is not only a matter of personal ambition but the central issues around which the modern democratic and republican nature of nation state hinges. The birth of modern welfare state was the result of the well being consideration of the citizens of a country. In modern times governments are formed and unformed based on their economic performance and provision of public utilities, reduction of poverty and control of economic crisis.

After the World War Second, the issue of development—economically, socially and of course militarily—was the central concern of the developing countries who achieved their independence from the imperial Europe. Since the market mechanism was quite insufficient for the realisation of these ends, these nation states embarked on a conscious effort in the form of planning to further the cause of their economic progress. Market would fail to provide employment, infrastructure, public utilities, and basic necessities at subsidised price as well as control emergence of monopolistic power. All these insufficiencies on part of the private market were termed **market failure.** Therefore, most of the economies adopted planning as the main instrument of transition from lower to higher state of development. The planning strategy in developing countries mainly focused on the industrial sector development to achieve self sufficiency in capital goods production.

However, achievements of the planning in developing economies at the aggregate level were quite moderate: neither uniform across these countries nor extraordinary in their magnitude, as was supposed at the beginning of this process. In many countries, the increased role of the state due to planning even created more problems than it solved through increased corruption and bureaucratisation of the economy. This was famously called as government failure and became part of the mainstream theoretical economics. Therefore markets were emphasised to be more efficient, particularly by neo-classical and neo-liberal economists. The international economic institutions like International Monetary Fund, World Bank and World Trade Organisation supported the market driven economic arrangement in developing countries. As a result, countries moved to a more market determined economic arrangement after the 1980s.

However, this too did not bring increase in growth of the developing countries as a whole. In case it did, there was an acute exclusion or substantial under provision to the economically marginalised sections of the society. Thus, the notion of market failure came to the forefront of the policy debate once more.

The dilemma of growth or economic performance for the developing countries has been more complex than was earlier thought to be. For example, according to Jose Antonio et al, in developing countries with the exception of East Asia, 'a much larger number of countries have seen erratic or declining growth with long-lasting impacts on living conditions. In the 1960s and 1970s, nearly 50 out of a sample of 106 developing countries experienced one or more prolonged episodes of sustained and high per capita income growth of more than 2 per cent per year. Since 1980, however, only 20 developing countries have enjoyed periods of sustained growth. In contrast, no less than 40 developing countries have suffered growth collapses, or periods of five years or longer during which there was no growth or decline in per capita income. During the 1980s and 1990s, this phenomenon increased, and the cases of successful growth diminished with some notable exceptions, mainly in Asia' (*Growth Divergences*, United Nations, pp. 3-5). According to a study, in spite of heavy policy reforms from 1980s to 1998, the median growth of per capita income of developing countries was a tragic zero (W. Easterly, Journal of Economic Growth, 2001).

Thus the quest for growth and development by the developing countries has confronted significant theoretical and empirical challenges as depicted by the above mentioned state of affairs. While many of the developing countries faced either stagnation or outright collapse in socio-economic terms, a few also experienced stupendous economic expansion and social development. Worth mentioning is the case of the East Asian economies. These economies are better helpful in studying the nature of successful economic development on the one hand and the dynamics of economic failures on the other. Among the successful economies from the last quarter of the twentieth century, the People's Republic of China is of particular importance.

China stands as an outstanding example of sustained growth during the last three decades. This success in the backdrop of the increasing growth failures experienced by the world economy makes the case of China particularly special. Constantly and speedily expanding national output had significant implications for the people of China. Further, being home to almost 20 per cent of the world population what happened in China also made a well felt impact on the profile of development and welfare of the global population. By its sheer population magnitude China always has stronger global implications than other nations. An attempt has been made in the present study to understand the causes and the impact of China's economic rise. Particular focus has been the rural sector of the Chinese economy.

1.2. Rural Transformation

Rural transformation is a phenomenon by which countries make a substantial shift in their level of social-economic state in the rural sector from lower stage of development to a higher one. It is the process of rural change which enables the rural citizens of an economy to enjoy much better standards of living than they are previously entitled to. Rural transformation on the one hand is the process of positive institutional and technical change and on the other a successful outcome of that change. Thus it not only involves a positive change in the production system of the rural sector but also social transformation of the countryside. Rural transformation can be said to have occurred if the development indicators like income, literacy, health, productivity, exports, technology, infrastructure and other institutional indicators undergo a positive, perceptible and well realised change. Concomitantly indicators like poverty, illiteracy, inequality, gender disparity, corruption, etc., experience a reduction in their magnitude.

1.3. Importance of Rural Sector

Despite the fact that the world population is divided between two equal halves, in developing countries the majority live in countryside. As per the World Development Report 2008, Countries like Burundi, Cambodia, Chad, Ethiopia, Malawi, Niger, Rwanda, Sri Lanka, and Uganda have more than eighty per cent of their population living in countryside. Other countries like Bangladesh, India, Kenya, Madagascar, Tajikistan, Tanzania, Vietnam, and Yemen have more than seventy per cent of their population as rural. Similarly, countries including, China, Central African

Republic, Pakistan, Thailand, Uzbekistan, and Zimbabwe have more than sixty per cent of their population as rural.

Thus in most of the developing countries, a much larger proportion of people live in rural than in urban areas. This demographic differential has substantial impact on the process and policy of development. One way to look at this is that an inclusive and people centric development strategy has to be more a rural than an urban phenomenon. Thus, the focus of the development policy has to be the rural sector. The relative emphasis on the rural sector would depend on the relative magnitude of the population residing in rural areas. If the state of wellbeing of the countryside is improved its impact on the development indicators like Human Development Index would be systematically more than the urban improvement because of the larger share of the population residing there.

The other aspect of looking at the same issue is that urban biased policies produce migration which on the one hand congest the urban centers reducing their capacity to provide public amenities while simultaneously giving rise to urban unemployment and thus reverse migration. This results into social and political instability as well as economic loss. As a result the governments are forced to renew their rural policies and reduce urban bias by providing increased share of their budgets to rural development.

1.4. Statement of the Study

Rural transformation lies at the heart of any economic reform programme especially in developing countries. These developing economies, including India, have a common feature of being predominantly agriculture oriented with more than three-fourth of land occupied by rural areas and having more than two thirds population as rural and more than one third employment generated by agricultural sector. The importance of a dynamic agriculture sector in the industrialisation of a developing economy cannot be under emphasised. It is well known historical fact that agricultural revolution has preceded the industrial revolution in the developed countries.

The transformation of China's rural economy from a relatively under-developed (in terms of per capita income, infrastructure, productivity, etc.) to the most successfully developing one has been one of the most important economic phenomenon of the last three decades. China's reform effort had two important consequences. First, enhanced incentives to the farmers brought a significant increase in productivity and in total output. Second, the increasing rate of savings translated into further change in rural industry.

In comparison to China, India is having much higher poverty rates. In particular the rural sector of Indian economy is much weaker. The divergence in the state of development—social and economic—between the two countries started assuming larger magnitude since China implemented reforms in late 1970s. Till then the comparative state of development did not exhibit much divergence. The reforms started in early 1990s, in India largely bypassed the rural/agricultural sector in stark contrast to China's reform policy. Although the two countries differ in their social, economic and political structure yet there are important common features.

Since China's rural reform has been a very successful programme and a hot debate it will be very pertinent to study its various phases and dimensions, their impact on various macroeconomic indicators and their relevance to Indian economy.

1.5. Literature Review

A host of literature exists on the Chinese economic transformation. Most of these works discuss the changes in the rural economy, its impact and determinants in the post-reform period. However, the subject of rural transformation is much broader in scope and provides a platform for the analysis of the previous theoretical literature on economic transformation with particular emphasis on the role of the rural or agriculture sector of an economy.

An outline of the typology of development strategies on the basis of growth performance and equity consideration is equally capable of providing a theoretical background for approaches to rural transformation. Four categories of development strategies have been the focus of vast literature produced on the subject. The first category may be characterised as *"grow first, then redistribute"*, emphasising on growth and markets or the famous trickle-down effect. The second, as believed and actually tried by communist or socialist groups, is "*redistribute first, then grow";* as done by China in early 1950s. The land reforms in developing countries were part of this strategy. The third, as a mid-way to the former two, may be called *"distribution with growth"*, which emphasises asset creation for poor in a growing economy though different means. Finally, catering the needs of the marginalised, considering the glaring market failures, as well as recognising the right to life and survival as basic, another strategy called "*basic human needs approach*" has been emphasised by many economists and public activists. (Perkins et al Economics of Development, Norton 2001)

The present literature review begins with the theoretical contribution of William Arthur Lewis and Fie-Ranis.

(i) Economic Development with Unlimited Supplies of Labour by William Arthur Lewis, *The Manchester School,* 1954.

This study is an important contribution to the dynamics of structural change which involved the agriculture sector of an economy. Customarily, the economy was of a dualist nature in which the modern capitalistic sector is characterised by high productivity of labour. The other sector was the subsistence sector, mainly traditional agriculture, characterised by low productivity and abundance of labour force. The productivity may fall to the level that creates disguised unemployment in this sector. Therefore, the process of economic transformation involves investment in and expansion of the modern capitalist sector. Since there is abundance of labour in the subsistence sector, therefore, labour for the capitalist sector is virtually unlimited at the subsistence wages, with some margin for inducement cost by which the labour is attracted. Since the labour is cheap, the increased savings are reinvested by the capitalists that allow almost an unlimited expansion of the capitalist sector till it is stopped by the exhaustion of the excess labour. Thus, the process of transformation is complete in this way.

(ii) *Development of the Labour Surplus* by John C. H. Fei and Gustav Ranis; Homewood Illions: Richard D Irvin, Inc., 1964.

This is an improvement over the Lewis' model. It is also is based on a dualist economy in which a large primitive agricultural sector co-exists with small but growing industrial sector. As the former is overpopulated, it provides cheap labour for the latter. The savings of the industrial sector being high due to low wages, their reinvested in the capital formation resulting into almost a self-perpetuating expansion of the capitalistic sector of the economy. The food and agricultural input to the industrial sector is provided by the agricultural sector. As the transfer of labour from agriculture to industrial sector takes place, the productivity of the agriculture labour marginally but progressively increases. Therefore, the forces that set in motion the migration of the labour into the industrial sector also set in motion the forces that retard its pace. In this way a structural change resulting into the development of an economy occurs.

(iii) *Are China's Rural Enterprises Outperforming State Enterprises? Estimation of the Pure Ownership Effect* by Gary H. Jefferson, Enterprise Reform in China: Ownership Transition and Performance, ed. Gary H. Jefferson and Inderjit Singh, the World Bank/Oxford University Press, 1999.

The author looks into the causality of the higher performance of the rural enterprises compared to the state enterprises. The author analysis the two hypothesis generally made regarding the performance, i.e., catch-up hypotheses and the overtaking hypothesis. Controlling for various policy variables, including the level of supervision, marketisation, management system, contractors, and the level of commitment of collateral, and enterprise-specific conditions, including scale and non-industrialisation inputs, as per the author, allows for a more accurate calibration of the pure ownership effect of state and collective ownership. The principal results of the study made by the author include: (a) if the above conditions are not controlled rural productivity was generally higher than state sector and (b) controlling for policy and enterprise-specific factors, ownership had no unambiguous impact. Thus a host of factor rather the simple change of ownership has played their part in the economic performance of rural industry in China.

(iv) *Chinese Rural Industrialisation in the Context of the East Asian Miracle,* by Justin Yifu Lin and Yang Yao, Enterprise Reform in China: Ownership Transition and Performance, ed. Gary H. Jefferson and Inderjit Singh, the World Bank/ Oxford University Press, 1999.

The authors begin by surveying various rationales provided for the growth of China rural industry. These include: (a) culture theory which focuses the positive role of cooperative culture in Chinese village, (b) new growth theory, which emphasises the positive externality created by the accumulation of knowledge and social capital, (c) property rights approach that takes into consideration the role of local governments facilitating access to material and financial resources, and (d) the classical comparative advantage theory focusing on the cheap labour available for an effective industrial transformation. They make a study of different explanations provided for the excellent performance of the rural industry by building hypotheses, centering on some basic ingredient of central importance. Variations in the performance of the provinces in China furnish the raw material to analyse basic factors determining economic success of the rural enterprises. These hypotheses include: (a) initial conditions, (b) market conditions, (c) human capital, (d) interaction with SOEs, (e) economic reforms, (f) factor endowments and (g) public ownership.

All these conditions played their role in the development of rural enterprises. However, their role through the reform period has not been consistent. For example, the role of public ownership during the period, 1987-97 was negative. But it is positive for the period 1970-77.

The authors also sketch some salient features of the rural enterprise development in their study. These include: (a) the capital first emerged from the agricultural surplus and later form accumulation of rural enterprises, (b) to begin with rural enterprises were overwhelmingly concentrated in labour- and resource-intensive industries, (c) rural enterprises were characterised by a wide range of ownership types, (d) these were tied to urban industry in various ways, and (e) rural enterprises development was distributed unevenly across the country.

From their overall analysis the authors make following conclusions: (a) rural industrialisation has been largely an unintended consequence that is mainly induced by China's land, capital, labour endowment, and relatively good rural infrastructure, the result of its recent history of collectivisation; (b) the rapid growth of the rural enterprise sector has been facilitated by the market-oriented reforms carried out in past 20 years, (c) urban light manufacturing industry helped the growth of the rural enterprises in the early years, and (d) in the course of its development, the rural enterprise sector has gradually abandoned public ownership and hardened the financial discipline on firms.

(v) *China's Economic Transformation*, by Gregory C. Chow, Blackwell Publishing, 2007.

The author discusses agriculture reform in third chapter of his book. His emphasises the appropriate decision making and correct incentive structure of the post reform period as causing agents of the economic boom in the rural economy. Further the opening of markets or a move toward market economy made the progressive expansion of the rural economy possible. The author further emphasises the role of reforms in price, banking sector, foreign trade, institutions and infrastructure as supporting a rural transformation.

(vi) *Plan and Market in China's Agriculture Commerce* by Terry Sicular, Growth without Miracles: Readings on the Chinese Economy in the Era of Reform, ed. Ross Garnaut and Yiping Huang; Oxford University Press, 2001.

The author looks into the role of market since the reform in late 1970s, and explores the possibilities of success of a mixed economy. The paper delves into the interaction of market and state in case of Chinese agriculture and an optimal mix of the same. The central conclusions of the analysis are: (a) markets place pressure on the state to choose planned prices so that they do not deviate too far from market prices, (b) in the presence of markets, state-planned prices and quotas will not, except in certain cases, directly affect levels of production and consumption, (c) however, they will affect them indirectly through their effects on the distribution of income and equilibrium.

Thus, author's theoretical analysis yields many conclusions regarding the nature of a mixed plan and market system like that of China. Accordingly commercial planning need not cause inefficiency or Pareto-inferior allocation of resources. Since planning causes lump-sum transfers among agents and between agents and the state, it can be used as an efficient means to pursue distribution of tax objectives.

(vii) Rural Development: Learning from China, by Sartaj Aziz; the Macmillan Press, 1978.

The author has covered much of the pre-reform communist China in its rural dimension. In the pre-reform period many achievements on the economic, social and infrastructural level were made. The author starts from the successful land distribution campaign in early 1950s through Great Leap Forward effort to Cultural Revolution in late 1970s and recounts the socio-economic change in China with special emphasis on technological advancement during this period. While discussing the central role of cooperatives replaced later by communes and further by production units in their chronological order, the author has placed great emphasis on the institutional side of the pre-reform period.

(viii) *The Role of Property Rights in China's Rural Reform and Development: A Review of Facts and Issues*, by James Kai-sing Kung; in China's Development Miracle; Origins, Transformation, and Challenges, ed. Alvin Y. So M. E. Sharpe, New York, 2003.

In this contribution, the author explores the role of property rights in the economic success of China. The author attributes much of the problems faced in the pre-reform period to the lack of an effective incentive system in the country. But with a change in the institutional setup in the direction of providing more incentives to the farmers, the productivity of the farms increased speedily. According to the author, "there is little dispute that property rights played a distinctively important role in the reform process: regardless of what was ultimately responsible for the incentive problem in collectivised agriculture, the reassignment of "residual" income right to the peasant household was by any measure a powerful institutional change that brought about the sharp increase in both farm income and crop output". However, according to the author, future success of China much depends upon making legal rights on land more transparent and farmer oriented.

(ix) *The Chinese Economy: Changes and Challenges in the Post-Mao Era*, by Kalipada Deb, Sterling Publishers Private Limited, 1993.

Two of the chapters by the author deal specifically with the rural economy; one titled "The Rural Economy: A General Survey" and "Development of Agriculture". In the first of these chapters the author makes some important conclusions: (a) the growth of the rural income in the post-Mao era was indeed remarkable, (b) there was a structural change in the rural economy in which the role of agriculture decreased while that of the industry increased measurably, (c) the organisation of the rural production changed; households and farmers share in output increased, (d) institutional and policy changes of far reaching consequences were adopted by government which changed the institutional structure of the economy on one hand, and altered the direction of government investment on the other, (e) however, there was a negative side to the reforms as well, like unequal income distribution, reduction in the farm output as employment and land use shifted, to the reforms as well.

The author further emphasises many dimensions of development in the agriculture including increased productivity, more production of industrial crops and significant contribution by animal husbandry. However, the provision of inputs, the state of irrigation and water conservancy work were not satisfactory.

(x) *Economic Growth, Income Distribution and Poverty Reduction in Contemporary China*, by Shujie Yao; Routledge Curzon Taylors and Francis Group, London and New York, 2005.

The book discusses the performances and problems of the economy of contemporary China from different perspectives. Chapter 3 is devoted to agriculture and rural development. The chapter discusses the experience of agriculture and rural development in China with special emphasis on the declining share of agriculture in the national output; this in the background of the high employment share of the sector. The author explains this paradox of low income and high employment share of the primary sector to the urban biased policies started by Mao and carried forward into the reform period by later planners. As a result the speedy growth of productivity and income in the primary sector was short lived and only sustained for six years from 1978 to 1984.

According to the author, the continuation of the urban biased policy, corruption and legacy of rural-urban separation are the main reasons for the ever rising urban-rural divide, making poverty reduction increasingly difficult. China has changed from a very egalitarian society to one of the world's most unequal nations as a result of economic reforms. However, if the institutions supporting property rights are not reformed, farmers will continue to suffer and the fundamental problems cannot be solved. The latest documents, according to the author, contain no blueprint for such reform.

(xi) *An Essay on Economic Reforms and Social Change in China* by Assar Lindbeck, the Policy Research Working Paper, 4057, the World Bank Development Research Group, Office of the Director November 2006.

In this essay the author discusses the economic and social change of China since the reforms in 1970s. The author describes the gradual transformation of the country's economy in terms of a nine dimensional vector including: (i), (ii) ownership (of firms and assets), (iii) level of centralisation, (iv) the mix of administrative processes and markets, (v) (vi) level of economic and non-economic incentives (for firms and individuals), (vii) (viii) level of cooperation/collusion or competition (for firms and individuals), and (ix) level of autarky and internationalisation of the economy.

Each of these parameters has experienced a substantial change from the time of reforms towards market oriented, deregulated, decentralised economy. As a result of these institutional changes China experienced substantial positive impact on its economic and social dimensions. However, China has much to gain by continuation of the reforms in the earlier or experienced direction. Therefore any resistance toward the trend by officials, like in case of demand for more transparent property rights, is uncalled for.

(xii) *Non-farm Activity and Rural Income Inequality: A Case Study of Two Provinces in China*, by Nong Zhu and Xubei Luo, Policy Research Working Paper, 3811, The World Bank, Development Economics, 2006.

In this paper the author focuses on the role of the non-farm activity in the reduction of poverty and inequality in rural China. The author case study include Hubei and Liaoning provinces for the three years; 1995 to 1997. The results suggest that non-farm activity reduces rural inequality. The poor households would have suffered a relatively larger income loss than the rich households if they were not allowed to participate in non-farm activity. Although the distribution of non-farm income is more unequal than farm income, with higher participation rate of poor households, non-farm activity reduces rural inequality.

Non-farm activity plays an increasingly important role in sustainable development and poverty reduction: it increases overall economic activity and employment; functions as a social safety net through diversifying income sources; enhances household's capability of overcoming negative shocks and investing in farm activity; mitigates income fluctuation; and prevents rapid or excessive urbanisation.

(xiii) *Poverty, Inequality, and Social Disparities during China's Economic Reform*, by David Dollar, Policy Research Working Paper, 4253, the World Bank, 2007.

The author focuses on the concomitant disparities on the social and economic front that the reform process with its unique success has brought to China. Growing disparities, and policy measures that might mitigate them, are the main focus of the paper. The factors that contribute to the emergence of these disparities include: (a) the household registration system which prevents migration to cities and thus the possibility for rural people to benefit from urban jobs, (b) weak tenure over rural land that limits the ability of peasants to benefit from their primary assets, (c) China's uniquely decentralised system in which poor localities are not able to provide for different socio-economic services provided by rich localities, and (d) emergence of large trade surplus that stimulates urban manufacturing sector, which is already relatively well off.

The policy recommendation that the author suggests for reduction of disparities in China include: (a) facilitate rather than retard rural-urban migration, (b) ensure adequate funding for basic education and health in all rural areas, (c) stronger equalising transfers among locations to move toward the relatively small level of disparity observed in most middle-income and advanced economies, (d) apart from increasing funds reforming the incentive in rural public health, (e) introducing a more transparent and effective progressive taxation and social protection system, and (f) rebalancing the export sector towards the domestic market by reducing the stimulated exports through competitive exchange rates.

(xiv) *Understanding and Interpreting Chinese Economic Reform*, Jinglian Wu, Thomson South-Western Ohio, USA, 2005.

The book is devoted to the evolution and nature of reforms and their impact on the economy of China. Chapter 3 deals with rural reforms. The author makes the case of family farm system as the best institutional arrangement for agricultural production, because: (a) agricultural production processes are integrated with life processes of animals and plants that requires the producer to make regular and appropriate interventions, and (b) production is greatly affected by climate and other natural processes, which requires the producers to possess total control to make decision of his choice. Further, advantages of the household operations include: (a) little transaction cost, (b) low decision-making cost, (c) higher capacity to bear risk, (d) simplified distribution system, and (e) low management cost. The existing problems in the rural economy include stagnant rural economy, poor rural residents, and backward rural society.

A move towards household production system therefore resulted into substantial economic expansion of the rural economy. Furthermore the author makes a case for the implementing a substantial change in the existing arrangement of land system. It needs to be made simple, people centered and transparent as well as secure so to realise the optimum potential output from the side of farmers.

The author also differentiates between different forms of contracting procedures which are usually treated as one in most of the books on China. Accordingly, the responsibility system adopted at the time of reforms could be categorised into three major ways: (a) *job contracting*: giving out a contract for a quantity of work to the work group, (b) *output-quota contracting*: give plots to farmers under contracts stipulating output quotas; the quota part of the output is handed in to the production team, and the above quota part is retained by the household or shared collectively by the production team and household, and (c) *responsibility contracting*: collective contracts the plots to families according to the number of persons or the number of labourers; households fulfill their quota and tax obligations and retain the rest for personal disposal or to be sold in the market.

(xv) Responsiveness, Flexibility, and Market Liberalisation in China's Agriculture, by Alan de Brauw, Jikun Huang, Scott Rozelle, *American Journal of Agriculture Economics*, Vol. 82, No. 5, Proceedings Issue. (Dec., 2001), pp. 1133-1139

The authors attempt to construct more effective technique to measure how market liberalisation affects the behavior of producers in transition economies on the basis of the case study of China. According to them, the methods previously used to measure the behavioural changes of producers have not fully captured the effects of market liberalisation. This is particularly true for the second part of the rural reform (1985 onwards). Building on the adjustment-cost literature, the authors generate two measures of change in producer behavior that arise during periods of market liberalisation: *changes to flexibility* and *changes to responsiveness*. The former is measured by own-price elasticities of labour and fertiliser, the latter by faster adjustment of land and labour by producers because of better markets. Their econometric results show that the reforms have increased both the flexibility and responsiveness of the Chinese agriculture producers in the later half of the reforms. However their effects were fairly minor. Moderate changes in behavior have also translated into moderate gains in late reform period.

(xvi) Two Decades of Rural Reform in China: An Overview and Assessment, by Jean C. Oi. *The China Quarterly*, No. 159, Special Issue: the Peoples Republic of China after 50 Years. (Sep., 1999), pp. 616-628.

This paper provides an overview and assessment of the major rural reforms of the first two decades of reform from the perspective of the social, political and economic goals of the regime. Though initially the reforms had been immensely successful bringing much of the rural society out of absolute poverty, yet the problems faced by further reforms are quite serious. This dilemma emerges as a result of incomplete reform as well as the consequences of its success.

As more lucrative opportunities emerged for rural labour, shift in occupation led to drop in the grain production in late 1980s. Further, even the township and village enterprises began to show serious problems by the early 1990s. Development of some region and stagnation of others led to pronounced regional inequalities. After a decade of transition, by 1990s, the "trickle-down" theory underlying Deng's policy of "let some get rich first" has come under increasing criticism as those who have fallen behind in the first phase of reform become more anxious and those who have failed to benefit lose patience. To overcome the consequent discontent, China faces the problem of consolidation of reforms, which may be even more difficult than initiation of the reforms in late 1970s.

1.6. Methodology and Data

The data utilised for the study of above two hypotheses is secondary in nature usually derived from China's official statistic census and those regularly published by international agencies like World Bank, UN agencies, IMF, OECD, and other important agencies. Important economic variables like rural-GDP, per capita income, investment, savings, employment, productivity and their respective compositions are utilised in conjunction with conventional economic understanding regarding trends in growth and composition of these variables. This helped to explain the impact of reforms on the overall socio-economic indicators of the rural sector as well as to study the structural change.

The approach of analysis in the study has been multidimensional. While analysis has been statistical or quantitative as well as historical in approach, however, analytical or theoretical dimension of the analysis has been equally emphasised. The chapter entitled "pre-reform period" has been more of a historical research. This is because much of the statistics that are available are rather speculative in nature because the official statistics stopped to be published after the Great Leap failure. The data developed later for the period has been relied upon for a quantitative approach. A lot of literature on the subject has been used to develop an outline and analysis of the pre-reform period. Such an approach of extensive survey into the period was necessary for looking into the magnitude and the sprawl of change that has occurred in the post-reform period.

An outline of reform and its impact at the aggregate level of the economy in the post-reform period was necessary prelude to the main focus of the research. The approach used in the chapter "Post-Reform Period" is statistical or quantitative in which the time series data with growth rates and changes in the per centage of different variables in the overall composition has been presented.

The main chapter of the study, "Rural Transformation" has combined both the simple quantitative and analytical methods to record the exact nature of the transformation. Compound growth rates of a spectrum of variables associated with the rural development have been obtained and analysed in the light of the conventional economic understanding. Change in the proportion of different variables in the total output and their disaggregated components are also developed to analyse the structural change in the economy.

The last chapter "Relevance of China's Reform Experience for India" uses the comparative time series data of different variables and projects the divergence in the state of development in the historical context. The difference in the development scenario is then analysed in the background of the different policy procedures adopted in the two countries. Some of the important positive institutional and technical dimensions of China's rural economy are recommended for India.

The overall scheme of research is neither vigorously analytical in the technical sense of the word, using numerous statistical and econometric techniques like regression, correlation nor historical, in the sense of looking to the process of transformation from a historical perspective and developing chronological sequence and data for the transformation.

1.7. Limitations of the Study

The subject dealt in the present study is having many dimensions among which choice made has been to present a case of economic and social transformation. However, the exact nature and measures of transformation are fraught with significant theoretical and empirical difficulties. Therefore, a simple approach to portray a case of transformation has been attempted. Such a simplification however, entails forgoing many of the potential theoretical and empirical dimensions of the study.

As the study had to take pre-reform period as its starting point, the data for the same is rather an approximation by both official and non-official institutes. Thus, to rely on the same with significant confidence is not possible. So is the accuracy and interpretation of the policy outcomes compromised.

Not all the variables that could have been part of the present study are available to the possible reach of the research student conducting the present study. Therefore, absence of some dimensions from the scene has marginally narrowed the outline of the study.

The study mostly uses the official statistics which have not been taken that easily across the sections of the economists. Chinese statistics have been at times thought to be simpleton exaggerations. However, there is no unanimity on the same. Further, progressively the statistics are thought to be better reliable than before. This controversy regarding the statistics casts a shadow of doubts on any attempt at measuring accurately the economic changes that have occurred in the country. Hopefully, the official measurements rather approximate to the real situation in China.

2

Pre-Reform Period

2.1. China in 1949: A Profile

On October 1, 1949, Mao Zedong proclaimed the Peoples Republic of China. 'For over a century (since the Opium War[1] in 1839-42), China had experienced the agonies of foreign invasion and domestic turmoil. Worst of all had been Japanese invasion of China (1937-45) and the subsequent four years of civil war between the Guomindang government of President Chaing Kai-shek and the revolutionary movement led by the Chinese Communist Party'.[2] 'While China had never been absorbed into the various European colonial empires, its situation as a "semi-colony" became increasingly obvious to everyone following the Opium Wars. Foreign power extorted a series of "unequal" treaties, concessions, and extraterritorial rights from the Chinese government. In addition to this, and in plain discrimination against all Chinese, various supervisory powers over purely Chinese institutions such as the postal service had to be granted to foreigners'.[3] After the fall of monarchy in 1911 affected by revolutionary military uprising for the establishment of a republic, it were the military governors turned war lords who ruled China up to 1928 when the Nationalist Government took control[4]. China was nominally unified under Chaing [the Nationalist leader], but his control on China was weak[5].

The main factions before the formation of a single government, in 1949, were the Nationalist Party, Kuomintang (KMT) led by Chaing Kai-shek and the Communist Party of China (CPC)—formed in 1921—led by Mao Zedong. The history of the two factions prior to the proclamation passed through different phases of fragile cooperation and violent conflict. 'Notwithstanding all efforts at mediation by American diplomats the failure in 1945 of the coalition negotiations, which even Moscow had demanded, brought about a renewal of the civil war. This resulted in Mao Zedong's victory, while Chaing Kai-shek was forced to retreat to Taiwan[6].'

Before liberation in 1949, China was a land of abysmal poverty and glaring inequalities. The Gross National Product as per the US government estimates was US$59 billion at 1978 prices but as per the Chinese government estimates it was only US$ 30.9 billion at 1979 prices[7]. The population of the country was 541.67 millions.[8] With a per capita net domestic product of US$57, at 1979 prices, China belonged to the poorest group among the underdeveloped countries of the world[9]. About three-fourths of this meager income was spent on food and housing leaving little for other necessities and investment requirements[10]. In the first half of the twentieth century it witnessed wars and civil unrest which led to decline in per capita Gross Domestic Product at an annual rate of -0.6 per cent from 1913 to 1950[11]. In 1949, output of food grain was about 75 per cent of 1936.[12]

With almost one quarter of the world population, China had only seven per cent of the world's cultivated area[13]. Though the average population was 157 persons per square mile, in North and South China, where 95 per cent of the Chinese lived, the density was as high as 332 and 334 persons per square miles respectively. With vast areas of the country unsuitable for cultivation (only about 1/10th of the total area in China is cultivated), the cultivated area per person was extremely low—0.35 acres[14]. Grain available per capita per annum was just 209 kg. 90 per cent of the population was concentrated in just 15 per cent of the total area[15]. The recurrent floods and droughts claimed millions of lives. In spite of a very high birth rate (around 40 per 1000) the population between 1850 and 1953 grew only by 0.3 per cent annually[16].

'At the end of its civil war, in 1949, industrial production had fallen to about half its previous recorded peak in 1941-1943; in consumer goods the drop was about 25 per cent, but in producers it was about two-thirds, and in certain basic materials such as pig-iron and steel the cuts amounted to 85 to 90 per cent'.[17]

The state of social services was almost nonexistent and poverty from the social perspective was at its highest level. In case of education and literacy almost 80 per cent of the population was illiterate. The number of primary schools, secondary schools, and colleges and universities was 24391, 1268, and 117 respectively. China had 21 thousand college graduates, with 4 colleges per 100,000 inhabitants. The total number of teachers was 932 thousand[18]. The enrollment figures in 1949 were 24.4 million at the primary level, 1.27 million at the secondary level and 0.117 million at the higher level, which comes to roughly 4.5 per cent, 0.23 per cent and 0.021 per cent of the total population respectively.[19] Less than 25 per cent of the Chinese children in the school going age (5-14 years) were going to schools in 1949[20].

The life expectancy at birth in 1949 was only 35 years while infant mortality (per thousand live births) was 117. The number of physicians was almost 38 thousand and each of them would be on an average required to serve 14250 people. The total number of health personnel was 505 thousand with 80 thousand hospital beds the population per bed was as high as 6770[21]. Eighty-five per cent of the population living in the rural areas was almost without modern medical facilities of any kind because doctors and hospitals were concentrated almost exclusively in the cities. Some 25 million people were affected by malaria and some 10 million were victims of schistosomiasis[22].

'In 1949, China's transport system was marked by extreme backwardness'.[23] It had a rail network of 22 thousand km with a transport volume of 56 million tones. There were only 2300 locomotives and 40 thousand cars[24]. The road network was 80.77 thousand km with transport performance of just 0.81 billion ton-kilometer. The number of trucks was 30 thousand[25]. China in 1949 had 73.62 thousand km of inland waterways with 454 ships[26]. 'At a density of 2.3 kilometers of railways, 8.4 kilometers of highways and 7.7 kilometers of inland waterways per thousand square kilometers of territory, China was less well provided with transport facilities than any other large country in the world'. Besides, there was a particularly marked dichotomy between the few areas of continuous accessibility and vast areas of limited or no accessibility'.[27]

General Economic History of the Period

The period from the declaration of the Republic in October 1949 to late 1970s can be divided into seven sub-periods which we discuss. The classification of six sub-periods is as: (a) Rehabilitation Phase: 1949-52, (b) First Plan 1953-57: Soviet Model, (c) Second Five Year Plan: Great Leap Forward, 1958-62, (d) Readjustment Period:1963-65, (d) Third Five Year Plan 1966-70: Cultural Revolution—1, (e) Fourth Five Year Plan 1971-75: Cultural Revolution—2, and (f) Post Revolution Period; 1976 and 1977.

2.2. The Rehabilitation Phase: 1949-52

2.2.1. Introduction

After assuming power in October 1949, the first challenge to the new government was the rehabilitation of the economy as it had gone through a long period of war, internal conflicts and instability. There was a pressing need of recovery from the abysmal economic scenario and China devoted its first few years to achieve this objective. There was an urgent need to curb inflation and attain fiscal and financial stability. Also, since the Communist Party by its ideology was committed to socialism initially and communism in the long run it required certain fundamental institutional changes which would goad the economy in that direction. Therefore the first priority for the authorities was restoration of productive capacity in economy and socialisation of the means of production. However the line of demarcation of these objectives was never clear as both these objectives could be achieved with same set of policies.

The reconstruction phase restored the economy to progress and on many dimensions there were considerable improvements. Most important of all was the institutional transformation of the economy which prepared it for a sustained development in the coming years. National income from 1949 to 1952 increased by more than 67 per cent and per capita income by almost 60 per cent.[28] There were satisfactory improvements in health care and education as well as infrastructure of the economy. 'Recovery in industry and agriculture brought about a large increase in the supplies of consumer goods and thereby permitted an increase in personal consumption... The redistribution of income resulting from nationalisation of industry and land reform was a contributing factor. Between 1950 and 1952, the considerable increase in the real wage bill was mainly due to the rise in average earnings, since employment rose only moderately. The rise in real income of peasants reflected the gradual completion of the agrarian reforms.'[29]

'The relative success of the measures adopted during these years—in the realm of monetary policy, taxation, restoration of communications, and even in the turbulent land-reform campaign—when considered together with the amazingly swift establishment of political control and relative order, may go far toward explaining the sense of legitimacy which the People's Republic has continued to enjoy through all the crisis of its later history'.[30] 'The new government provided various welfare schemes; these included relief for 1.2 million people, creating jobs for 0.24 million unemployed people and 0.44 million prostitutes, beggars and offenders, and taking care of 0.11 million old, handicapped or impoverished persons and orphans. Such welfare initiatives had never been seen under the previous Nationalist government'.[31] 'The destruction of the old [rural] elite at this time removed a major obstacle in the path of China's state-building efforts and appeared to resolve the long-standing struggle between centralising and decentralising forces in Chinese polity.'[32]

2.2.2. Macroeconomic Indicators[33]

In 1952 China's total GDP was 155,548 million yuan at 1987 prices or $231,550 million at 1990 GK $[34]. Agriculture contributed 112,038 million yuan or 72.02 per cent of GDP, industry and construction 14,769 million yuan or 9.49 per cent and services 28741 million yuan or 18.47 per cent.[35] In terms of employment, primary sector contributed 82.54 of the total employment, secondary sector 6.98 per cent and tertiary sector 10.47 per cent in 1952.[36]

2.2.3. Institutional Change

In this period a major land reform programme was completed in which land ownership was drastically transformed. 'The Agrarian Reform Law was promulgated in June, 1950 in order to introduce a peasant proprietorship by redistributing land'[37]. 'Before the reform, about one-half of the land was owned by landlords, who rented it to tenant farmers. These farmers and hired labourers constituted about two-thirds of the rural population. As a result of land redistribution, a large proportion of the population became independent peasants'[38]. Almost 46.6 million hectares of land was distributed to 300 million peasants[39] that transformed the agrarian structure of the economy. A substantial share of national income, variously estimated as 15 to 30 per cent, had previously gone to landlords, rich gentry, money-lenders, merchants, and others. Land reform redistributed this income, on the first ground, among the peasant population[40]. The programme of agrarian reform was pursued with great commitment. 'By the spring of 1952, the agrarian reform was complete for more than 90 per cent of the total rural population'.[41]

The reform process was also extended to cooperation in the community for increased production. This was because the capital base in terms of equipments and human resource was either low or dispersed and required streamlining and maximum use. This was done through the agency of mutual teams established on voluntary bases in the rehabilitation period. 'By 1951 there were reported to be some 4,300,000 mutual-aid teams of various kinds in the country, over twenty per cent of China's peasant households being members of such units'.[42]

'Planning was limited in general to the allocation of only a few key commodities in short supply and to the formulation of annual targets for specific industries'.[43] Industrialists were allowed to continue the operation of their enterprises[44]. The entire modern transport sector and about one-third of the industrial enterprises were already under state supervision before the establishment of the People's Republic in 1949. These were nationalised and made state-owned enterprises.[45] However there was a steep progression toward state ownership in this phase as in 1952, 56 per cent of the industrial output originated from the state owned enterprises and 27 per cent from joint state-private firms (or State capitalistic enterprise) as compared to 34.7 and 9.5 per cent in 1949 respectively. Output share of private enterprises decreased from 56 to 17 per cent in the same period[46]. However state ownership was not always achieved through direct nationalisation of private enterprises by confiscation or remuneration but indirectly, thereby reducing the possibility of resistance and conflict with the industrialists at a fledgling state of the Republic. 'An attempt [was] made to absorb the private sector of industry into planning process through such indirect measures as the placing of orders, the allocation of raw materials and the granting of bank credits on a selective basis'[47].

2.2.4. Agriculture

China being an underdeveloped economy with huge population relied heavily on its agriculture sector to feed its population and supply surplus food as well as raw material for industrial sector. Total grain production in 1949 was just 113 million tones in which the principal contributor were rice (43 per cent), wheat (12.22 per cent), corn (10.35 per cent), tubers (8.71 per cent), soybeans (4.51 per cent), sugar cane (2.33 per cent), and peanuts (1.12 per cent). Up to 1952 grain production increased to 164 million tones that is an overall increase of 45.13 per cent in the period. Livestock production also increased in the period. The index of agriculture and livestock production recorded an increase of 33 percentage points during this period.[48] Taking 1953 as base year agricultural production in the period increased from 65 per cent in 1949 to 91 per cent in 1952.[49] Agriculture tax as percentage of national agricultural output decreased from 13.89 per cent in 1949 to 13.20 per cent in 1952.[50] On the technological front, proportion of area machine ploughed in 1952 was a mere 0.1 per cent and chemical fertilisers used per hectare (kg) were negligible.[51]

2.2.5. Industry

The rehabilitation phase restored existing industry to its optimal course which was in disarray in preceding years. Taking 1953 as the base year, industrial production increased from 30 per cent in 1949 to 76 per cent in 1952.[52] Thus industrial production in the period from 1949 to 1952 increased by 150.6 per cent.[53] At the end of the period total industrial production exceeded the previously recorded peak level'.[54] 'Up to 1953 the major part of investment was devoted to restoration and reconstruction of existing capacity, leading to quick increase in output'.[55] 'Output of producers goods rose at a much faster rate than that of consumers goods and their share in total output rose from 29 per cent in 1949 to 40 per cent in 1952. Annual average growth of light industry was 29 per cent while heavy industry experienced an annual average growth of 48.9 per cent.[56] 'By 1952, ...,output of the major heavy industrial products had attained levels surpassing the highest rates achieved in Manchuria and rest of mainland China combined during the pre-Communist period'.[57]

2.2.6. Education

The number of primary schools increased from 346.8 thousand in 1942 to 527 thousand in 1952. Total enrollment in primary schools increased from 24.4 million in 1949 to 51.1 million in 1952. In 1952

China had 4.3 thousand secondary schools against four thousand in 1949. Total enrollment in secondary schools increased from one million in 1949 to 2.5 million in 1952.[58] The number of years of education per person aged 15 and older was 1.70 years in 1952.[59] Apart from this formal education structure, the mass literacy campaigns for adults also contributed to the dissemination of basic literacy. The number of adult participants and graduates in anti-illiteracy classes in the rehabilitation years was 4.06 million according to official statistics.[60]

2.2.7. Health

The number of physicians in the period increased from 38 thousand in 1949 to 52 thousand in 1952. Population per physician in the same period decreased from 14250 to 11050.[61] Life expectancy at birth attained a value of 38 years.[62] Death rate per thousand decreased from 20 in 1949 to 17 in 1952.[63]

2.2.8. Infrastructure

The rehabilitation period witnessed good growth of transport infrastructure. Highways in operation increased by 56.76 per cent with an annual compound growth rate of 16.16 per cent in the period. Total highways network increased from 80.76 thousand km in 1949 to 126.6 thousand km in 1952. Waterways network recorded an increase of 29.07 per cent in the period with 73.6 thousand km in 1949 and 95 thousand km in 1952. Airways increased by 15.18 per cent increasing from 11.39 thousand km in 1949 to 13.12 thousand km in 1952. Growth in railways was comparatively slower which increased by only 5 per cent in the rehabilitation period. The total rail strength increased from 21.8 thousand km in 1949 to 22.9 thousand km in 1952.[64] The area of irrigated land in this period increased to 22 million hectares which represented 23.25 per cent of the total arable land.[65] Energy production infrastructure also improved leading positive trends in energy production. The production of raw coal increased from 32.43 million metric tones in 1949 to 66.4 million metric tones in 1952, recording an annual average compound growth of 27.03 per cent. Crude oil production increased from 0.12 million metric tones in 1949 to 0.44 million metric tones in 1952. Electricity generation increased from 4.31 billion kilowatt-hours in 1949 to 7.26 billion kilowatt-hours in 1952.[66]

2.2.9. External Sector

In 1950 China's merchandise exports valued US$ 550 million (at current exchange rates) while its imports were US$ 580 million leaving US$ 30 million deficit in its balance of trade. In 1952 exports were equal to US$ 820 million while imports were US$ 1120 million with net trade deficit reaching to US$ 300 million.[67] 'By 1950, the trade of China began to play an important part in the trade of the centrally planned economies'.[68] To increase its political clout it extended loans to other countries as early as 1951'.[69] 'The ratio of net imports to fixed investment was much higher in the beginning of the period, amounting to about 13 per cent of fixed investment in 1950-53'.[70] 'For 1950 to 1952, net foreign borrowing amounted to some 15 per cent of fixed investment'.[71]

2.3. The First Five Year Plan, 1953-57: Soviet Model

2.3.1. Introduction

After the rehabilitation phase China embarked on its First Five Year Plan in 1953. 'The Chinese First Plan was not officially adopted and promulgated until 1955, but it covered the whole period from 1953 to 1957 and so included the temporary economic programmes of 1953 and 1954'.[72] 'The First Plan was due to finish at the end of 1957 and was actually declared fulfilled at the end of 1956'.[73]

'The strategy of development envisaged in the First Plan was greatly influenced by the Soviet Model of development'.[74] 'The entire planning ... was directed to the urgent industrialisation of China. A model was found without much difference of opinion in the first two Soviet Five Year Plans of the Stalin era (1928-37). This Soviet concept, which derived from Preobrazhenski, provided for an unusually large share of the GNP's being used for investments'.[75] 'In less than thirty years, the USSR became the second largest of the world's industrial nations'.[76] '[China's] own relative backwardness and inexperience, and her dependence on the Soviet Union for technical know-how, etc., further inclined them to follow the Soviet pattern of development and planning'.[77] However, 'during the First Five Plan, the Soviet credit available for new investment constituted merely three per cent of the total state investment'.[78]

'According to the Communist theory of industrialisation, economic development is contingent above all on the growth of heavy industry, including fuels, electric power, iron and steel, machinery and chemicals'.[79] 'The Stalinist model involves not only collectivisation of agriculture, but also total subordination of the agricultural sector of the economy to the needs of rapid industrial development and the lopsided priority of heavy and capital-goods industry over light industry and consumer-goods industry'.[80]

'China adopted two key sets of guiding principles behind the Soviet development strategy: (a) the Marxist principles of common ownership with the state as trustee, and of generalised egalitarianism; and (b) the Stalinist practices of central planning for resource allocation, suppression of light industries and services in favor of heavy industries, and minimising trade and financial linkages with the capitalist economies. Mao added a third guiding principle to China's economic policy making, the principle of regional economic self-sufficiency, a region should be self-sufficient not only in food production but also in industrial goods as well.'[81]

The principal areas of operation for the Five Year Plan were five in number: Northeast China (Manchuria), North China (with its center in Tienstsin area), Shanghai complex, Wuhan complex, and Northwest China.[82] '[It] allocated 56 per cent of state investment to the interior provinces'.[83] 'The fact that perspective details of the First Five Year Plan were only published in 1955 indicates that only then was the regime confident enough to announce its long-range economic goals'.[84]

'On the eve of her First Five-Year Plan China was economically far weaker than Soviet Union of the late 1920s'.[85] 'On eve of their respective First Five Year Plans (1952 for China and 1928 for the USSR), Soviet output was greater, perhaps by a half or more. By 1957, however, Chinese output had become significantly larger than the Russian output of 1928'.[86] 'A large and sudden increase in agriculture output of this sort would, of course, strengthen the political position of the regime, both at the home and abroad. It could be held forth as a justification for the vast exercise of compulsion practiced by the communists'.[87]

'China avoided the massive disruption of production that accompanied the collectivisation of agriculture in the USSR, with its adverse effects on real wages and the morale of the industrial labour force. The Chinese have also had a greater, if incomplete, success in controlling the inflation of money wages in industry'.[88] 'Sectoral imbalance was not present during most of the period in any substantial degree. This was partly due to the existence of large amounts of unused capacity at the current plan. Shortages of certain industrial materials began to appear during the latter part of 1956 as a result of the extremely high increase in investment during the year, but... no serious bottlenecks because of drawing upon government stocks of these materials accumulated previously'.[89] 'The First Plan had a number of noteworthy achievements: some five hundred major industrial plants were built, steel production reached four million tons, and about 60 per cent of the machinery and equipment for the Plan was produced'.[90] 'By the end of the Chinese plan, therefore, Chinas output of the major heavy industrial products was two or three times that of India'.[91]

'The substantial increase in food output during years was barely sufficient to make up for the decline in output during the war and the continued growth of population. In consequence, per capita output in 1955-57 did not exceed the pre-war level'.[92] 'The relatively low rate of growth in agriculture during 1956 and 1957 raised doubts about the possibility of maintaining a rapid rate of industrialisation as envisaged by the First Five Year Plan. At the same time the danger of politically alienating the peasants loomed on the horizon'.[93]

'Following many expression of popular discontent, large wage increases were affected in 1956: on an average by 13 per cent in government employment, 16 per cent in heavy industry, 12 per cent in light industry and 11 per cent in other-. The budget that year, for the first time since the 'Liberation', showed a substantial deficit of 7.3 per cent of total expenditure'.[94]

'In China, which was able only in 1950 to halt the hyper-inflation inherited from the civil war, prices declined by 20 to 30 per cent during that year, but from 1950 to 1956 they increased again by about 20 per cent'.[95] Between 1952 and 1956, real income of labour in relation to industrial production declined by 25 per cent.[96] 'The rate of expansion in national product ... slowed down ...exclusively due to the sharp decline in the rate of increase in industrial production'.[97]

The First Five-Year Plan was broadly fulfilled, in fact, one year ahead of schedule. But there a multitude of difficulties and discrepancies appeared; especially in 1955 and 1956... serious shortages and irregularities occurred, especially in the supply of consumer goods. Distribution was sometimes unsatisfactory; quality was very variable and generally declining'.[98]

2.3.2. Macroeconomic Indicators

The GDP in this period increased from $ 231550 million[99] in 1952 to 322640 million dollars in 1957, an increase of 39.33 per cent. The average annual compound growth rate of the period was 6.86 per cent. The contribution of primary sector to GDP decreased from 72.02 per cent in 1952 to 62.34 per cent that of secondary sector increased from 9.49 per cent to 16.66 per cent and increased for services sector from 18.87 per cent to 20.99 per cent in the First Plan.[100] Primary sector employed 79.84 per cent of labour force in 1957 against 82.54 per cent in 1952; the comparative figures for secondary sector were 9.62 per cent in 1957 and 6.98 per cent in 1952, and for tertiary sector it is 10.53 per cent in 1957 and 10.47 per cent in 1952.[101] State investment in capital construction by sector in the First Five Year Plan was: industry, 45 per cent; construction, 3.7 per cent; agriculture 7.1 per cent; transport, 15.3 per cent; commerce 3.6 per cent and; others 27.3 per cent.[102]

2.3.3. Institutional Change

'Within the framework of the general line of the transitional period the socialist transformation of agriculture and industry as well as of trade and handicrafts was essentially completed'.[103] During 1953, an increase of over 10,000 agricultural cooperatives was reported'[104] and 'higher level cooperatives were begun on an experimental basis'.[105] 'The farmers were organised into cooperatives under the pretense that this would improve production and marketing, but they were soon forced to surrender their produce to government procurement agencies'.[106] 'Various forms of cooperatives began even before the completion of the land reform programme. Of the three major form of cooperatives up to 1955, the most famous was the "mutual aid team", in which four or five neighbouring households pooled their labour, farm tools, and draft animals for peak seasons on a temporary or permanent basis. .. .the second form was "elementary cooperatives", in which 20-30 neighbouring households combined their assets in a unified scheme. .. The third form was the collective farm, or the "advanced cooperatives", in which all means of production, were collectivised. Remuneration in a collective was based solely on labour contribution and took the form of work points'.[107]

'Until 1955, Chinese agriculture was operated primarily by individual peasant households. In the latter year, a bumper harvest emboldened the regime to force through, with unusual speed, that desideratum of modern communism, the collectivisation of agriculture. The tiny fields of the individual peasant holdings were merged and the work of cultivation was greatly intensified through collective operation'.[108] 'In 1956 the Chinese communists had organised virtually all farm households into collectives'.[109] 'By 1957, 96 per cent of all peasant households had been organised in higher level APCs'.[110] 'In a further measure of state control, the Agriculture Bank of China was established on March 25, 1955, under the overall direction of the state owned Chinese People's Bank'.[111]

'The wages and employment policy of the urban sector, which started in the First Five-Year Plan period, was one of "full employment with low wages." This policy, in turn, was essentially one of egalitarianism in providing both work opportunity and remuneration, though for the latter a principle of "payment by work" was adhered to'.[112]

'Apart from constructing the socio-economic hegemony that suffocated the market activities, the other main tactic was to adopt a gradualist approach towards private entrepreneurs, through sequential policies of "utilisation", 'restriction', and 'transformation'.... The first step was 'utilisation' (1949-52), when the state provided the private sector a range of preferential measures. ... the second step was 'restriction' (1952-53)..., [through which], private sector would be allowed to operate on condition that private enterprises submitted their complete plans of production and sales for state approval... the final step was 'transformation' (1954-57)[in which] the State Council promulgated its Provisional Regulations for Joint State-Private Industrial Enterprises. This defined 'mixed state-private enterprises' as the 'advanced forms of state capitalism', and required private enterprises to work with state investments or other mixed state-private enterprises, under the joint direction of capitalists and state-appointed functionaries.'[113]

'In the wake of the unparalleled centralisation achieved during the early and mid-1950s, Mao and other Chinese leaders became convinced that the "democracy" component of the democratic centralism principle needed strengthening. The result was a significant devolution of decision-making power from the center to the provinces in the late 1957'.[114] 'Some efforts [at decentralisation] were discernable as early as 1956 with such moves by the state as the removing of a variety of lesser products from direct allocation by state commercial departments and distributing them instead through the market'.[115]

Towards the end of the First Plan major institutional transformation had taken place. As per the official statistics output share of the state owned industry had increased from 43.04 per cent in 1953 to 53.77 per cent in 1957. Output share of the collective industries had gone up from 3.87 per cent in 1953 to 19.03 per cent in 1957. Ownership of the individual industry changed drastically producing 19.26 per cent of industrial output in 1953 which decreased to 0.83 per cent in 1957. Share of the other industries which included joint state-collective, state-individual, collective-individual, domestic-foreign ventures decreased from 33.83 per cent in 1953 to 26.37 per cent in 1957.[116]

Significant institutional transformation of the retail market also occurred in the First Plan. In 1952, as per the official figures, state was the source of 34.6 per cent of the total retail sale which increased considerably to 73.9 per cent in 1957. In the same period the share of collectives in the total retail sale increased from 0 per cent to 19.5 per cent. The share of individuals recorded a significant decrease from 61.2 per cent in 1952 to 3.2 per cent in 1957. Peasant sales to non-agrarian population also witnessed a decrease from 4.3 per cent of total retail sale in 1952 to 3.3 per cent in 1957.[117]

2.3.4. Agriculture

In the First Five Year Plan agriculture exhibited moderate growth. In absolute terms, agriculture GDP increased from 155548 million yuan in 1952 to 135118 million yuan in 1957. The total growth of the sector was 20.60 per cent in the period with an average annual growth rate of 3.81 per cent. Industrial growth rates were almost five times greater than agriculture.[118] This reflected the policy priority of the economy in the First Five Year Plan. However, over the Plan period terms of trade for farm and sideline products against industrial products improved from 110.8 to 130.4. The purchase price of farm and sideline products increased from

121.6 in 1952 to 146.18 in 1957 while as price index of industrial products sold in rural areas increased from 112.7 in 1952 to 118.4 in 1957.[119] Agricultural tax as percentage of national agricultural output decreased from 13.20 per cent in 1952 to 11.51 per cent in 1957.[120] Gross value of agricultural output by sector in 1957 exhibited the following pattern: crop farming 80.65 per cent; forestry 1.7 per cent; animal husbandry 12.9 per cent; subsidiaries 4.3 per cent; and fisheries 0.5 per cent.[121] The proportion of area machine ploughed in 1957 was 2.6 per cent against 0.1 per cent in 1952; however, there were no measurable improvements in use of chemical fertilisers per hectare (in kg) in this period.[122]

'Government policy towards agriculture differed in many essential aspects from that of other centrally planned economies. First, no extensive mechanisation (was) contemplated before the full development of the tractor producing industry during the Second Five Year Plan beginning in 1958. Second, although government policy aims at complete collectivisation that is to proceed by stages'.[123] 'With the possible exception of improved seeds, agricultural modernisation of mechanisation played only a minor role'.[124] 'Methods embodied in the plan for promoting the increase of agricultural production include[ed] expansion of agricultural credit, improvement of irrigation by government water conservation projects, supplying of cheap fertilisers and agricultural implements, and expanding scope of mutual aid teams, which were to be transformed gradually into agricultural producers cooperatives'.[125]

'Agriculture was to function as the accumulation base for the development of industry'.[126] 'Agriculture prices were set at a very low level relative to industrial prices. This naturally reduced the peasants' incentive to produce as well as invest'.[127] 'During 1953-56, 51.7 per cent of the gross industrial output came from industries using raw materials from agricultural sector.... This substantial direct dependence of industry on agriculture was increased two indirect factors. First, need to import heavy equipment and certain basic materials for industrial expansion had to be met chiefly by the export of agricultural commodities. Second, the scale of industrial investment was, to a fairly large extent, determined by the performance of agricultural sector in the preceding year in as much as agricultural surplus has constituted a major source of investment resource in the Chinese economy'.[128]

'Despite the enormous reclamation efforts, increase in cultivated area could hardly keep up with population increase. Total sown area, however, increased substantially, about 11 per cent from 1952 to 1957; the multiple cropping index increased from 131 in 1952 to 141 in 1957. There was even a slight increase of sown area per capita of farming population'.[129] 'Probably most important source of increase in yield was irrigation. The irrigated area increased to 63 per cent in 1957'.[130]

'There was no "agricultural revolution" in the technical sense as the Chinese Communist strategy of developing agriculture was one of agricultural reorganisation (from land distribution, mutual-aid teams, elementary cooperatives to advanced cooperatives). This strategy achieved its purpose in the utilisation of labour, but it had its limitations'.[131] 'The ...experience of ... mainland China ...indicate that agricultural output could have been substantially raised in the past despite the need to devote a rising proportion of resources to industry'. ... The sharp increases in yields were largely due to the extension of irrigation works, at little cost to the government, by a fuller utilisation of agricultural manpower'.[132]

'The agricultural sector provides raw material, food, labour, markets, foreign exchange, and sometimes saving for the industrial sector. Some 80-855 of the raw materials for "light" industry, encompassing essentially the manufacture of consumer goods, were supplied by the agricultural sector in 1950s. The failure of this sector to grow sufficiently in relation to the industrial sector created the prospect of increasing serious underutilisation of plant capacity'. [133]

2.3.5. Industry

In the First Plan industry exhibited remarkable growth. Industrial GDP increased from 14769 million yuan in 1952 to 36127 million yuan in 1957. The total growth of the sector was 144.6 per cent over the period with an average annual compound growth rate of 19.59 per cent.[134] The reason for this remarkable growth was the central place given to the industrial sector in the development planning by the government which made agriculture subservient to the needs of industry. In the industrial sector itself heavy industry was given a very high priority. Of the total fixed investment of 25.03 billion yuan at current prices heavy industry received 85 per cent against 15 per cent to light industry.[135] The average annual growth of the light industry in this period was 12.9 per cent while heavy industry experienced a growth rate of 25.4 per cent.[136]

'At the beginning of it's the First Five Year Plan, China's heavy industry was still in its infancy. This does not mean, however, that production was negligible. The Japanese had built a respectable industrial center in Manchuria. This plan was inherited by the Chinese Communists, albeit in a rather shoddy condition caused by Soviet looting after the Japanese surrender'.[137] 'The new investment programme under the First-Five Year Plan, which began in late 1953, concentrated on constructing new large scale heavy industries, based to a large extent on capital equipment imported from the Union of Soviet Socialist Republics'.[138] 'The central theme of the First Five-Year Plan of development of China (was) concentration on investment in large-scale heavy industry, with the intention of providing a foundation for future rapid development'.[139] 'The term 'heavy industry' is used here, as in Communist parlance, to refer to extractive industries, electric power generation, timbering, and that part of manufacturing devoted to munitions and producers goods, such as metals, machinery, and building materials'.[140]

'On the eve of the launching of the First Five Year Plan, consumer goods were relatively more important than capital goods in terms of their gross value output. At the completion of the plan, however, the relative importance was reversed'.[141] The priority built-up of industry resulted partially in remarkable growth rates'.[142] This growth varied considerably from year to year, largely because of industry's substantial dependence upon agriculture and because of uneven performance in the agricultural sector of the economy'. The composition of industrial output also changed considerably during this period'.[143] 'During the Plan, the average rate of accumulation was 24.2 per cent—about the same percentage as that of the Soviet Union during its First Five-Year Plan'.[144] 'Toward the end of 1956 it became evident that the rate of increase in the supply of pig-iron, steel and lumber had fallen behind the rate of increase of demand. The increase in demand for these goods was the result of increase in investment in fixed capital'.[145] 'The much more rapid increase in investment than in national income and in retail sales leave no doubt that there was a shift in allocation of national income in favor of investment'.[146]

2.3.6. Health

In the First Plan China attained good success in improving the health conditions compared to 1949 position. Redistribution of land seems to have been fundamental for food security. Also improvement in asset distribution thereby guaranteed basic medicine to those with relatively good share of land. Combined with good growth rate and direct medical facilities by authorities, this equity creating redistribution effort led to improved access to health facilities. Total health expenditure in the First Plan was 1.455 million yuan which was 1.08 per cent of the total state expenditure.[147] As a result death rate per thousand decreased from 17 in 1952 to 10.80 in 1957[148] and average life expectancy at birth reached 57 years in 1957.[149]

2.3.7. Education

The number of primary schools increased from 527 thousand in 1952 to 547.3 thousand in 1957. Total enrollment in the same period increased from 51.1 million to 64.3 million. In 1957 the number of secondary schools had reached 11.1 thousand against 4.3 thousand in 1952. Total enrollment increased from 2.5 million in 1952 to 6.3 million in 1957.[150] 'Educational institutions were reorganised. All private universities ceased operation and were incorporated into state universities modeled after the Soviet education system'.[151] Furthermore, 'early educational reforms of the 1950s attempted to get rid of the influence of the Western education model'.[152]

2.3.8. Infrastructure

In terms of transportation infrastructure, the First Five Year Plan was the best in the entire pre-reform (1949-78) China in terms of growth. The average annual compound growth of railways was 3.11 per cent with 22.9 thousand km in 1952 and 26.7 thousand km in 1957. In case of highways, road strength increased from 126.6 thousand km in 1952 to 254.6 thousand km in 1957; the average annual growth rate being 14.99 per cent. Waterways in operation increased from 95 thousand km in 1952 to 144.1 thousand km in 1957; an average annual increase of 8.68 per cent. Airways strength increased by an annual average of 15.04 per cent in this period which increasing from 13.12 thousand km in 1952 to 26.44 thousand km in 1957.[153] The irrigated area increased to 27 million hectare in 1957 from 22 million hectare in 1952 and represented 26.17 per cent of the arable area.[154] In energy sector, raw coal production increased from 66.49 million metric tones in 1952 to 130.73 million metric tones in 1957 with an average annual growth rate of 14.47 per cent. Crude oil production increased from 0.44 million metric tones in 1952 to 1.47 million metric tones in 1957. Electricity recorded an overall increase of 166.39 per cent in the period increasing from 7.26 billion kilowatt-hours in 1952 to 19.34 billion kilowatt-hours in 1957. China also started to produce natural gas in this plan with total production of 0.33 billion cubic meters in 1957.[155]

'During the Plan, the Chinese made strenuous efforts to introduce and expand a rational system of transport for such important materials as coal, grain and timber. As such, a sum of 8210 million yuan was invested in capital construction for transport, postal and telecommunication services. Of this amount 69 per cent was used for railway construction. Railways were thus recognised as the key sector of national transport...the main efforts in highway building was concentrated in minority nationalities areas in Southwest China, in the border areas and along the coast'.[156] 'Transportation construction was undertaken to attain the following aims: to disperse the industrial base; to improve the defense support system; to reduce the regional disparities; and to facilitate the central government control over the entire country'.[157] 'The increase in irrigated area was primarily a product of intensive use of labour. It is reported that of the increased irrigated area in 1953-56, 91 per cent was the result of the work of masses with practically no investment by the government'.[158]

2.3.9. External Sector

China's merchandise trade showed a considerable increase with total turnover increasing from US$ 1940 million in 1952 to US$ 3100 million in 1957. Merchandise exports in 1957 were US$ 1600 million while imports were US$ 1500 million, recording a trade surplus of US$ 100 million.[159] 'The importance of imports to Chinese economic growth during the First Plan may be judged from the fact that they accounted for about 40 per cent of domestic requirements for machinery, about two-thirds of domestic petroleum and chemical fertiliser consumption, and virtually all rubber consumption'.[160]

'The sharp decline in the export surplus of mainland China ensued mainly from Western Europe to over 100 million dollars in 1957 as against less than 40 million in 1956, and from a decline in the net export to Asia and the Far East from about 190 million in 1956 to nearly 170 million in 1957'.[161] 'Despite the relatively poor performance of livestock production, there was a substantial increase in exports of meat and eggs from this country, compared with the pre-war level'.[162] 'Soviet Union became a net importer from China as early as 1956'.[163]

2.4. The Second Five Year Plan: Great Leap Forward, 1958-62

2.4.1. Introduction

'China had no Second Five-Year Plan (1958-62) only five ad hoc annual plans during the period. In basic construction and industrial production a great leap forward did take place in the first three years, only to be followed by collapse and readjustment in the last two years. In agriculture, the period started with an unprecedented bumper crop in the first year, after which there commenced an agricultural crisis that grew in intensity from year to year until 1962 when the output of food grains green vegetables began to show recovery'.[164]

'The Great Leap was largely an attempt to introduce a series of drastically new policy measures replacing the existing ones... without first making a sufficient test of their validity and effectiveness'.[165] 'Virtually all formal rules were abandoned, and the resulting anarchy... made a major contribution to the economic difficulties of 1960 and 1961'.[166] 'Problems were compounded by the ideological dispute with the Soviet Union leading to the Sino-Soviet split, the termination of Soviet aid, and the precipitate withdrawal of all Soviet engineers and technicians from China, carrying with them the blueprints for factories and engineering projects still under construction'.[167] 'The leap years (1958-60) represent a boom period followed by a severe depression'.[168] 'The expansion of the country's economy in 1958 was such that several of the targets set for 1962 had been reached or exceeded and, therefore, the Five-Year Plan became obsolete'.[169]

'The general consequences of the Great Leap Forward are well known by now: overproduction, overinvestment, especially in economically unsound projects, shortages, breakdown and clogging in the transportation system, financial chaos, serious decline in central budgetary revenues, plus all the moral, political, and social consequences of these conditions'.[170] [However], 68 per cent of new large-scale metallurgical projects undertaken between 1949 and 1964 were begun after 1958 (with the vast majority built during the leap years), whereas over 36 per cent of all steel-making capacity put in place between 1950 and 1970 was constructed in 1958-1960'.[171]

'In spite of the enormous concentration of attention in the agricultural sector and on small industries and handicrafts during 1958 and 1959, it was expected that the most spectacular leap forward would take place in the advanced industrial sector and that agriculture would continue to rely on organising human energy without the diversion of material capital'.[172] 'China, despite its size and natural resource endowment, continued to have much less freedom of choice because, in the present stage of its development, the utilisation of its natural resources (was) still largely dependent on imports of machinery and equipment'.[173]

'The Tenth Plenum of the Chinese Communist Party in 1962 adopted an "agriculture first" policy which included priority for state investment in the agricultural sector, an increase in chemical fertiliser imports, greater production of farm machinery, and importation of grains'.[174]

2.4.2. Macroeconomic Variables

In the period there was a net decline of both GDP and per capita income. GDP decreased from $322640 million to $271381 million; a net decrease of 15.88 per cent over the period i.e., an annual average compound growth rate of "3.40 per cent.[175] In 1962 agriculture contributed 55.55 per cent of GDP while secondary and tertiary sectors contribute 20.01 and 24.42 per cent respectively. Thus in total GDP, primary sectors contribution declined by 6.79 percentage points, industrial sector's contribution increased by 3.35 percentage points and tertiary sectors contribution to GDP increased by 3.43 percentage points. In employment, the primary sector contributed 78.67 per cent, secondary sector 9.31 per cent and tertiary sector 12.01 per cent.[176] State investment in capital construction by sector in the Second Five Year Plan was: industry 60.4 per cent; construction 1.4 per cent; agriculture 11.3 per cent; transport 13.5 per cent; commerce 1.9 per cent; and others 11.5 per cent.[177]

'Under the impact of improvements in agricultural output and of a more realistic reallocation of resources between various industries, a process of recovery from the reduced level of preceding two years was taking place [in 1962]'.[178] 'The rise in agricultural production and the stabilisation or a slight rise in industrial output of indicates that national income also increased in 1962'.[179]

'During the First Five Year Plan, 46.5 per cent of capital construction investment went to heavy industry. During the GLF years, 1958-60, the figures were 57 per cent and 56 per cent, and 53.3 per cent, respectively. Light industry had its investment share cut from 5.9 per cent during 1953-57, to 4.0 per cent in 1960. Agriculture received increased investment in the GLF years compared to the First Five-Year Plan, the relevant figures being 7.8 per cent for 1953-57, and 10.5 per cent for 1958-1959'.[180]

2.4.3. Institutional Changes

'During 1958, the institutional structure of the agricultural sector was profoundly changed ... [when] the movement for the country-wide formation of "communes" gathered momentum in August 1958, and by mid-December 740,000 collective farms, embracing 99 per cent of all peasant households, were reorganised into 26,000 communes'.[181] 'The average commune contained about 5000 households, 10,000 workers, and 10,000 acres. Remuneration in a commune was based mainly on the subsistence needs and only partly on the work performed by a peasant. Working on private plots and trading at rural fairs, which existed in the other forms of cooperatives, were prohibited'.[182] 'The new form of organisation [communes] apparently grew out of experience in the construction of large irrigation works in 1957 and 1958'.[183]

'Ownership of productive means, which included land as well as livestock, was transferred to commune. Private cultivation was no longer allowed. ... Economic management was divided into three levels. The lowest level, **the production team**, was responsible for the organisation of daily work. The next level, **the brigade**, which was the direct successor of the former APCs, had to control production. The final level, the planning of all economic activity and the controlling of lower levels, was carried out centrally by **the commune**'.[184] 'Three reforms of the management system were instituted in 1958. First, the various sets of rules and regulations were to be extensively revised to take into account "the interest of the masses". Second, workers were to be organised to participate in management at different levels of enterprise, while management was required to join the workers in physical labour. Third, a system of "close coordination among management, workers, technical personnel and administrative staff under the leadership of the enterprises' Party committee" was inaugurated'.[185]

'By early 1959 the regime was aware that subsidiary production had suffered heavily, at least because of over-tight commercial controls. ... . Consequently, the authorities began experimenting with reopening rural markets in particular areas—culminating in a directive on September 25, 1959, calling for nationwide adoption. ... .By the summer of 1960 the regime went a step further by encouraging the restoration of small private plots and of limits on the amount of labour time which the commune could require of its members'.[186] 'By the winter of 1960-61, the internal situation of China became so serious that the leadership decided to call a halt to the Great Leap Forward. ... in the fall of 1960, the leadership decided on a far-reaching alteration of the commune system, making the small production brigade the operative unit of planning, production, and accounting'.[187]

In 1961, the peasant economy was restructured on the basis of 'the so-called "three freedoms and one contract" (sanzi yibao), that is, the extension of plots for private use, the extension of free markets, the increase in the number of small enterprises that had sole responsibility for their own profits or losses, and the fixing of output quotas based on the individual households'.[188] 'Private plots, which had been confiscated in 1958, were returned and peasants were given permission to sell their products at rural trade fairs'.[189] 'Ownership and hence the calculation of profit and loss and wages was passed down to the production brigades'.[190] 'Thus after four years of experimenting with the larger units, the regime was back to a unit which may have been smaller than the one with which it started'.[191]

'The commune system was not abolished after this crisis; however, its functions were reduced to administration and coordination. Starting in 1962, resource ownership, responsibility for production management, and accounting for the purpose of income distribution were delegated to the small production team of 20-30 households. This new institution, in essence, was a hybrid of the elementary cooperative and advanced cooperative of 1950s'.[192]

2.4.4. Agriculture

In the Second Five Year Plan agriculture GDP decreased considerably; more than it had increased in the First Plan. It decreased from 135118 million yuan in 1957 to 101283 million yuan in 1962, a net decrease of 25.04 per cent over the period at 5.60 per cent annual average compound growth.[193] Agricultural tax as proportion of national agricultural output decreased steeply in this period; from 11.51 per cent in 1957 to 6.70 per cent in 1961.[194]

'During 1958, the outstanding development in agriculture was the striking increase in output of over 60 percent'.[195] 'The original plan provided for only slightly higher rates of increase than during the preceding plan, but the increase which took place in 1958 were more than double the expansion planned for 1958-1962'.[196] 'It is noteworthy that the rise in output was attained without any appreciable increase in the sown area.., mostly the result of technological improvements and more intensive methods of cultivation [including], extension of the irrigated area, increase in use of manure, deep ploughing method, extension of close planting, intensive use of fertilisers, increase in the use of pesticides and a considerable increase in the man-hours expended both on irrigation and on the cultivation of land'.[197]

The sector experienced steep depression due to wrong policies and natural calamities. 'Food production was greatly reduced, because of a lack of incentive for farmers working in communes: because of Mao's misguided policies of growing grain in inappropriate places and killing birds (causing insects to flourish); and because of bad weather'.[198]

'The disastrous situation created by the two consecutive bad harvests becomes particularly evident if one bears in mind from 1957 to 1961 the population of China increased by at least 60 million; in consequence, the per capita grain production in 1961 seems to have been about 10 per cent lower than 1957'.[199] 'The difficulties encountered in the industrial sector were largely influenced by the setback of agriculture. The shortfall of agricultural output had resulted in a decline in the supply of agricultural raw materials to industry, as well as in severe food shortages, which had an adverse effect on labour productivity'.[200]

'Overemphasis on machine building and neglect of agriculture, priorities that characterised the 1950s, were changed dramatically after 1960 to a then more appropriate emphasis on agriculture and chemicals'.[201] 'Since the late 1950s, as China abandoned the Soviet model and developed its own strategy of development, prices began to be changed in favor of agriculture'.[202] 'Before 1958, a higher rate of interest was charged on agricultural loans than on loans to state industrial and commercial enterprises. After 1958, the reverse was true'.[203] 'Agricultural production increased substantially after two years of disastrously low level of output'.[204]

'The efforts intended to overcome the effect of the fall in harvest included an enlargement of the acreage of under late autumn crops, transfer of manpower from the cities to the countryside and bringing new land under the plough... there was also a further reappraisal of the policy of collectivisation, continuing a trend which began in 1959. The role played by "communes" was further restricted in favour of "productive agricultural brigades", essentially similar to the collective farm existing in other [communist] countries. Brigades which formerly were to be closely integrated into the "commune" became independent economic and financial units'.[205]

2.4.5. Industry

After remarkable growth, the sector came to a complete standstill during this period. Industrial GDP slightly increased from 36127 million yuan in 1957 to 36491 million yuan in 1962. The total growth was 1.57 per cent in the period with 0.20 per cent annual average growth.[206] Industrial

GDP increased in first three years consistently but then declined substantially. However, overall it did not experience the disaster faced by agriculture sector in the period. The failure of industrial sector to grow was partly affected by the disaster witnessed by agriculture. Also, a shift of priority in the policy towards agriculture took place. The total fixed investment in industry was 72.83 billion yuan at current prices of which 89.9 per cent was allotted to heavy industry and 10.1 per cent to light industry.[207] The average annual growth rate of heavy industry declined significantly in this period to 6.6 per cent against 25.4 per cent in the previous plan. Light industry grew by a mere 1.1 per cent.[208]

'During the First Five Year Plan the planners followed a policy of holding increases in the labour force in the modern sectors to a minimum. In 1958 this policy was reversed and every effort was made to increase the labour force in construction and heavy industry'.[209] 'Although large-scale enterprises continued to be built, a major effort was made to develop new small-scale plants that would make better use of China's highly labour–intensive factor endowments'.[210]

The developments within the industrial sector were influenced by the changes which occurred in agriculture and foreign trade in the course of the year as well as by the cumulative results of certain developments in the industrial sector itself during the preceding years'.[211] 'Unusual expansion of industrial production resulted from the maturation of a large number of investment projects initiated during the Five-Year Plan for 1952-1957 and from the very great expansion of small-scale production that was made possible through the employment of great number of people in productive activities involving little capital outlay'.[212]

'In China centralised fixed investment had declined by 11 per cent in 1957 but increased by 115 per cent in 1958. Total fixed investment undoubtedly increased even more if account is also taken of a very steep increase in construction work organised at the local level which entailed relatively little additional state expenditure. The very extensive irrigation works, as well the construction of dams and artificial lakes for hydroelectric stations and for the prevention of floods, were achieved by the mobilisation of tens of millions of agricultural workers and peasants who, because of the seasonal character of agricultural work, had been previously occupied for only about two-thirds of the year'.[213]

'If heavy investment in 1956 and 1957 and substantial increase in the labour force accounted for the great expansion in industrial output from 1958 to 1960, the investment programme during these three years was a major factor bringing about the end of the Great Leap Forward. .. .the massive investment resulted in the production of large quantities of capital goods which could not be readily used in the economy for the lack of complementary factors'.[214]

'The further expansion of industry was hampered by imbalances and bottlenecks which had developed during the preceding period of rapid growth... defective planning and lack of coordination between complementary enterprises or industrial branches had resulted in shortages of machinery, equipment, spare parts and materials in some cases and involuntary stock accumulation in others'. In consequence, the degree of utilisation or plant capacity was considerably reduced, quality standards deteriorated and over-all efficiency declined'.[215] 'In short, the new policies [1961] meant that capital investment had to be reduced, consumer goods industries and industries producing goods for the agricultural sector were to be favored, and quality rather than quantity was to be emphasised'.[216]

2.4.6. Education

The number of primary schools in this period increased for first three years and subsequently decreased for another two years. However, there was an overall increase from 547.3 thousand in 1957 to 668.3 thousand in 1962. The same trend of first increasing and subsequently decreasing in the period was exhibited by total enrolment. Overall, it increased from 64.3 million in 1957 to 69.2 million in 1962. The trend of the period was also followed by secondary schools and enrolment therein. The number of secondary schools increased from 11.1 thousand in 1957 to 19.5 thousand in 1962. Total enrolment increased from 6.3 million to 7.5 million in secondary schools.[217]

'Communes and brigades founded at local level their own educational institutions according to their specific needs. Within short time factories, mines and cooperatives set up vocational or specialised schools which were often called colleges or even universities. Their predecessors were the evening schools. Workers and peasants were students and skilled workers functioned as lecturers. Aside from these there arose the "half-work/half-study" and "red and expert" universities'.[218]

2.4.7. Health

The Great Leap Forward policy combined with bad weather conditions resulted in large scale elimination of population. However, at the beginning and end the death rates per thousand were very normal, 10.80 in 1957 and 10 in 1962.[219] The in-term period witnessed the demographic disaster. State expenditure on health in this period was 2.345 million yuan which amounted to 1.02 per cent of the total state expenditure.[220]

2.4.8. Infrastructure

Despite the negative impact of Great Leap Forward on Chinese economy transport infrastructure continued to increase its network in this period. Railways network increased at 5.32 per cent annual average and total strength increased from 26.7 thousand km in 1957 to 34.6 thousand km in 1962. Highway road strength increased by 82 per cent; it increased from 254 thousand km in 1957 and 463.5 thousand km in 1962. Waterways and airways recorded increase of 12.35 and 33.50 respectively. In this period pipelines became operational for transport with only 100 km in operation.[221] Due to developments in irrigation infrastructure the irrigated area increased from 27 million hectares in 1957 to 31 million hectares in 1962 which was 32.94 per cent of the total arable area.[222] Raw coal production in 1962 reached to 180 million metric tones from 130.73 million metric tones in 1957. Crude oil production increased from 1.47 million metric tones to 6 million metric tones recording an increase of 308.16 per cent increase in the period. Production of electricity increased from 19.34 billion kilowatt-hours in 1957 to 30 billion kilowatt-hours in 1962. The production of natural gas reached to 3.27 billion cubic meters in 1962 from 0.33 billion cubic meters in 1957.[223]

'The Great Leap Forward Movement put great strain on transport facilities and as such failed to solve the problems of the transportation system. Hence in the early nineteen-sixties, the Chinese adopted a policy of consolidation, reinforcement and improvement in transport undertakings'.[224] 'The existing road system had been extended considerably. However, most of these new roads were simple country roads, poorly leveled, and neither paved nor graveled'.[225] 'Throughout the period of the Second Five-Year Plan, there was little progress in airway transport'.[226]

2.4.9. External Sector

In the Second Plan merchandise trade of China decreased from total turnover of US$ 3100 million in 1957 to US$ 2660 million in 1962. Merchandise exports were US$ 1490 million in 1962 while imports were US$ 1170 million. Trade balance recorded a surplus of US$ 320 million.[227] 'For 1950 to 1952, net foreign borrowing of mainland China amounted to some 15 per cent of fixed investment, but its position subsequently shifted to that of net capital exporter, and for the period 1950-1959 as a whole a net outflow equivalent to about one per cent of fixed investment was recorded'.[228] 'An important consequence of the shortage of agricultural supplies was a reduction of exports and an increase in imports of food, which reduced the country's ability to finance imports of raw materials and equipment for industrial sector'.[229]

2.5. The Readjustment Period: 1963-65

2.5.1. Introduction

'As Great Leap Forward economic policies were discredited by the Great Famine, leaders reverted to less radical strategies for economic development'.[230] The policies adopted, particularly centralisation of production decisions of industrial sector in the commune, lost their credibility and political apparatus looked for more relaxed policies. Mao Zedong lost ethical hold on the party due to disastrous consequences of his wild imagination and more moderate leaders assumed greater responsibilities to get the country back on track. The policy devisors launched the "readjustment" programme to redeem the loss incurred thus far. The programme turned out to be a very successful one and the economy resumed its lost position. Institutional and investment policies were aligned to utilise the existing potential of the economy rather than trying to enhance it.

The readjustment period was phase of robust growth in the pre-reform China. After a disaster of unimaginable proportions, which resulted in mass scale mortality, the steep recovery in this phase was impressive. That China was successfully able to realign its economy for better was in itself a daunting challenge in 1960-61. On the other hand, however, these years of rapid growth represented nothing more than recoveries from the economic disaster of "The Year of Great Leap Forward".[231]

2.5.2. Macroeconomic Indicators

GDP in the readjustment period following the failure of Great Leap Forward increased considerably. It increased form $271381 million to $398061 million dollars: an increase of 46.67 per cent in the period at an annual average compound growth rate of 13.62.[232] In 1965, primary sector contributed 52.20 per cent of GDP while secondary and tertiary sectors contributed 24.34 per cent and 23.45 per cent respectively. Thus both primary and tertiary sectors recorded a decrease of 3.35 and 0.97 percentage points respectively in their contribution to GDP; industrial sector's contribution increased by 4.33 percentage points. Employment-wise, primary, secondary and tertiary sectors contributed 80.95, 7.94, and 11.09 per cent respectively in 1965.[233] State investment in capital construction by sector in this period was: industry, 49.9 per cent; construction 2.1 per cent; agriculture 17.6 per cent; transport 12.7 per cent; commerce 2.5 per cent; others 14.4 per cent.[234]

2.5.3. Institutional Changes

'A more moderate government led by president Liu Shaoqi allowed the farmers to farm on private plots of land, while the commune system still existed nominally'.[235] 'After 1962, some experiments in improving the evaluation of work points were made; nevertheless, the production team system was maintained as the basic farming institution until the household-based farming system reform was instituted in 1979'.[236] 'Both the collectives and the county governments were encouraged to develop rural industries to serve agriculture'.[237]

Towards the end of the adjustment period the ownership of industry had moved still further in the earlier direction. The output share of the state owned enterprises had reached to its peak level of 90.07 per cent in 1965. The share of collectives had decreased from 19.03 per cent in 1957 to 9.93 per cent in 1965. Individually owned industrial units and joint ventures of various form ceased to contribute anything by 1965.[238] In the case of retail market, state's share increased from 73.9 per cent of the total retail sale to 83.3 per cent in 1965. The share of collectives in the retail share in the same period declined from 19.5 per cent to 12.9 per cent. The share of individual enterprises decreased from 3.2 to 1.9 per cent and that of peasant sales to non-agrarian population from 3.3 per cent to 1.9 per cent from 1957 to 1965.[239]

2.5.4. Agriculture

In the readjustment period agriculture GDP improved quite steeply. It increased from 101283 million yuan in 1962 to 139600 million yuan in 1965 recording a total increase of 37.83 per cent at an annual average growth rate of 11.28 per cent.[240] Gross value of agricultural output by sector in 1965 exhibited the following pattern: crop farming 75.8 per cent; forestry 2 per cent; animal husbandry 14 per cent; subsidiaries 6.5 per cent; and fisheries 1.7 per cent.[241]

The policies followed in this period were very relaxed compared to those adopted in the Great Leap drive. Also climatic conditioned in this period were not unfavourable like those of preceding period. The terms of trade at the end of the period had improved to 158.7 in 1965 for which the value in 1957 was 130.4. Purchase price for farm and sideline products had increased from 146.2 in 1957 to 187.9 in 1965 while that of industrial products sold in rural areas increased from 112.1 in 1957 to 118.4 in 1965.[242] From the technological perspective the proportion of area machine ploughed increased considerably from 2.6 per cent in 1957 to 15.6 per cent in 1965; while as the use of fertilisers also improved from negligible levels in 1957 to 19.4 kg per hectare in 1965.[243]

2.5.5. Industry

After reaching its lowest ebb in 1962 industry rebounded robustly in the readjustment period. Industrial GDP increased from 36491 million yuan in 1962 to 65097 million yuan in 1965. The total industrial growth of the period was 78.39 per cent and annual average compound growth rate was 21.28 per cent.[244] Such robust growth was affected by good growth of the agricultural sector, relaxed policies adopted in industry and completion and use of hitherto incomplete industrial projected initiated with the help of Soviet experts. Although rural industries were deemphasised after the failure of the Great Leap, interest in them was revived in 1963 as part of the "walking on two legs" (simultaneous development of modern and small rural industries) strategy of development'.[245] The total fixed investment was substantially reduced from 14.56 billion yuan per year in the Great Leap period to annual seven billion yuan in the readjustment period. Of the total 21.02 billion yuan, heavy industry received 92.2 per cent and light industry only 7.8 per cent.[246] However, light industry experienced higher growth than heavy industry; growth in the former was 21.2 per cent per year while in the latter it was 14.9 per cent.[247]

2.5.6. Education

In the readjustment phase significant improvements in primary education were made. The number of schools increased from 668.3 thousand in 1962 to 1681.9 thousand in 1965. Total enrollment increased from 69.2 million in 1962 to 116.2 million in 1965. In secondary education there was a net decrease of schools from 19.5 thousand in 1962 to 18.1 thousand in 1965. Total enrollment in secondary schools increased from 7.5 million in 1962 to 9.3 million in 1965.[248] 'Educational policies shifted toward an emphasis on expertise, and concerns with educational quality led to the closing of the substandard minban and other schools, particularly in rural areas'.[249]

2.5.7. Health

The death rate per thousand decreased marginally in this period from 10 per thousand in 1962 to 9.6 per thousand in 1965. However, in 1963 and 1964 it was higher at 10.1 and 11.5 respectively.[250] State expenditure on health in this period was 1.884 million yuan which was 1.56 per cent of the total state expenditure.[251] Despite many achievements from 1949, 'the health care system in China served only a very small proportion of the population, largely concentrated in big cities. Almost two-thirds of the doctors lived and worked in urban areas. ... .Health facilities were vastly superior in urban areas, which cornered the bulk of the allocation for the health facilities'.[252]

2.5.8. Infrastructure

In the readjustment period growth of transport infrastructure slackened. Railways increased only by 5.2 per cent with 1.70 average annual compound growth rates. Highways strength increased by only 11 per cent with 3.54 average annual growth rates. Waterways showed a negative average annual growth rate of 0.87 and decreased by 2.59 per cent in the period. There was an increase of 11.61 per cent and 300 per cent in airways and pipelines respectively.[253] Irrigated area increased from 31 to 33 million hectares from 1962 to 1965 representing 34.67 per cent of the arable area.[254] In energy sector production of raw coal increased from 180 million metric tones to 220 million metric tones with an average annual compound growth of 6.92 per cent. Crude oil production reached to 10.60 million metric tones in 1965 from six million metric tones in 1962 recording 308 per cent growth in the period. Natural gas production increased from 3.27 billion cubic meters in 1962 to 11.32 billion cubic meters in 1965. Electricity generation increased from 30 billion kilowatt-hours in 1963 to 42 billion kilowatt-hours in 1965.[255]

2.5.9. External Sector

Merchandise trade in this period increased significantly from a turnover of US$ 2660 million in 1962 to US$ 4250 million in 1965. Exports in 1965 were US$ 2230 million and imports US4 2020 million resulting in a net surplus of US$ 320 million in balance of trade.[256]

2.6. The Third Five Year Plan,1966-70: Cultural Revolution-1

2.6.1. Introduction

The Great Leap tragedy weakened Mao's hold on the party and the readjustment period brought many new faces like Liu Shaoqi with moderate persuasions to the forefront of the political apparatus. Either of these two developments, i.e., loss of political control or takeover of moderate policies was not to the likening of extremist communists. 'Mainly to regain his political power Mao initiated the Cultural Revolution in 1966'.[257] The stated purpose of the revolution was the purge of society from capitalist elements including the party. 'In August 1966 millions of youthful workers and students were mobilised into Red Guard units, as Mao's chosen instrument of political rectification'.[258]

'The Cultural Revolution represented a criticism of growing inequalities in Chinese society, particularly inequalities between the city and the countryside, and between professionalised, bureaucratic elite and the Chinese masses'.[259] Therefore, 'equalisation of economic differences between city and countryside remained an operative goal, with vigorous efforts undertaken to provide machinery, fertiliser, and construction materials to agriculture communes and to extend educational and public health services deeper into rural areas'.[260]

The process of the struggle for power during the Cultural Revolution had led to a fragmentation of political power, both among central leaders in Peking and between Peking and the provinces'.[261] 'Cultural Revolution was destructive above all of the elite, in contrast to, say, the Great Leap during which it was the masses who suffered most'.[262] 'The initial targets of the Cultural Revolution were the party leaders and cadres at different levels. ... By the winter of 1966-67 the attack was widened to include the factories and enterprises, and "poor" and "lower-middle" peasants were instructed to carry on similar "revolutionary activities" on the farms'.[263] 'Initially, the economy was isolated from disruptive effects from the Cultural

Revolution, but once the workers became active participants, serious disruptions in transportation and production soon followed'.[264]

The Cultural Revolution was a unique phenomenon for many reasons: in terms of its motivation, instruments and impact. The twin motives of power and ultra-leftist persuasion made the cadres, like Red Guards, as interested in seeking their objective as the leaders of Cultural Revolution. The instrument of mass mobilisation gave a strong momentum that even leaders like Liu Shaoqi—once at the helm of affairs—were helpless to resist the movement. Though its effects were discursive for the economy of China, however, its impact was not as wide and deep as that of the Great Leap Forward. The reason for it being that Cultural Revolution was more a political process than an economic one, and secondly, the conscious efforts were made for the rural economy to develop.

2.6.2. *Macroeconomic Variables*

GDP in the Third Plan increased from $398061 million in 1965 to $517301 million in 1970. This adds up to a net increase of 29.95 per cent over the period at an annual average compound growth rate of 5.38 per cent.[265] In 1970, the primary sector contributed 46.91 per cent, secondary sector 31.69 per cent, and tertiary sector 21.39 per cent of GDP. From 1965 it means a decrease of 5.29 and 2.06 percentage points in the contribution of primary and tertiary sectors respectively to GDP, while as contribution of secondary sector to GDP increased by 7.35 percentage points in this period. Employment contribution of primary, secondary and tertiary sector in 1970 was 80.39, 9.48 and 10.12 per cent respectively.[266] State investment in capital construction by sector in this period was: industry 55.5 per cent; construction 1.8 per cent; agriculture 10.7 per cent; transport 15.4 per cent; commerce 2.2 per cent; and; othe. 14.4 per cent.[267]

2.6.3. *Institutional Change*

The official figures are not available for the period because of Cultural Revolution. However, there seems to have been a slow retreat from earlier policies of magnifying state role in industry. This is borne by the later statistics. However state played a still dominant role in the retail market. On the whole the ownership pattern did not change at any perceptible level in this period. In the industries production the collectives seem to have been strengthened without any space for individual and joint ventures. In the retail market collectives seem to have been losing ground to the state. Same was the case of individuals. 'The cultural revolution witnessed the elimination of the piece-rate system, bonus and premiums, etc., a cut in the salary levels of the highest paid personnel, and a general watering down of the emphasis on material incentives and self-interest'.[268]

2.6.4. Agriculture

Agricultural growth in the Third Plan was very moderate. Agricultural GDP increased from 139600 million yuan in 1965 to 163016 million yuan in 1970. Total growth over the period was just 16.77 per cent with average annual compound growth rate equal to 3.14 per cent.[269] The reason for this slackened growth was the disruption caused by Cultural Revolution. Gross value of agricultural output by sector in 1970 exhibited the following pattern: crop farming 74.7 per cent ; forestry 2.2 per cent; animal husbandry 12.9 per cent; subsidiaries 8.7 per cent; and fisheries 1.5 per cent.[270] Agricultural tax as percentage of national agricultural output decreased from 6.7 per cent in 1961 to 6.0 per cent in 1970.[271]

2.6.5. Industry

In comparison to agriculture, industry grew at better pace in the period. Industrial GDP increased from 65097 million yuan in 1965 to 110140 million yuan in 1970. Therefore, total industrial growth in the period was 69.19 per cent with average annual compound growth rate of 11.09 per cent.[272] Total industrial fixed investment increased in this period to an annual average of 10.38 billion yuan against 7 billion yuan in the previous period. Of the 54.15 billion yuan fixed investment for the Third Plan heavy industry was allotted a share of 92.1 per cent and light industry received 7.9 per cent.[273] Due to disruptive effects of Cultural Revolution both the light and heavy industry experienced slower growth rates than the readjustment period.

2.6.6. Education

In the Cultural Revolution there was a net decrease in the number of schools and enrollment in the primary education. The number of schools decreased from 1681 thousand in 1965 to 961.1 thousand in 1970. Total enrollment decreased from 116.2 million in 1965 to 105.3 million in 1970. The case of secondary education, however, follows the opposite trend in the period. Though official data for 1966 to 1971 for the number of schools is not available, however, the number of schools increased from 18.1 thousand in 1965 to 93 thousand in 1972. Total secondary enrollment increased from 9.3 million in 1965 to 26.4 million in 1970.[274]

'Nowhere (was) the impact of the Cultural Revolution more marked than in higher education'.[275] 'For three or four years, most colleges and universities held no regular classes, and since they began opening again in 1969, they have operated at limited capacity, enrolling small classes, and tentatively experimenting with new procedures'.[276] 'While educational quality certainly suffered greatly during the Cultural Revolution, the policies of this period appear to have been effective in promoting mass education among underserved groups including rural population'.[277]

At the higher level, education system ceased to function and universities were closed'.[278] 'Still, it is obvious that advanced research continued, and progress was made in several lines. Examples include: the successful testing of hydrogen bomb; reported development of intermediate range ballistic missiles; production of the MIG-21 jet fighter; and great expansion of production of trucks and tractors'.[279] 'In 1966, Mao Zedong pushed a radical decree through the party's central committee proclaiming the start of a new educational era in which political recommendation and class background were the primary means of determining progress through the education system'.[280]

'The cultural revolution had three basic objectives in reforming the educational system. In terms of the content of education, the first objective was to intensify ideological education so as to raise the "political consciousness" of students. The second objective was to integrate theory and practice in the educational process in order to make education more responsive to the immediate production needs of the country. In terms of the scope of the educational system, the third objective was to popularise education, especially in the rural areas of China'.[281] From 1968, educated urban youth were sent to villages and far off areas to work in fields and develop industry and other infrastructure.

2.6.7. Health

'Since the Cultural Revolution, the health system in China has been completely revolutionised. The urban and elite bias which characterised it in the earlier has yielded place to a rural bias. Relatively greater resources of material and manpower have been made available to rural areas'.[282] Death rate per thousand decreased continuously from 9.6 in 1965 to 7.6 in 1970.[283] State expenditure on health in the first part of the Cultural Revolution was 3.835 million yuan amounting to 1.52 per cent of the total state expenditure.[284]

2.6.8. Infrastructure

In the Third Five Year Plan, transport infrastructure exhibited increasing trend in railways, highways, airways and pipelines but recorded a decline in waterways transport infrastructure. Railways increased from 36.4 thousand km in 1965 to 41 thousand km in 1970 recording an overall increase of 12.63 per cent and average annual compound growth of 2.40 per cent. Highways increased by 23.75 per cent in this period; from 514.5 thousand km in 1965 to 736.7 thousand km in 1970. Airways increased marginally by 3 per cent in the period while pipelines increased from 400 km in 1965 to 1200 km in 1970, an increase of 200 per cent. As opposite to these positive trends waterways again recorded a decline of 5.89 per cent. Waterways strength declined from 157.7 thousand km to

148.4 thousand km from 1965 to 1970.[285] Developments in irrigation infrastructure led to an increase of irrigated area from 33 million hectares in 1965 to 38 million in 1970, increasing the irrigated area to 38.80 per cent of arable land.[286] Energy infrastructure continued to improve in the period. Raw coal production increased from 220 million metric tones in 1965 to 300 million metric tones in 1970 recording an overall growth of 36.36 per cent in the period. Crude oil production recorded an overall increase of 149 per cent in the period increasing from 10.6 million metric tones in 1965 to 26.4 million metric tones in 1970. Natural gas production increased from 11.32 billion cubic meters in 1965 to 16 billion cubic meters in 1970. Electricity generation increased from 42 billion kilowatt-hours in 1965 to 60 billion kilowatt-hours in 1970.[287]

2.6.9. External Sector

Merchandise trade in 1970 recorded a total turnover of US$ 4590 million, an increase of just eight per cent over the 1965 turnover. China in this period also recorded deficit in its trade balance. Exports in 1970 valued US$ 2260 million while imports US$ 2330 million thus resulting in a trade deficit of US$ 70 million.[288]

2.7. The Fourth Five Year Plan, 1971-75: Cultural Revolution-2

2.7.1. Introduction

Much of the rigour and enthusiasm with which Cultural Revolution had been initiated and followed in the previous plan had faded away before the introduction of the Fourth Five Year Plan. Therefore, Cultural Revolution in its original intensity had ended by 1970. However, the hangover of the Revolution carried forward quite strongly even in this period. Though attempts were made to correct the extremes of the revolution but the basic policy pursued was the same. The course of events and the policy was not revised drastically in favor of post-Great Leap policies.

Since Cultural Revolution was a holistic phenomenon covering all facts of China's life, its impact was shared by different aspects of collective life. Its impact on the economy was relatively moderate, when compared to Great Leap strategy. Its political and cultural effects were relatively more pronounced, education being most significantly influenced.

'Partly because it was such a multi-dimensional event, touching people in so many ways, no established form of analysis is capable of embracing its totality. There was not one institution in the country, from the family and the school to the party and the government, which was not profoundly affected'.[289] However, two aspects rendered Cultural Revolution flexible resulting in less severe impact on the economy: the range and spectrum of human life it sought to influence and the fact that people, majority of them, were the supposed instrument of carrying it to its logical conclusion.

The former made it possible that only one aspect, like economy, does not bear the whole brunt of revolution, while as the latter made people active participants whose actions had a direct bearing on their own lives. Both these aspects brought about good moderation in the pace and depth of Cultural Revolution.

2.7.2. Macroeconomic Variables

In the Fourth Five Year Plan the GDP of the Chinese economy increased by 29.7 per cent at an annual compound growth rate of 5.34. It increased from $517301 million in 1970 to $67102 million in 1975. The contribution of primary, secondary, and tertiary sector to GDP was 42.27, 37.05 and 20.66 per cent respectively. Over the period, contribution of primary and tertiary sector to GDP decreased by 4.64 and 0.73 percentage points respectively, while industrial sector's contribution increased by 5.36 percentage points.[290] Contribution of employment by primary, secondary and tertiary sector was 76.95, 12.76, and 10.27 per cent respectively in 1975. Thus agriculture recorded a decrease of 3.44 percentage points, secondary and tertiary sector an increase of 3.28 and 0.15 percentage points respectively to employment.[291] State investment in capital construction by sector in the Fourth Five Year Plan was: industry 55.4 per cent; construction 1.6 per cent; agriculture 9.8 per cent; transport 18.0 per cent; commerce 2.9 per cent; and; others 12.3 per cent.[292]

2.7.3. Institutional Change

In the past decade there was some institutional shift in the industry which however did not allow the space to individuals and joint ventures. According to the official statistics, the role of the state was reduced in the industrial production while that of collectives increased to almost 1957 level. Output share of the state owned industries decreased from 90.07 per cent in 1965 to 81.09 per cent in 1975. Collectives produced 18.91 per cent of the total industrial output in 1975 against 9.93 per cent in 1965. Individuals and joint ventures were not allowed any space.[293] In case of the retail market the state assumed still larger role in this period, increasing steadily toward its peak level, for the entire pre-reform period, of 90.5 per cent retail share in 1978. The role of collectives in the retail market weakened still further and same was the case of individuals. Peasant sales to non-agrarian population seem to have retained their position of 1965 even at 1975.[294]

2.7.4. Agriculture

Agricultural sector maintained growth pace of the previous plan. Agricultural GDP increased from 163016 million yuan in 1970 to 190577 million yuan in 1975. This represents an overall increase of 16.90 per cent and annual average compound growth rate of 3.17 per cent.[295] This low growth over a decade implied deep policy failures and lack of appropriate incentives. Also with such low growth in agriculture the possibility of effective poverty reducing programmes diminishes substantially despite good industrial growth. Gross value of agricultural output by sector in 1976 exhibited the following pattern: crop farming 69.3 per cent; forestry 3.3 per cent; animal husbandry 13.9 per cent; subsidiaries 12 per cent; fisheries 1.5 per cent.[296]

The terms of trade for the farm and sideline products against industrial products sold in the rural areas continued to improve, though at a very slow pace, over last two plans; from 158.7 in 1965 to 185.9 in 1975.[297] Agricultural tax as percentage of national agricultural output decreased from 6 per cent in 1970 to 5 per cent in 1975.[298]

2.7.5. Industry

The industrial growth in this period slackened as compared to the previous Plan. Industrial output increased from 110140 million yuan in 1970 to 167022 million yuan in 1975. That is it increased by 51.64 per cent in the period with 8.68 per cent annual average compound growth rate.[299] Industrial fixed investment in the Fourth Plan was 97.79 billion yuan with an annual average of 19.55 billion yuan. Share of heavy industry in this investment was 89.5 per cent and that of light industry 10.5 per cent.[300]

2.7.6. Education

In this period the number of primary schools increased but did not come even closer to the 1965 maximum (1681 thousand). The number of schools increased from 961.1 thousand in 1970 to 1093 thousand in 1975. Total enrollment however crossed the earlier benchmark and increased from 105.3 million in 1970 to 150.9 million in 1975. The number of secondary schools increased from 93 thousand in 1972 to 123.5 thousand in 1975. Total enrollment increased from 26.4 million in 1970 to 44.7 million in 1975.[301] 'The first post-cultural revolution graduations took place in late 1973'.[302]

'Before the Cultural Revolution, enrollment was primarily by examination and all new students were higher middle school graduates.[303] 'Since 1972 enrollment procedures have been systematised into a four-step process: voluntary application; recommendation by the masses; approval by the local party committee; and examination by the school'.[304] 'Under this system a youth must have at least two years of "practical experience" before applying for admission, gain the backing of workers in his or her unit and the approval of the Party Committee, and finally face an examination administered by the university'.[305]

'In the wake of the cultural revolution in the mid-1960s, elementary education experienced a 10-year period of rapid and largely uncontrolled growth. ... .But the policy of "putting politics in charge," which brought about this dramatic increase in elementary schooling, was also responsible for a significant decline in the quality of schooling'.[306]

'High level, abstract research, even pure research with no immediate application, (was) not ignored in China despite the emphasis on practice. But for the most part it is undertaken in various research institutes rather than in universities'.[307]

2.7.7. Health

The average life expectancy of the period was 63.2 years. Infant mortality rate, under-five mortality rate, and maternal mortality rate in the period was 85, 120, and 55 respectively.[308] State expenditure on health in the Fourth Five Year Plan was 6.562 million yuan amounting to 1.67 per cent of total state expenditure.[309] Death rate in this period decreased marginally from 7.6 per thousand in 1970 to 7.3 per thousand in 1975.[310]

2.7.8. Infrastructure

In case of railways, highways and waterways this period followed the earlier trend. However, in case of airways and pipelines the pace of improvement was significant. Railways by increasing from 41.0 thousand km in 1970 to 46 thousand km in 1975 recorded an overall increase of 12.19 per cent. Highways increased by 23 per cent in the same period; from 636.7 thousand km in 1970 to 738 thousand km in 1975. Airways improved significantly by 107.3 per cent in this period; from 40.6 thousand in 1970 to 84.2 thousand n 1975. Pipelines recorded an increase of 341.6 per cent in the period; from 1.2 thousand km in 1970 to 5.3 thousand km in 1975. Waterways continued its declining trend and decreased by 8.62 per cent in the fourth plan; from 148.4 thousand km in 1970 to 135.6 thousand km in 1975.[311] In this plan irrigated area increased from 38 million hectares to 43 million hectares which represented 47.60 per cent of the total arable land.[312] In this period there was a substantial increase in the electricity production which increased to 108 billion kilowatt-hours 1974 from 60 billion kilowatt-hours in 1970; an average increase of 15.83 per cent per annum. Natural gas production increased from 16 billion cubic meters in 1970 to 35 billion cubic meters in 1974 representing an annual average compound growth of 21.69 per cent. Crude oil production increased from 26.40 million metric tones in 1970 to 63.6 million metric tones in 1974. Raw coal production increased from 300 to 399 million metric tones in this period of four years.[313]

2.7.9. External Sector

In the Fourth Plan China's merchandise trade increased considerably with total turnover increasing from US$ 4590 million in 1970 to

US$ 14750 million in 1975—an increase of 3.21 times from 1970 level. Exports amounted to US$ 7260 million in 1975 and imports US$ 7490 million with a resultant trade deficit of US$ 230 million.[314]

2.8. Post Revolution Period: 1976-77

2.8.1. Introduction

The period following Cultural Revolution up to reforms was a period of uncertainty. Death of Mao created a political vacuum which could have been exploited either by the extremist communists or the moderates. The arrest of the 'Gang of Four' provided space for moderates to be in charge. The two years of 1976 and 1977 represented the concluding phase of the extremist policies. There was good deal of rethinking in this period and people were ready for alternatives which served their development aspirations without being too much addicted to ideological persuasions. The extremist faction, who in 1975-76, called for increased levels of collectivisation and restriction on sideline occupations and village markets'[315], was losing ground and the moderates were steadily taking over the reins of the administration.

'The traumatic year for China was 1976. First, in January, came the death of Premier Zhou Enlai, and later, in April, the Tian Men demonstrations (sometimes called the April 5th Movement) in support of Premier Zhou and against the policies and power of Jiang Qing (Mao's wife), Zhang Chunqiao (a deputy premier), and others in the group which would later be called the gang of four. During the summer the old veteran and acting head-of-state Zhu De died, and one of the most destructive earthquakes in history killed 240,000 people in Tangshan. Finally, in September, Chairman Mao died, and final stage in the process of leadership succession began. In October, the gang of four was arrested, and during the following year, a new leadership was formed around Hua Guofeng, supposedly chosen by Mao to succeed him; Ye Jianying, a veteran cadre closely linked to the military; and Deng Xiaoping, once again rehabilitated to become the mainstay of the new regime'.[316]

The political leadership of China was facing enormous crisis in this period to begin with. However, general criticism to continuation of Cultural Revolution policies, death of Mao and succession of moderates to the national political stage in 1977 proved later a watershed in Chinese economic history. The economy in the period was in serious difficulties facing almost stagnation and prospects of better life were dwindling seriously. Despite many achievements in the previous decades absolute poverty—income and non-income—was high. As majority of the people depended on primary sector there was no immediate hope for them without a massive revival of the sector. However, the sector was facing negative growth rates in these years. The policies pursued in the previous decade had arrived at the saturation level and were not yielding positive results. The dominance of the moderates at the center was the result of the failure of these policies. China at the end of 1977 was left with no option but to exercise new and better policies that would bring momentum to its stagnant economy.

2.8.2. Macroeconomic Indicators

In this period of two years GDP increased from $671024 million in 1975 to $699016 million in 1977. This is a cumulative increase of 4.17 per cent at an annual compound growth rate of 2.06 per cent.[317] In 1977 agriculture contributed 38.98 while secondary and tertiary sector contributed 39.21 and 21.80 per cent respectively. Compared to previous plan there was a decrease of 3.29, an increase of 2.16 and 1.14 percentage points in primary, secondary and tertiary sector respectively. In 1977, of the total employment primary sector contributed 74.46 per cent while secondary and tertiary sector contributed 14.19 and 11.24 per cent respectively. Over these two years primary sectors share in employment decreased by 2.49 percentage points while secondary and tertiary sector recorded an increase of 1.43 and 0.97 percentage points respectively.[318]

2.8.3. Institutional Change

The earlier policies of decreasing the role of state in industrial production were continued in this period as well. Collectives were given more space in the economy. However there was no space for individuals and joint ventures. In case of the retail market the share of the state reached its peak in 1978. Its share in the total retail share was 90.5 per cent. Therefore the period witnessed a slight increase of the role of the state in this period. The role of collectives decreased in the retail market.[319]

2.8.4. Agriculture

Agriculture sector performance deteriorated still further and in these two years exhibited negative growth. Agricultural production decreased from 190577 million yuan in 1975 to 183071 million yuan in 1977. This represents a net decrease of 3.93 per cent and average annual compound growth rate of 1.98 per cent.[320] The policy and institutional structure of agriculture had already crossed the saturation point and resulted in negative growth. Gross value of the agricultural output in 1977 exhibited the following pattern: crop farming 67.5 per cent; forestry 3.25 per cent; animal husbandry 13.1 per cent; subsidiaries 14.1 per cent; and; fisheries 1.5 per cent.[321]

Over the last more than decade China's agriculture witnessed technological transformation of sizeable magnitude. Proportion of machine ploughed area increased from 15.6 per cent in 1965 to 40.7 per cent in

1978, while as use of chemical fertilisers per hectare increased from 19.4 kg in 1965 to 89 kg in 1978.[322]

2.8.5. Industry

Industry in these two years continued decelerating and was following the decreasing trend of agriculture though the rates per se were not negative. Industrial GDP increased from 167022 million yuan in 1975 to 184135 million yuan in 1977. Therefore, it recorded an increase of 10.24 per cent in two years with average annual growth rate of 4.99 per cent.[323] After the Great Leap disaster it was the lowest growth that the sector had witnessed. Annual average fixed investment for the period was 23.31 billion yuan which was the highest level of average fixed investment in the pre-reform period. The light industry received a share of 10.6 per cent and heavy industry 89.4 per cent.[324] The average growth rate of light industry after the readjustment period, till reforms in 1978, was 8.3 per cent while heavy industry in the same period experienced a growth rate of 11.8 per cent.[325]

2.8.6. Education

In these two years both the number of schools as well as enrollment in primary education decreased in absolute terms. The number of schools decreased from 1093.3 thousand in 1975 to 982 thousand in 1977. Total enrollment declined from 150.9 million in 1975 to 146.2 million in 1977. The number of secondary schools however increased significantly from 123.5 thousand in 1975 to 201.3 thousand in 1977. Total enrollment followed the same trend and increased from 44.7 million to 67.8 million.[326]

2.8.7. Health

The health status of the Chinese people by the end of the 1970s was remarkably good for a country at China's income level. The gains, although partly the result of sound health policies, were largely due to rising income and what that means for diet, education, access to clean water and sanitation, and the like.... . Life expectancy reached to about 65 years in 1977.[327] Death rate per thousand in these two years decreased from 7.36 in 1975 to 6.91 in 1977.[328] State expenditure on health was about 2.17 per cent of the total state expenditure.[329]

2.8.8. Infrastructure

In these two years growth rates of transport infrastructure were low compared to the Fourth Plan. Railways increased at an average annual growth rate of 1.50—the lowest in the pre-reform era. Highways increased from 783.6 thousand km in 1975 to 855.6 thousand km in 1977, thus recording an overall growth of 9.18 per cent. Airways in operation increased by an overall 56.88 per cent in these two years; from 84.2 thousand km in 1975 to 132.1 thousand km in 1977. From the readjustment period pipelines recorded the lowest growth in this period. It increased at an annual rate of 12.43 per cent; from 5.3 thousand km in 1975 to 6.7 thousand km in 1977.[330]

2.8.9. External Sector

Merchandise trade in these two years increased slighily to a turnover of US$ 14800 million in 1977. Exports amounted to US$ 7590 million in 1977 and imports US$ 7210 million leaving a surplus of US$ 380 million dollars.[331]

2.9. Comments

At the time of its proclamation, China was a deeply backward country with a very poor socio-economic profile. Till the reforms in 1978 policy fluctuated quite widely and so were the results on the economic and social aspects of collective life. The euphoria with revolution and experimentation had deep consequences; negative and positive, immediate and long-lasting. The overall moderate growth of the GDP in the period partly indicated failure of the policies targeted for speedy economic transformation of the economy. Simultaneously, developments in other fields like infrastructure, education and health were impressive and could crucially affect efforts to take-off to better growth.

From the institutional side there was almost a complete transformation of the economy in this period. From the promulgation of the Agrarian Reform Law in 1950, aimed at large-scale ownership change of land, through mutual aid teams, elementary cooperatives, advanced cooperatives and finally the communes the socialist transformation of the agriculture was essentially completed in 1958. In case of industry, the same formulae of step wise transformation to sate and collective ownership through direct and indirect means were adopted. The policy of utilisation, restriction and transformation was adopted. The retail market was also subjected to same procedure in which the role of state and collectives took over the role of private individual commercial units.

Some relaxations to the role of state and collective ownership and management were institutionalised at times, like after Great Leap disaster, but were exceptional and marginal enough to be ignored. The only substantial change that occurred after the Great Leap debacle was that the production brigade rather than the commune was instituted as the basic operative unit of planning, production and accounting. The role of the commune was that of administration and coordination.

The annual growth rate of GDP in the period was just 4.51 per cent. Agriculture growth in the period was quite low at about 2 per cent. Comparatively industry growth rate of 10.61 per cent was much better. Growth rate of services sector was 5.21 per cent for the period.

Apart from the fact that the government inherited a backward agricultural system, the priority to the industry at the cost of agriculture made it always lag behind. The main focus of the First Plan was development of heavy industry, for which agriculture was to play a subservient role. However, after the First Plan there was growing recognition that developments in primary sector have very strong implications on the industry and social indicators. Therefore some efforts at providing different inputs to agriculture were contemplated more seriously. These included providing increasing number of tractors for ploughing land, chemical fertilisers, better irrigation, better seeds and handier farm tools. However, notwithstanding these positive developments, the institutional side of agriculture was so weak that towards the end of the pre-reform period it experienced negative growth rates.

Industry, to begin with, was no better than agriculture. However, constant emphasis through the Plans led to robust growth rates. In particular the heavy industry was focus of attention and investment. The consequences of Great Leaf failure were relatively less severe on industry as these were on agriculture. Efforts to develop small-scale labour intensive industry as part of "walking on two legs" also led the spread of industry to rural areas. An overall high rate of industry led to development of a good industrial sector by the end of the period. However, lack of coordination and overinvestment led to severe bottlenecks at times and towards the concluding part of the concerned period the growth rates of industry were the lowest after Great Leap disaster.

Complementarities of industry and agriculture were perceptible in the period, particularly in the Great Leap Forward phase when the failure of agriculture led to severe plunge of industry into lowest growth rates of the period. Though the main focus of the planners was heavy industry even after the Great Leap debacle, its limits of success were determined by health of the agriculture sector. The impact of agriculture was both on the demand and supply side: on the supply side it provided raw materials for different sectors of industry and on the demand side the demand for industrial products was limited by the performance of the agriculture. Industry provided the tools, tractors and infrastructure for agricultural development as well as supply of fertilisers. Also it was the main source of demand for raw material.

In the pre-reform period, China made good progress in the field of health and literacy and education. Life expectancy at birth increased from a mere 35 years in 1949 to almost 65 years in 1978. Death rate more than halved during the period from 13 in 1954 to 6 in 1979. Both infant and child mortality rates reduced substantially. For the world's most populated country with underdeveloped health care facilities meeting this challenge was an enormous success. To achieve this China used very ingenious methods like bare feet doctors and oriented its healthcare system toward rural areas particularly during and after Cultural Revolution. Similar achievements were made in the field of literacy and education. Though education faced enormous political interference which at times resulted in closing of schools and universities, however achievements in the field of mass literacy were very great. The spread of basic literacy to all sections of society, adult and young, women and labourer, remote and urban was again done quite ingeniously through communes, factory schools, and adult literacy campaigns apart from the formal schools. Research through specialised research institutions resulted in good scientific and technological development.

One of the crucial areas that China did not neglect in spite of policy oscillations was infrastructure. Despite bad impact of many policy alternatives on the economy, it continuously kept upgrading its infrastructure. Transportation infrastructure including railways, highways, waterways, airways and pipelines was expanded considerably. Energy sector including raw coal, crude oil, natural gas, and electricity also recorded good improvement. Improvement in irrigation system doubled the irrigated area in the period. All this placed Chinese economy at an advantageous position despite many bottlenecks.

The important lessons from pre-reform China with important policy implications is that despite moderate growth rates in the period, significant improvements were made in certain social indicators like health and education. Four features of the planning seem to have played important role in the Chinese case which explains the possibility of low growth and high social development. The first is the Chinese perspective of human resource development. The thrust on pragmatism in education to serve the immediate needs of the economy made educated people direct contributors to economy rather than white collar experts. Education and training was more about solving ones immediate problems rather than abstract intellectual exercises.

Second, continuous efforts at infrastructure and energy development provided an important universal input to the production process as well as basic facility for general public use which effectively improved the standard of living. Third, decentralised planning with respectable autonomy meant decentralised governance which made planners and officials more receptive to local problems and local solutions with little lags in implementation. Fourth, pro-rural policies, particularly in Rehabilitation Period (land distribution) and Cultural Revolution improved the effective asset base and health and education facilities for common masses resulting in improvements in social indicators.

Despite many achievements to its credit, the pre-reform period was not successful to bring poverty rate down to a reasonable level. China at the end of this period had enormous poverty particularly in rural areas. Per capita income was very low and other indicators of development like infant mortality, child mortality, literacy, maternal mortality, sanitation, and infrastructure and energy per capita, were considerably unfavourable by the developed country standards.

References

1. The Opium Wars, also called Anglo-Chinese Wars, lasted from 1839-42 and 1856-60. The immediate cause was British smuggling of opium from British India into China in violation of China's drug laws. China was defeated in both the wars and forced to sign the treaties of Nanjing and Tianjin. Theses became popular as the *Unequal Treaties* for heavy trade concessions and annexation of Hong Kong to Britain.
2. Ness, Peter Van, (Ed). 1989. *Market Reforms in Socialist Societies: Comparing China and Hungary*. Lynne Rienner Publishers London, p. 149.
3. Kraus, Willy. 1982. *Economic Development and Social Change in the Peoples Republic of China*. Springer-Verlag New York Inc., p. 1.
4. Pritchard, Earl H. 1951. The Political Ferment in China 1911-1951, *Annals of The American Academy of Political and Social Science*, Vol. 227, Report on China, pp.1-12.
5. Chow, Gregory C. 2007.*China's Economic Transformation*. Blackwell Publishing, USA.
6. Kraus, Willy. 1982. *op. cit.* p. 4.
7. *Ibid.,* p. 326.
8. *Ibid.,* p. 326.
9. *Ibid.,* p. 326.
10. Clark, Colin. 1965. Economic Growth in Communist China. *China quarterly*, No. 21 in Ajit Kumar Singh (1985) *Economic Development and Inequalities in Communist China 1949-1975*, Himalaya Publishing House Bombay.
11. Maddison, Angus. *The World Economy: A Millennial Perspective*. OECD/ Academic Foundation 2006.
12. United Nations. 1956. *World Ecoromic Report, 1955*. United Nations Department of Economic Affairs, New York.
13. Singh, Ajit Kumar. 1985. *Economic Development and Inequalities in Communist China 1949-1975*. Himalaya Publishing House Bombay, p.19.
14. *Ibid.,* p. 21.
15. *Ibid.,* p. 157.

16. *Ibid.*, pp. 20-21.
17. United Nations. 1956. *World Economic Report 1955. op. cit.*
18. Kraus, Willy. 1982. *op. cit.*
19. State Statistical Bureau. 1960. *Ten Great Years*. Foreign Exchange Press, Peking. p. 196.
20. Singh, Ajit Kumar. 1985. *op. cit.*, p. 22.
21. Kraus, Willy. 1982. *op. cit.*
22. Singh, Ajit Kumar. 1985. *op. cit.*
23. Comtois, Claude. 1990. Transport and Territorial Development in China 1949-1985. *Modern Asian Studies*, Vol. 24, No. 4 (Oct): 784.
24. Kraus, Willy. 1982. *op. cit.* p. 345.
25. *Ibid.*, p. 346.
26. Kraus, Willy. 1982. *op. cit.* p. 348.
27. Comtois, Claude. 1990. *op. cit.*
28. Kraus, Willy. 1982. *op. cit.* This is supported by both the Chinese and US government estimates.
29. United Nations. 1953. *World Economic Report 1951-52*. United Nations Department of Economic Affairs, New York.
30. Schwartz, Benjamin. 1973. China's Development Experience 1949-72. *Proceedings of the Academy of Political Science*, Vol. 31, No. 1, China's Development Experience. (Mar.).
31. Ho, Toby. 2000. Managing Risk: The Suppression of Private Entrepreneurs in China in the 1950s. *Risk Management*, Vol. 2, No. 2, pp. 29-38.
32. Cohen, Paul A. 1988. The Post-Mao Reforms In Historical Perspective. *The Journal of Asian Studies,* Vol. 47, No. 3. (Aug.): pp. 524-25.
33. All the statistics are official unless cited otherwise.
34. After several necessary adjustments to the Ren (1997) International-comparison-programme-type estimate of comparative Chinese/US real expenditure levels for 1986, Maddison has developed a comparative basis to the 1990 multilateral Geary-Khamis purchasing power parities. For details see Maddison, *Chinese Economic Development in the Long Run: 960-2030* AD.
35. SSB and Hitotsubash University Institute of Economic Research. 1997. *The Historical National Accounts of the People's Republic of China, 1952-1990*, Tokyo, in Maddison, Angus. *op. cit.* 2007, pp. 159-160.
36. *State Statistical Bureau. 1993.* China Statistical Yearbook, *pp. 100-101 in Maddison, Angus. op. cit.* 2007.
37. Datta, K.L. *Central Planning: A Case Study of China*. Concept Publishing Company, New Delhi, p. 33.
38. United Nations. 1952. *World Economic Report, 1950-51*. United Nations Department of Economic Affairs, New York, April.
39. Datta, K.L. *op. cit.*

40. Lloyd, G Reynolds. 1975. China as a Less Developed Economy, *The American Economic Review*, Vol. 65, No. 3 (Jun.).
41. United Nations. 1953. *World Economic Report, 1951-52. op. cit.*
42. Thomas, S. B. 1956. Communist China's Agrarian Policy: 1954-56. *Pacific Affairs,* Vol. 29, No. 2 (Jun.).
43. United Nations. 1956. *World Economic Report, 1955. op. cit.*
44. Chow, Gregory C. 2007. *op. cit.*
45. Datta, K.L. op. cit p. 4.
46. Kraus, Willy. 1982. *op. cit.*
47. United Nations. 1951. *Economic Report, 1949-50.* United Nations Department World of Economic Affairs, New York, April 19.
48. Kraus, Willy. 1982. *op. cit.* pp. 335-336.
49. United Nations. 1958. *World Economic Report, 1957.* United Nations Department of Economic Affairs, New York.
50. Hsu, Robert C. 1982. Agricultural Financial Polices in China, 1949-80. *Asian Surve*y, Vol. 22, No. 7 (Jul.,).
51. Griffin, Keith, (Ed.). 1984. *op. cit.* (Official figures)
52. United Nations. 1958. *World Economic Report, 1957. op. cit.*
53. Kraus, Willy. 1982. *op. cit.* p.46.
54. United Nations. 1956. *World Economic Report 1955. op. cit.*
55. *Ibid.*
56. Griffin, Keith (Ed.). 1984. *op. cit.*
57. Moorsteen, Richard. 1959. Economic Prospects for Communist China. *World Politics*, Vol. 11, No. 2 (Jan.).
58. *Ministry of Education, Department of Planning (Ed.),* Achievement of Education in China: Statistics, 1949-1983 *(Beijing: People's Education Press, 1985),* pp. 184-85, 197, 213, 220; *State Education Commission (Ed.),* Achievement of Education in China: Statistics, 1986-1990 *(Beijing: People's Education Press, 1991),* pp. 59, 66, 74, 76; *in Emily Hannum. Political Change and the Urban-Rural Gap in Basic Education in China, 1949-1990.* Comparative Education Review, Vol. 43, No. 2 (May, 1999), p. 196.
59. Maddison, Angus. 2007. *Chinese Economic Performance in the Long Run.* Development Center Studies OECD.
60. Stites, Regie and Semali, Ladislaus. 1991. Adult Literacy for Social Equality or Economic Growth? Changing Agendas for Mass Literacy in China and Tanzania. *Comparative Education Review*, Vol. 35, No. 1, Feb.
61. Kraus, Willy. 1982. *op. cit.*
62. Maddison, Angus. 2007. *op. cit.*
63. Jowett, A. J. 1984. The Growth of Chinas Population: 1949-1982 (With Special Reference to the Demographic Disaster of 1960-61). *The Geographical Journal,* Vol. 150, No. 2 (Jul.,).

64. Comtois, Claude. 1990. *op. cit.* pp. 786-87.

65. Fan, Shenggen, Zhang, Linxiu, and Zhang, Xiaobo. 2002. *Growth, Inequality, and Poverty in Rural China; the Role of Public Investments.* Research Report 125 International Food Policy Research Institute Washington, D.C.

66. Smil, Vaclav. Energy in China: Achievements and Prospects. *The China Quarterly*, No. 65 (Mar., 1976): pp. 62-63.

67. Maddison, Angus. 2007. *op. cit.*

68. United Nations. 1956. *World Economic Report 1955. op. cit.*

69. United Nations. 1961. *World Economic Report, 1960.* United Nations Department of Economic Affairs, New York.

70. United Nations. 1962. *World Economic Report, 1961.* United Nations Department of Economic Affairs, New York.

71. *Ibid.*

72. Brodsgaard, Kjeld Erik. 1983. Pragmatic change: Readjustment and Reform in the Chinese Economy, 1953-1981, part 1. *Modern China*, Vol. 9, No. 1 (Jan.).

73. Kirby, E. Stuart. 1958. Economic Planning and Policy in Communist China. *International Affairs* (Royal Institute of International Affairs 1944-), Vol. 34, No. 2, (Apr.,).

74. Singh, Ajit Kumar. 1985. *op. cit.* p. 69.

75. Kraus, Willy. 1982. *op. cit.*

76. Moorsteen, Richard. 1959. op. cit.

77. Singh, Ajit Kumar. 1985. *op. cit.* p. 69.

78. Lippit, Victor D. 1975. The Great Leap Forward Reconsidered. *Modern China*, Vol. 1. (Jan.).

79. Shabad, Theodore. 1955. Communist China's Five Year Plan. *Far Eastern Survey* Vol. 24, No. 12 (Dec.).

80. Schwartz, Benjamin. 1973. pp. 17-26.

81. Woo, Wing Thye and Bao, Shuming. 2003. *China: Case Study on Human Development Progress towards the Millennium Development Goals at the Sub-National Level.* Background Paper for HDR UNDP: pp. 7-8.

82. Rosse, Robert M. 1954. The Working of Communist China's Five Year Plan. *Pacific Affairs*, Vol. 27, No. 1 (Mar.).

83. *Ibid.*

84. Schurmann, Franz. 1963. Economic Policy and Political Power in Communist China. *Annals of American Academy of Political and Social Science*, Vol. 349, Communist China and the Soviet Bloc (Sep.).

85. Brodsgaard, Kjeld Erik. 1983. *op. cit.*

86. Moorsteen, Richard. 1959. *op. cit.*

87. Moorsteen, Richard. 1959. *op. cit.*

88. *Ibid.*

89. United Nations. 1957. *World Economic Report 1956.* United Nations Department of Economic Affairs, New York.

90. Shih, Joseph Anderson. 1972. *op. cit.*
91. Moorsteen, Richard. 1959. *op. cit.*
92. United Nations. 1959. *World Economic Report 1958*. United Nations Department of Economic Affairs, New York.
93. Brodsgaard, Kjeld Erik. 1983. *op. cit.*
94. Kirby, E. Stuart. 1958. *op. cit.*
95. United Nations. 1958. *World Economic Report, 1957*. United Nations Department of Economic Affairs, New York.
96. *Ibid.*
97. *Ibid.*
98. Kirby, E. Stuart. 1958. *op. cit.*
99. The figures in dollars used are invariably in 1990 international dollars, except where mentioned.
100. SSB and Hitotsubash University Institute of Economic Research. 1997. *op. cit.* In Maddison, Angus. *op. cit.* 2007, pp. 159-160.
101. *State Statistical Bureau. 1993.* China Statistical Yearbook, pp. 100-101 in Maddison, Angus. *op. cit.* 2007, p. 170.
102. Powell, Simon G. 1992. *op. cit.*
103. Kraus, Willy. 1982. *op. cit.*
104. Hisa, Ronald. 1954. The Chinese Economy under Communist Planning. *Pacific Affairs*, Vol. 27, No. 2 (Jun.).
105. Thomas S. B. 1956. Communist Chinas Agricultural Policy, 1954-56. *Pacific Affairs*, Vol. 29, No. 2 (Jan.).
106. Chow, Gregory C. 2007. *op. cit.* p. 26.
107. Lin, Justin Yifu. 1990. *op. cit.*
108. Moorsteen, Richard. 1959. *op. cit.*
109. Hollister, William W. 1964. *op. cit.*
110. Kraus, Willy. 1982. *op. cit.*
111. Thomas, S. B. 1956. Communist Chinas Agricultural Policy, 1954-56. *Pacific Affairs*, Vol. 29, No. 2 (Jan.).
112. Ishikawa, Shigeru. 1983. China's Economic Growth Since 1949—An Assessment. *The China Quarterly*, No. 94 (Jun.): p. 260.
113. Ho, Toby. 2000. Managing Risk: The Suppression of Private Entrepreneurs in China in the 1950s. *Risk Management*, Vol. 2, No. 2, pp. 34-35.
114. Cohen, Paul A. 1988. Post-Mao Reforms in Historical Perspective. *The Journal of Asian Studies*, Vol. 47, No. 3, (Aug.): pp. 518-540.
115. Perkins, Dwight H. 1973. Plans and their Implementation in the People's Republic of China. *The American Economic Review*, Vol. 63, No 2, Papers and Proceedings of the Eighty-fifth Annual Meeting of the American Economic Association (May).
116. Wu, Yanrui. 1996. *op. cit.*

117. Powell, Simon G. 1992. *op. cit.*
118. SSB and Hitotsubash University Institute of Economic Research. 1997. *op. cit.* In Maddison, Angus. *op. cit.* 2007.
119. Hsu, Robert C. 1982. *op. cit.*
120. *Ibid.*
121. *Jingji Yanjiu Ziliao. 70 (May 1980) in O'Leary, Greg and Andrew Watson. The Role of Peoples Commune in Rural Development in China.* Pacific Affairs, Vol. 55, No. 4. (Winter, 1982-83).
122. Griffin, Keith (Ed.). 1984. *op. cit.* (Official figures).
123. United Nations. 1956. *World Economic Report, 1955. op. cit.* p. 106.
124. Hou, Ching-Ming. 1968. *op. cit.*
125. United Nations. 1954. *World Economic Report 1952-53.* United Nations Department of Economic Affairs, New York.
126. Brodsgaard, Kjeld Erik. 1983. Pragmatic change: Readjustment and Reform in the Chinese Economy, 1953-1981, part 1. *Modern China*, Vol. 9, No. 1 (Jan.).
127. Hsu, Robert C. 1982. Agricultural Financial Policies in China, 1949-80. *Asian Survey,* Vol. 22, No. 7 (Jul.).
128. Hisa, Ronald. 1959. China's Industrial Growth, 1953-57. *Annals of American Academy of Political and Social Science*, Vol. 321, Contemporary China and the Chinese (Jan.).
129. Hou, Ching-Ming. 1968. Sources of Agricultural Growth in Communist China. *The Journal of Asian Studies*, Vol. 27, No. 4(Aug.): pp. 734-724.
130. *Ibid.*
131. *Ibid.*
132. United Nations, 1959. *World Economic Report 1958.* United Nations Department of Economic Affairs, New York, 1959.
133. Lippit, Victor D. 1975. *op. cit.*, pp. 97-98.
134. SSB and Hitotsubash University Institute of Economic Research. 1997. *op. cit.* In Maddison, Angus. *op. cit.* 2007, pp. 159-160.
135. Lin, Cai and Li (1994: 62) Quoted by Justin Yifu Lin And Yang Yao in *Enterprise Reform in China Ownership, Transition, and Performance.* Ed. Gary H. Jefferson and Inderjit Singh. Oxford University Press/World Bank.
136. Griffin, Keith (Ed.). 1984. *op. cit.*
137. Moorsteen, Richard. 1959. *op. cit.*
138. United Nations. 1955. *World Economic Report, 1953-54.* United Nations Department of Economic Affairs, New York, pp. 47.
139. United Nations. 1956. *World Economic Report, 1955. op. cit.*
140. Moorsteen, Richard. 1959. *op. cit.*
141. Hisa, Ronald. 1959. *op. cit.*
142. Kraus, Willy. 1982. *op. cit.*

143. Schurmann, Franz. 1963. Economic Policy and Political Power in Communist China. *Annals of American Academy of Political and Social Science*, Vol. 349, Communist China and the Soviet Bloc (Sep.).
144. Brodsgaard, Kjeld Erik. 1983. *op. cit.*
145. United Nations. 1957. *World Economic Report, 1956*. United Nations Department of Economic Affairs, New York.
146. *Ibid.*, 241.
147. *China Health Yearbook*, Beijing: The Peoples Medical Publishing House, 1985, pp. 59 in *Chinas Economic Reforms: Costs and Benefits of Incrementalism.* Ed. Qimiao Fan and Peter Nolan, Macmillan.
148. Jowett, A. J. 1984. The Growth of Chinas Population, 1949-1982 (with Special Reference to the Demographic Disaster of 1960-61). *The Geographical Journal*, Vol. 150, No. 2 (Jul.).
149. *China Human Development Report 2007/08. Access for All: Basic Public Services for 1.3 Billion People*. China Translation and Publishing Corporation, 2008.
150. *Ministry of Education, Department of Planning (Ed.),* Achievement of Education in China: Statistics, 1949-1983 (Beijing: People's Education Press, 1985), pp. 184-85, 197, 213, 220; State Education Commission (Ed.), Achievement of Education in China: Statistics, 1986-1990 (Beijing: People's Education Press, 1991), pp. 59, 66, 74, 76; *in Emily Hannum. Political Change and the Urban-Rural Gap in Basic Education in China, 1949-1990.* Comparative Education Review, Vol. 43, No. 2 (May, 1999).
151. Chow, Gregory C. 2007. *op. cit.*
152. Shih, Joseph Anderson. 1972. Science and Technology in China. *Asian Survey*, Vol. 12, No. 8 (Aug.).
153. Comtois, Claude. 1990. *op. cit.* pp
154. Fan, Shenggen and Zhang, Linxiu and Zhang, Xiaobo. 2002. *op. cit.* pp. 21.
155. Smil, Vaclav. 1976. Energy in China: Achievements and Prospects. *The China Quarterly*, No. 65 (Mar.): pp. 62-63.
156. Comtois, Claude. 1990. *op. cit.* pp. 787-788.
157. *Ibid.*
158. Hou, Ching-Ming. 1968. *op. cit.*
159. Maddison, Angus. 2007. *op. cit.*
160. Moorsteen, Richard. 1959. *op. cit.*
161. United Nations. 1958. *World Economic Report, 1957*. United Nations Department of Economic Affairs, New York.
162. United Nations. 1959. *World Economic Report, 1958*. United Nations Department of Economic Affairs, New York.
163. Fan, Liang-Shing. 1973. The Economy and Foreign Trade of China. *Law and Contemporary Problems*, Vol. 38, No. 2, Trade with China (Summer-Autumn,).

164. Li, Choh-Ming. 1964. Chinas Industrial Development, 1958-63. *The China Quarterly*, No. 17 (Jan-Mar.).
165. Ishikawa, Shigeru. 1983. *op. cit.*
166. Perkins, Dwight H. 1973. Plans and their Implementation in the People's Republic of China. *The American Economic Review*, Vol. 63, No 2, Papers and Proceedings of the Eighty-fifth Annual Meeting of the American Economic Association (May,).
167. Shih, Joseph Anderson. 1972. *op. cit.*
168. Hollister, William W. 1964. Capital Formation in Communist China. *The China Quarterly*, No. 17 (Jan.-Mar.).
169. United Nations. 1959. *op. cit.*
170. Schurmann, Franz. 1963. *op. cit.*
171. Joseph, William A. 1986. A Tragedy of Good Intentions: Post-Mao Views of the Great Leap Forward. *Modern China*, Vol. 12 No. 4 (Oct.,).
172. Schwartz, Benjamin. 1973. China's Development Experience 1949-72. *Proceedings of the Academy of Political Science*, Vol. 31, No. 1, China's Development Experience, (Mar.).
173. United Nations. 1962. *op. cit.*
174. Fan, Liang-Shing. 1973. *op. cit.*
175. SSB and Hitotsubash University Institute of Economic Research. 1997. *op. cit.* in Maddison, Angus. *op. cit.* 2007, pp. 159-160.
176. *State Statistical Bureau. 1993.* China Statistical Yearbook, pp. 100-101, *in Maddison, Angus. op. cit.* 2007.
177. Powell, Simon G. 1992. In China: From Communes to Commodity Economy 1978-1990. *Studies on East Asia,* Manchester University Press.
178. United Nations. 1963. *World Economic Report, 1961*: Current Economic Developments. United Nations Department of Economic Affairs New York.
179. *Ibid.*
180. Brodsgaard, Kjeld Erik. Pragmatic change: Readjustment and Reform in the Chinese Economy, 1953-1981, part 1. *Modern China*, Vol. 9, No. 1 (Jan., 1983).
181. United Nations. 1959. *World Economic Report, 1958*. United Nations Department of Economic Affairs, New York.
182. Lin, Justin Yifu. 1990. Collectivisation and China's Agricultural Crisis In 1959-1961. *The Journal of Political Economy*, Vol. 98, No. 6 (Dec.): pp. 1234.
183. United Nations. 1959. *op. cit.*
184. Kraus, Willy. 1982. *op. cit.* pp. 128-29.
185. Li, Choh-Ming. 1964. *op. cit.*
186. Perkins, Dwight K. 1964. *op. cit.*
187. Schurmann, Franz. 1963. *op. cit.*

188. Brodsgaard, Kjeld Erik. 1983. *op. cit.*
189. *Ibid.*
190. Perkins, Dwight K. 1964. *op. cit.*
191. Perkins, Dwight K. 1964. *op. cit.*
192. Lin, Justin Yifu. 1990. *op. cit.*
193. SSB and Hitotsubash University Institute of Economic Research. 1997. *op. cit.* in Maddison, Angus. *op. cit.* 2007, pp. 159-160.
194. Hsu, Robert C. 1982. Agricultural Financial Polices in China, 1949-80. *Asian Survey*, Vol. 22, No. 7 (Jul.,).
195. United Nations. 1959. *op. cit.*
196. *Ibid.*, p. 290.
197. United Nations. 1959. *op. cit.*, pp. 261-62.
198. Chow, Gregory C. 2007. *op. cit.*
199. United Nations. 1962. *op. cit.*
200. United Nations, 1962. *World Economic Report 1961*. United Nations Department of Economic Affairs New York, 1962.
201. Perkins, Dwight H. 1973. *op. cit.*
202. Hsu, Robert C. 1982. *op. cit.*
203. *Ibid.*
204. United Nations. 1963. *World Economic Report, 1961: Current Economic Developments*. United Nations Department of Economic Affairs New York.
205. United Nations. 1961. *World Economic Report, 1960*. United Nations Department of Economic Affairs, New York.
206. SSB and Hitotsubash University Institute of Economic Research. 1997. *op. cit.* in Maddison, Angus. *op. cit.* 2007.
207. Lin, Cai and Li (1994: 62) Quoted By Justin Yifu Lin and Yang Yao in *Enterprise Reform in China Ownership, Transition, and Performance*. Ed. Gary H. Jefferson and Inderjit Singh. Oxford University Press/World Bank.
208. Griffin, Keith (Ed.) 1984. *Institutional Reform and Economic Development in the Chinese Countryside*. The Macmillan Press Ltd.
209. Hollister, William W. 1964. *op. cit.*
210. Perkins, Dwight H. 1973. Plans and their Implementation in the People's Republic of China. *The American Economic Review*, Vol. 63, No. 2, Papers and Proceedings of the Eighty-fifth Annual Meeting of the American Economic Association (May,).
211. United Nations. 1963. *World Economic Report, 1962*: Current Economic Developments. United Nations Department of Economic Affairs, New York.
212. United Nations. 1959. *op. cit.*, p. 266.
213. *Ibid.*, p. 271.
214. Li, Choh-Ming. 1964. Chinas Industrial Development, 1958-63. *The China Quarterly*, No. 17 (Jan-Mar.), p. 20.
215. United Nations. 1962. *op. cit.*
216. Brodsgaard, Kjeld Erik. 1983. *op. cit.*

217. *Ministry of Education, Department of Planning (Ed.),* Achievement of Education in China: Statistics, 1949-1983 (Beijing: People's Education Press, 1985), pp. 184-85, 197, 213, 220; *State Education Commission (Ed.),* Achievement of Education in China: Statistics, 1986-1990 (Beijing: People's Education Press, 1991), pp. 59, 66, 74, 76; *in Emily Hannum. Political Change and the Urban-Rural Gap in Basic Education in China, 1949-1990.* Comparative Education Review, Vol. 43, No. 2 (May, 1999).
218. Kraus, Willy. 1982. *op. cit.*
219. Jowett A. J. 1984. Growth of Chinas Population, 1949-1982 (with Special Reference to the Demographic Disaster of 1960-61). *The Geographical Journal*, Vol. 150, No. 2 (Jul.): p. 158.
220. *China Health Yearbook*, Beijing. 1985. The Peoples Medical Publishing House.
221. Comtois, Claude. 1990. Transport and Territorial Development in China 1949-1985. *Modern Asian Studies*, Vol. 24, No. 4 (Oct.): pp. 786-87.
222. Fan, Shenggen, Linxiu Zhang, Xiaobo Zhang. 2002. *op. cit.*
223. Smil, Vaclav. 1976. *op. cit.* pp. 62-63.
224. Comtois, Claude. 1990. *op. cit.*
225. Kraus, Willy. 1982. *op. cit.*
226. Comtois, Claude. 1990. *op. cit.*
227. Maddison, Angus. 2007. *op. cit.*
228. United Nations. 1962. *op. cit.*
229. *Ibid.*
230. Hannum, Emily. 1999. Political Change and the Rural-Urban Gap in Education in China, 1949-90. *Comparative Education Review*, Vol. 43, No. 2 (May).
231. Clark, Colin. 1976. Economic Development in Communist China. *The Journal of Political Economy*, Vol. 84, No. 2 (Apr.).
232. SSB and Hitotsubash University Institute of Economic Research. 1997. *op. cit.* in Maddison, Angus. *op. cit.* 2007, pp. 159-160.
233. *State Statistical Bureau. 1993.* China Statistical Yearbook, pp. 100-101 *in Maddison, Angus. op. cit.* 2007.
234. Powell, Simon G. 1992. *op. cit.*
235. Chow, Gregory C. 2007. *op. cit.*
236. Lin, Justin Yifu. 1990. *op. cit.*
237. Hsu, Robert C. 1982. Agricultural Financial Policies in China, 1949-80. *Asian Survey*, Vol. 22, No. 7 (Jul.).
238. *Wu, Yanrui. 1996.* Productive Performance of Chinese Enterprises: An Empirical Study. *Macmillan Press Ltd.*
239. Powell, Simon G. 1992. *op. cit.*
240. SSB and Hitotsubash University Institute of Economic Research. 1997. *op. cit.* in Maddison, Angus. *op. cit.* 2007, pp. 159-160.

241. *Jingji Yanjiu Ziliao, 70 (May 1980), Quoted By, Greg O'Leary; Andrew Watson. The Role of Peoples Commune in Rural Development in China.* Pacific Affairs, Vol. 55, No. 4. (Winter, 1982-83).
242. Hsu, Robert C. 1982. *op. cit.*
243. Griffin, Keith (Ed.) 1984. *Institutional Reform and Economic Development in the Chinese Countryside*. The Macmillan Press Ltd.
244. Maddison, Angus. 2007. *op. cit.* pp. 159-160.
245. Hsu, Robert C. 1982. *op. cit.*
246. Lin, Cai and Li (1994: 62) Quoted By Justin Yifu Lin And Yang Yao in *Enterprise Reform In China Ownership, Transition, and Performance*. Ed. Gary H. Jefferson and Inderjit Singh. Oxford University Press/World Bank.
247. Griffin, Keith (Ed.) 1984. *op. cit.*
248. *Ministry of Education, Department of Planning (Ed.),* Achievement of Education in China: Statistics, 1949-1983 (Beijing: People's Education Press, 1985), pp. 184-85, 197, 213, 220; *State Education Commission (Ed.),* Achievement of Education in China: Statistics, 1986-1990 (Beijing: People's Education Press, 1991), pp. 59, 66, 74, 76; *in Emily Hannum. Political Change and the Urban-Rural Gap in Basic Education in China, 1949-1990.* Comparative Education Review, Vol. 43, No. 2 (May, 1999).
249. Hannum, Emily. 1999. *op. cit.*
250. Jowett, A. J. 1984. Growth of Chinas Population, 1949-1982 (with Special Reference to the Demographic Disaster of 1960-61). *The Geographical Journal*, Vol. 150, No. 2 (Jul.).
251. *China Health Yearbook*, Beijing: the Peoples Medical Publishing House, 1985, p. 59 cited by Chinas Economic Reforms: Costs and Benefits of Incrementalism. Ed. Qimiao Fan and Peter Nolan, Macmillan, p. 205.
252. Singh, Ajit Kumar. 1985. *op. cit.*
253. Comtois, Claude. 1990. *op. cit.* pp. 786-87.
254. Fan, Shenggen, Linxiu Zhang and Xiaobo Zhang. 2002. *op. cit.*
255. Smil, Vaclav. 1976. *op. cit.* pp. 62-63.
256. Maddison, Angus. 2007. *op. cit.*
257. Chow Gregory C. 2007. *op. cit.*
258. Field, Robert Michael. 1986. The Performance of Industry during the Cultural Revolution: Second Thoughts. *The China Quarterly*, No. 108 (Dec.).
259. Harding, Harry. 1972. Political Trends in China since Cultural Revolution. *Annals of the American Academy of Political and Social Science*, Vol. 402, China in the World Today (Jul.,).
260. *Ibid.*
261. *Ibid.*
262. Pye, Lucian W. 1986. Reassessing the Cultural Revolution. *The China Quarterly* No. 108 (Dec.,).
263. Wu, Yuan-Li. 1968. Ideology and Cultural Revolution. *Asian Survey*, Vol. 8, No. 3 (Mar.): pp. 230-31.

264. Durenberger, Robert F. 1972. Radical Ideology and Economic Development in China: The Cultural Revolution and its Impact on the Economy. *Asian Survey*, Vol. 12, No. 12, The Cultural Revolution and its Aftermath (Dec.,).
265. SSB and Hitotsubash University Institute of Economic Research. 1997. *op. cit.* in Maddison, Angus. *op. cit.* 2007, pp. 159-160.
266. *State Statistical Bureau. 1993.* China Statistical Yearbook, pp. 100-101 *in Maddison, Angus. op. cit.* 2007.
267. Powell, Simon G. 1992. *op. cit.*
268. Singh, Ajit Kumar. 1985. *op. cit.*
269. SSB and Hitotsubash University Institute of Economic Research. 1997. *op. cit.* in Maddison, Angus. *op. cit.* 2007, pp. 159-160.
270. *Jingji Yanjiu Ziliao, 70 (May 1980) Quoted By, Greg O'Leary; Andrew Watson. The Role of Peoples Commune in Rural Development in China.* Pacific Affairs, Vol. 55, No. 4. (Winter, 1982-83).
271. Hsu, Robert C. 1982. *op. cit.*
272. SSB and Hitotsubash University Institute of Economic Research. 1997. *op. cit.* in Maddison, Angus. *op. cit.* 2007, pp. 159-160.
273. Lin, Cai and Li (1994: 62) Quoted By Justin Yifu Lin And Yang Yao in *Enterprise Reform In China Ownership, Transition, and Performance*. Ed. Gary H. Jefferson and Inderjit Singh. Oxford University Press/World Bank.
274. *Ministry of Education, Department of Planning (Ed.),* Achievement of Education in China: Statistics, 1949-1983 (Beijing: People's Education Press, 1985), pp. 184-85, 197, 213, 220; *State Education Commission (Ed.),* Achievement of Education in China: Statistics, 1986-1990 (Beijing: People's Education Press, 1991), pp. 59, 66, 74, 76; *in Emily Hannum. Political Change and the Urban-Rural Gap in Basic Education in China, 1949-1990.* Comparative Education Review, Vol. 43, No. 2 (May, 1999).
275. Teiwes, Frederick C. 1974. Before and After the Cultural Revolution. *The China Quarterly*, No. 58 (Apr.-Jun.).
276. Seybolt, Peter J. 1974. Higher Education in China. *Higher Education*, Vol. 3, No. 3 (Aug.).
277. Hannum, Emily. 1999. *op. cit.*
278. Chow, Gregory C. 2007. *op. cit.* p. 28.
279. Shih, Joseph Anderson. 1972. *op. cit.*
280. Hannum, Emily. 1999. *op. cit.*
281. Wang, Robert S. 1975. Educational Reforms and the Cultural Revolution: The Chinese Evaluation Process. *Asian Survey,* Vol. 15., No. 9 (Sep.).
282. Singh, Ajit Kumar. 1985. *op. cit.*
283. Jowett, A. J. 1984. *op. cit.*
284. *China Health Yearbook*, Beijing: the Peoples Medical Publishing House, 1985, pp. 59 cited by Chinas Economic Reforms: Costs and Benefits of Incrementalism. Ed. Qimiao Fan and Peter Nolan, Macmillan,
285. Comtois, Claude. 1990. *op. cit.* pp 786-87.

286. Shenggen Fan, Linxiu Zhang, Xiaobo Zhang. 2002. *Growth, Inequality, and Poverty in Rural China: the Role of Public Investments*. Research Report 125 International Food Policy Research Institute Washington, D.C.
287. Smil, Vaciav. 1976. *op. cit*. pp. 62-63.
288. Maddison, Angus. 2007. *op. cit*.
289. Pye, Lucian W. 1986. *op. cit*.
290. SSB and Hitotsubash University Institute of Economic Research. 1997. *op. cit.* in Maddison, Angus. *op. cit.* 2007, pp. 159-160.
291. *State Statistical Bureau. 1993.* China Statistical Yearbook, pp. 100-101 *in Maddison, Angus. op. cit.* 2007.
292. Powell, Simon G. 1992. *op. cit*.
293. Wu, Yanrui. 1996. *op. cit*.
294. Powell, Simon G. 1992. *op. cit*.
295. SSB and Hitotsubash University Institute of Economic Research. 1997. *op. cit.* in Maddison, Angus. *op. cit.* 2007, pp. 159-160.
296. *Jingji Yanjiu Ziliao, 70 (May 1980) Quoted By, Greg O'Leary; Andrew Watson. The Role of Peoples Commune in Rural Development in China.* Pacific Affairs, Vol. 55, No. 4. (Winter, 1982-83).
297. Hsu, Robert C. 1982. *op. cit*.
298. *Ibid.*
299. SSB and Hitotsubash University Institute of Economic Research. 1997. *op. cit.* in Maddison, Angus. *op. cit.* 2007, pp. 159-160.
300. Lin, Cai and Li (1994: 62) Quoted By Justin Yifu Lin And Yang Yao in *Enterprise Reform In China Ownership, Transition, and Performance*. Ed. Gary H. Jefferson and Inderjit Singh. Oxford University Press/World Bank.
301. *Ministry of Education, Department of Planning (Ed.),* Achievement of Education in China: Statistics, 1949-1983 (Beijing: People's Education Press, 1985), pp. 184-85, 197, 213, 220; *State Education Commission (Ed.),* Achievement of Education in China: Statistics, 1986-1990 (Beijing: People's Education Press, 1991), pp. 59, 66, 74, 76; *in Emily Hannum. Political Change and the Urban-Rural Gap in Basic Education in China, 1949-1990.* Comparative Education Review, Vol. 43, No. 2 (May, 1999).
302. Teiwes, Frederick C. 1974. *op. cit*.
303. *Ibid.*, p. 340.
304. Seybolt, Peter J. 1974. *op. cit*.
305. Teiwes, Frederick C. 1974. *op. cit*.
306. Hawkins, John N. and Regie Stites. 1991. Strengthening the Future's Foundation: Elementary Education Reform in the People's Republic of China. *The Elementary School Journal*, Vol. 92, No. 1, Special Issue: International Education (Sep.).
307. Seybolt, J. 1974. *op. cit*.
308. United Nations. 2002. *Human Development Report 2002: Deepening Democracy in Fragmented World*. United Nations Development Programme.

309. *China Health Yearbook,* 1985. Beijing: the Peoples Medical Publishing House, pp. 59 in Chinas Economic Reforms: Costs and Benefits of Incrementalism. Ed. Qimiao Fan and Peter Nolan, Macmillan.
310. Jowett, A. J. 1984. *op. cit.*
311. Comtois, Claude. 1990. *op. cit.* pp. 786-87.
312. Shenggen Fan, Linxiu Zhang, Xiaobo Zhang. 2002. *op. cit.*
313. Smil, Vaclav. 1976. *op. cit.* pp. 62-63.
314. Maddison, Angus. 2007. *op. cit.*
315. Domes, Jurgen. 1982. New Policies in the Communes: Notes on Rural Societal Structure in China, 1976-81. *The Journal of Asian Studies*, Vol. 41, No. 2 (Feb.).
316. Ness, Peter Van (Ed.). 1989. *Market Reforms in Socialist Societies: Comparing China and Hungary*. Lynne Rienner Publishers London.
317. SSB and Hitotsubash University Institute of Economic Research. 1997. *op. cit.* in Maddison, Angus. *op. cit.* 2007, pp. 159-160.
318. *State Statistical Bureau. 1993.* China Statistical Yearbook, pp. 100-101 *in Maddison, Angus. op. cit.* 2007.
319. Powell, Simon G. 1992. *op. cit.*
320. SSB and Hitotsubash University Institute of Economic Research. 1997. *op. cit.* in Maddison, Angus. *op. cit.* 2007, pp. 159-160.
321. *Jingji Yanjiu Ziliao, 70 (May 1980) in Greg O'Leary; Andrew Watson. The Role of Peoples Commune in Rural Development in China.* Pacific Affairs, Vol. 55, No. 4. (Winter, 1982-83), pp. 604.
322. Griffin, Keith (Ed.) 1984. *op. cit.*
323. SSB and Hitotsubash University Institute of Economic Research. 1997. *op. cit.* in Maddison, Angus. *op. cit.* 2007, pp. 159-160.
324. Lin, Cai and Li (1994: 62) in Justin Yifu Lin And Yang Yao in *Enterprise Reform In China Ownership, Transition, and Performance*. Ed. Gary H. Jefferson and Inderjit Singh. Oxford University Press/World Bank.
325. Griffin, Keith (Ed.) 1984. *op. cit.*
326. *Ministry of Education, Department of Planning (Ed.),* Achievement of Education in China: Statistics, 1949-1983 (Beijing: People's Education Press, 1985), pp. 184-85, 197, 213, 220; *State Education Commission (Ed.),* Achievement of Education in China: Statistics, 1986-1990 *(Beijing: People's Education Press, 1991),* pp. 59, 66, 74, 76; *in Emily Hannum. Political Change and the Urban-Rural Gap in Basic Education in China, 1949-1990.* Comparative Education Review, Vol. 43, No. 2 (May, 1999).
327. UNDP/China Development Research Foundation. 2005. *China Human Development Report 2005: Development with Equity*. China Translation and Publication Corporation. *Human Development Report 2002: Deepening Democracy in Fragmented World*. UNDP.

328. Jowett, A. J. 1984. Growth of Chinas Population, 1949-1982 (with Special Reference to the Demographic Disaster of 1960-61). *The Geographical Journal*, Vol. 150, No. 2 (July).
329. *China Health Yearbook*, 1985. Beijing, the Peoples Medical Publishing House, pp. 59 in Chinas Economic Reforms: Costs and Benefits of Incrementalism. Ed. Qimiao Fan and Peter Nolan, Macmillan.
330. Comtois, Claude. 1990. *op. cit.* pp. 786-87.
331. Maddison, Angus. 2007. *op. cit.*

3

Post-reform Period

3.1 Introduction

In the past three decades China was the fastest growing economy of the world. This was the result of a stream of reforms initiated in late 1970s. Towards the concluding phase of the pre-reform period, policy effectiveness had reached its saturation level and economy was undergoing a state of complete stagnation. The introduction of reforms changed the whole scenario, brought significant vitality to the economy which approximated 10 per cent annual growth since then. The reforms started with relaxing the rules of central planning and progressed continuously to affect a more market oriented economy. Performance of the economy not only resulted from the reforms but also lead to further reforms. Thus reforms and economic performance were mutually reinforcing continuum of processes.

Impressive economic performance of the past three decades was largely a result of the institutional changes in the economy juxtaposed with appropriate macroeconomic policies. The former considerably changed the property right regime which furnished the necessary incentives for hard work, efficiency, and investment. In the initial phase this was particularly important for the primary sector. Macroeconomic policies were regularly adjusted to maintain a high growth propensity while taking care of the stability. Variations in the growth performance reveal that the policy was more effective in the former than the latter. Sustained growth over this duration was maintained by constantly enhancing the supply side potential while maintaining a growing demand. The former notably involved building infrastructure and the latter the institutionalisation of the role of domestic and international market.

The reforms in China had many peculiar characteristics which were not shared by other transition economies and which had a large impact on the outcome of the reforms. The process of liberalisation, privatisation and globalisation played a significant role in laying the foundations of a vibrant economy. However, China's approach in this regard was quite different from other centrally planned economies, either communist or otherwise, which opted to switch over to market based or capitalist arrangement.

Before a quantitative assessment and presentation of the macroeconomic dimensions and performance, a brief discussion of the qualitative aspects of the reform process is inevitable.

3.2 Nature of Reforms

By way of reforms, Russia and other transition economies went for an abrupt departure from their command economy arrangement and made considerable institutional changes within a very short span of time. As a result of this *shock-therapy approach* most of these nations faced economic crisis of enormous magnitude and dimensions. Following reforms, these destabilised economies experienced deterioration in their socio-economic indicators, like growth of GDP, per capita income, external balance, employment, poverty reduction etc.

China's transition process differed from most of the centrally planned economies essentially in three respects. The first concerned the pace and magnitude with which reforms were pursued. The second related to the overall strategy. The third difference is associated with the initial focus and base of the reforms.

China's transition process to market was very slow as compared to other economies. The process of reforms followed many stages and institutional changes aimed at liberalisation were quite gradual. Markets were opened gradually by deregulating the prices in a phased manner. Firms were privatised only after going through many intermediate stages between administrative planning and market mechanism. Gradualism was also followed in other sectors of the economy as well.

Secondly, the reforms were initiated at the very gross root level by the local leaders, following a bottom-up approach, and were not designed by the central authorities. These were based on experimentation rather than on a preconceived blueprint. Reforms were initiated in certain experimental places and extended, if successful, to rest of the country. Furthermore, the scope of flexibility was left intact to accommodate the variation in regions.

Both the gradualist approach and bottom-up strategy helped the economy to overcome the limitations of and possible damage from the policies designed at the central level on a preconceived blueprint, devised on many occasions by experts less aware about local conditions. It also allowed the flexibility to move to alternative policy options without any measurable loss and without changing the larger objectives of the reforms. In fact, contrary to other transition economies, the design was decided by the course of the economy and not by any specific model of transition. As a result, China's success of three decades was without complete privatisation, liberalisation and democratisation, supposed to be vital for efficiency of the economy.

The third important dimension of the reforms was their rural focus and agriculture origin. The reforms in China started in rural sector or the primary sector. Prior to the reforms, the agricultural and allied sectors' production was determined by the different hierarchies of the government, which farmers were required to comply. There was no scope for private production which had heavy disincentive impact on the performance of the sector. Therefore, in the late 1970s, agriculture production experienced negative growth rate.

The main reform in this sector was the introduction of the *Household Responsibility System*. According to this, land was allotted to the farmers on long term basis for the production of crops. However, farmers were not given the ownership of the land. They were allowed to produce crops as they would find convenient and profitable and sell it in the private market, but subject to the fulfillment of certain quota requirements. The quota requirement was later dropped and agriculture sector became market driven. Furthermore, the farmers were allowed to retain or accumulate wealth through this process which was not allowed before reforms. Later other sectors of the economy were brought into the ambit of the reforms.

Being an underdeveloped and agrarian economy, most of the people in China lived in rural areas and depended on the primary sector. According to World Development Report 2008, even as late as 2003-05, rural population as a percentage of total population was 60.5 per cent. Therefore, the peculiar type of privatisation that China adopted, despite absence of ownership of land, resulted in the increase of the farmers' economic standards by substantial amount. China's impressive record of poverty reduction in the earlier phase is largely attributed to the reforms in the rural sector of the economy.

3.3 Institutional/Historical Change in the Post-reform Period

3.3.1. Introduction

The decision to shift the focus of policy from class struggle to economic development in the Third Plenum of the Eleventh Chinese Communist Party Congress held in December 1978 is the beginning of the reform period. This shift demonstrated move toward pragmatism in policies evaluated in terms of economic outcomes. Market was recognised as an indispensable tool for economic development because it ensured efficiency in resource allocation and provided incentive for entrepreneurs. However, to avoid the costs of sudden and significant departure from the complete planning to market economy, planning was still to play a dominant role. Therefore, the idea of "planning as a principal part and market as a supplementary part"[1] dominated the policy discourse in the initial phase.

The first stage of the economic reform program (1978–84) focused mainly on the rural sector. The government aimed at expanding agricultural production, diversifying the rural economy, improving the rural standard of living, and promoting new technologies. Several important experimental initiatives were intended to enlarge enterprise autonomy and to expand the role of financial incentives within the traditional economic structure. These measures included introduction of profit retention for enterprises and performance-related bonuses for workers. They also permitted state enterprises to produce more than what the state plan mandated. Furthermore, the enterprises involved in exportation were allowed to retain part of their foreign exchange earnings for use at their own discretion.[2]

In the second stage (1984-1986), the emphasis shifted to formalising the financial obligations of the state enterprises to the government and exposing these enterprises to market influences. In 1983, a tax on profits replaced profit remittances to the government. A year later, the government allowed state enterprises to sell output in excess of plan quotas at negotiated prices and to plan their production accordingly, thereby establishing a dual-track price system.[3] During the third stage (1987-1992), a contractual system was formalised and widely adopted. It clarified the authority and responsibilities of enterprise managers. The last stage (1993-present) attempted to introduce the modern corporate system to the state enterprises.[4]

3.3.2. Dual-Track Price Reform

'China's price reform began in late 1978, implementing a dual-track system in which the share of production subject to state procurement continuously declined, and more and more prices were subjected to varying degrees of market guidance. The reforms began in agriculture and spread slowly, first to consumer goods and later to intermediate goods industries. In each case a free market developed in parallel with the controlled market, where state supply was kept unchanged at the (lower) price. Supply in the free market track grew rapidly, so its share in total output rose steadily. Meanwhile the planned price was raised incrementally until it approached the market price. By the end of the 1994 this dual track system had led to the decontrol of more than 90 per cent of retail prices and between 80 to 90 per cent of agricultural and intermediate product prices, all of which are now market determined.'[5]

3.3.3. Agriculture

Commune leaders in some regions recognised that they could fulfill their output quotas for delivery to the government procurement departments by reorganising the commune internally following and improving upon practices in the 1950's. In essence, each farm household was assigned a piece of land and was held responsible for delivering a given quantity of a certain product to satisfy the procurement requirement. After fulfilling the delivery quota, the farm household would be free to keep products for its own consumption or sale in the market at market prices. This "responsibility system" is similar to private farming in a market economy, with each farm household leasing its land and paying the delivery quota as rent. This system was officially adopted by the Fourth Plenum of the Eleventh Central Committee of the Communist Party in September 1979.[6]

However, the Party started to actively promote the household responsibility system only in early 1982. By the end of 1982, 80 per cent of households adopted the household responsibility system nationwide, and by 1984, almost all of them had done so. By that time, the contracts of the household responsibility system were all extended to a period of 15 years.[7]

3.3.4. Industry

In October 1978, Sichuan Province selected six enterprises to undertake an experiment with the theme of ***expanding enterprise autonomy*** and introducing profit retention. In the following year about 100 industrial enterprises in Sichuan joined the experiment. In July 1979, the central government issued five documents to promote Sichuan's experience nationwide, but still on an experimental basis. By 1980, about 60 per cent of SOEs (in terms of output value) joined the experiments and obtained some limited autonomy. In April 1981, the first document implementing the "**Economic Responsibility System**" in industrial SOEs was issued.[8]

In 1984 commune and brigade enterprises became **township and village enterprises** (TVEs). Townships and villages reappeared as administrative units. The old commune administration was replaced by separate township governments, township party committees and economic association committees. The government also sanctioned the development of private rural enterprise.[9] In the same year, the government officially permitted the *market track* alongside with the planned track for industrial goods, but with a restriction of price ranges of the market track to be within 20 per cent of the planned price. In February 1985, such a restriction was removed and the **"dual-track"** was formally in place.[10]

But the autonomy was rather limited and profit retention was negotiated on an annual basis. To address the financial incentive problem, starting in

January 1987 the government promoted the "**contract responsibility system**" (*chengbao zhi*). Under this system, contracts lasted for at least three years to avoid annual bargaining. Compared with the previous rounds of enterprise reform, the contract responsibility system delegated more control rights to managers. But its main focus was the increased retained profits to enterprises and an adoption of various ways for dividing cash flow between the enterprises and the government. The contract responsibility system had a political advantage because it had something for all parties-enterprises, local governments, and the central government. By the end of 1987, about 80 per cent of large and medium-sized SOEs adopted the contract responsibility system, and by 1989, almost all SOEs adopted it which continued through 1993.[11]

Rural Township and Village Enterprises (TVEs) actually had their roots in earlier programmes of rural industrialisation, but in 1984 local governments were given permission to pursue a TVE-based development strategy to help absorb labour released by the agricultural reforms. Together with growth of urban collectives, the explosion of TVE activity resulted in progressive diversification of industrial ownership away from the SOEs in favor of the so-called non-state sector, although most of this was still within the public domain.[12]

Privatisation of SOEs and layoffs of state workers began to occur on a large scale in 1995. Privatisation of SOEs started initially by local governments as experiments in a few provinces, such as Shandong, Guangdong, and Sichuan.[13] By the end of 1996, up to 70 per cent of small SOEs had been privatised in pioneering provinces and about half were privatised in many other provinces. In addition, about ten million workers from SOEs and urban collectives were laid off by the end of 1996, and an additional 11.5 million workers were laid off in 1997. This layoff itself was a big achievement for reform: never before had state employees been laid off and state enterprises closed down.[14]

The Fifteenth Party Congress held in September 1997 made a major breakthrough on ownership issues: State ownership was downgraded to a "pillar of the economy" and private ownership was elevated to an "important component of the economy."[15]

3.3.5. Fiscal Policy

In 1980, a major fiscal reform concerning the central and provincial relationship began, known as the "***fiscal contracting system***" under the nickname of "eating from separate kitchens" (*fenzao chifan*). Under the fiscal contracting system, budgetary revenue income was first divided between "central fixed revenue," all of which was remitted to the center, and "local revenue," which was shared. The contractual sharing rates varied from province to province.[16] The fiscal contracting system greatly strengthened the link between local revenue and expenditures, and it gave local governments at all levels the authority and incentives to develop their local economies because the revenue they were able to retain was linked closely to local economic prosperity. Fiscal decentralisation has created multiple power centers, and it has had a lasting economic and political effect on other reforms.[17]

In 1986, central government entered into a "**fiscal contract responsibility system**" with local governments, which had in fact long been responsible for the collection of almost all taxes.[18] On January 1, 1994, China introduced major tax and fiscal reforms more aligned with international practices. This reform introduced a clear distinction between national and local taxes and established a national tax bureau and local tax bureaus, each responsible for its own tax collections.[19]

The direct role of government in financing and controlling development was dramatically reduced. The previous budgetary contribution to state enterprises disappeared and was replaced by large net subsidies. Most taxes are now collected by local authorities which have a strong financial interest in the profitability of the enterprises they run. They grant large tax relief and tax incentives for such activity, which is the second major reason for the proportionate fall in government revenue. The proportionate size of government revenue in 2005 had fallen to 17 per cent of GDP compared with 31 per cent in 1978.[20]

3.3.6. Banking

Until 1978, the Peoples' Bank of China was part of the Ministry of Finance and controlled virtually all financial and insurance transactions. Since 1978, the government has created a much more complex banking structure. The Peoples' Bank is now a Central Bank; there are four big commercial banks, a larger number of investment banks, insurance companies, and urban and rural credit co-operatives. The banks attract customers by paying interest on deposits and expanding the branch network.

In 1981 *bond* issues were initiated. The Shanghai Stock Exchange had been closed in 1949 and was reopened in 1990; the new Shenzhen Exchange followed in 1991. In 2006, the Shanghai Exchange, together with the Hong Kong Exchange (whose capitalisation is bigger), launched a successful IPO and sold $21.9 billion shares in the Industrial and Commercial Bank of China[21].

Before 1993, 70 per cent of the Central Bank's loans to State Banks were made by the Central Bank's local branches, which were heavily influenced by the local governments. In 1993, the Central Bank centralised its operation after Vice Premier Zhu Rongji became its governor. Since then, its local branches have been supervised only by the headquarters of the Central Bank, not as before also by the local government of the region in which they reside. In 1995 China passed the "Central Bank Law" to give the Central Bank the mandate for monetary policy independent of the local government.[22]

Before 1998, the state always bailed out troubled financial institutions, but for the first time in 1998, several high profile banks and investment companies, such as Hainan Development Bank and Guangdong International Trust Investment Company, closed down or went bankrupt. This signaled an important change on the part of the government: it was determined to discipline state financial institutions.[23]

3.3.7. Legal Institutions

In late 1978, the Chinese leadership stressed the importance of law for its modernisation drive at the historic Third Plenum of the Eleventh Central Committee of the Chinese Communist Party. Since then, the Chinese government has embarked on one of history's most concerted programmes of constructing a socialist legal system with Chinese characteristics.[24] In December 1982, a new state constitution was adopted by the National People's Congress (NPC) codifying the new state policy on socialist democracy and the rule of law.[25]

In 1988, the Constitution was amended, permitting private firms to operate as a complement to the socialist economy. Previously, only individual firms employing no more than seven people as assistants were allowed to operate."[26] Private ownership and the rule of law were incorporated into the Chinese Constitution in March 1999. An amendment of Article 11 of the Constitution places private businesses on an equal footing with the public sector by changing the original clause "the private economy is a supplement to public ownership" to "the non-public sector, including individual and private businesses, is an important component of the socialist market economy" (*China Daily*, March 16, 1999).[27] On February 28, 2001, the NPC Standing Committee ratified the International Covenant on Economic, Social and Cultural Rights (ICESCR) with a statement that serves as a reservation to Article 8 regarding workers' rights to organise independent trade union federations.[28]

The government started to take initial steps towards labour market reform in mid 1980s. The Tentative Stipulations on the SOEs Labour Contract System, which was later replaced by the Labour Law (1994), the Regulation on Unemployment Insurance for State Enterprise Employees (1991) and Resolution on Unified Enterprise Basic Pension Insurance System (1997), was promulgated in July 1986 to terminate the permanent employment system in SOEs. However, the new labour contract system applied only to new employees, until the first half of the 1990s, most employees in the SOEs still retained lifetime employment (Wu Zengxian, Europe-Asia Studies, Nov. 1997).[29]

China has undertaken considerable reforms in its legal system. Between 1978 and early 2008, the NPC passed 229 new national-level laws and revised the constitution four times. Only eight pre-1978 laws are still in use. Some of the most important laws establish contract and property rights, the right of citizens to sue the government in cases of abuse or loss as a result of government action, tax obligations, the rights and responsibilities of company managers and shareholders, the legislative process, and the rights of workers.[30]

3.3.8. Foreign Trade

From the early 1970s onwards, opportunities to participate in world trade on a more or less normal basis improved steadily. In 1971, China joined the United Nations. In 1972 relations with Japan and the United States were transformed by state visits, leading to diplomatic recognition by Japan and *de facto* recognition by the United States. The US embargo on trade and transactions was lifted. China joined the IMF and the World Bank in 1980, and the Asian Development Bank in 1986. In 1982, it was granted observer status in the GATT and began a long battle for membership of the World Trade Organisation (WTO) which ended successfully in 2001.[31]

In 1979 the government decided to expand foreign trade and welcome foreign investment. Two provinces, Guangdong and Fujian, were in the forefront of the opening up process because of their geographic location. In July 1979, the central government decided that the two provinces should pursue reform "one step ahead" of other regions in the country, allowing them to adopt "special policies" (*teshu zhengce*) and to implement "flexible measures" (*linghuo cuoshi*). In 1980 China established four special economic zones: Shenzhen, Zhuhai, and Shantou adjacent to Hong Kong in Guangdong Province, and Xiamen in Fujian Province across the Taiwan Straits. Not only did these zones enjoy lower tax rates, but more importantly, they enjoyed a special institutional and policy environment and gained more authority over their economic development.[32]

The success of Guangdong and Fujian Provinces and the four special economic zones led the central government in 1984 to declare additional fourteen coastal cities as "coastal open cities," which gave them new authority similar to that of the special economic zones. Two coastal open cities, Shanghai and Tianjin, obtained authority to approve foreign investment up to $30 million; Dalian up to $10 million; and the remaining 11 cities up to $5 million. In 1988, Hainan was added as the largest special economic zone when it became a separate province.[33]

In 1994 the two-tiered exchange rate system is unified to reflect market forces. The former official rate was abolished and a new, single floating rate is adopted, based on swap centers' exchange rates. Shanghai prepares to open the National Foreign Exchange Trading Center that will electronically link China's major swap markets.[34]

3.4. Macroeconomic Variables

3.4.1. Gross Domestic Product

In the last twenty-five years (1978-2003) Chinese economy experienced unprecedented growth which had enormous implications for the people of China in particular and global economy as a whole. Though, the over all high growth sustained in this period, however, there was lack of uniformity in the growth rate through the entire period. This makes it possible to look at the complete period through different growth phases with alternative crusts and troughs or phases of relatively high and low growth.

In 1978, when the process of reform was first unleashed, the GDP of China was 517055 million yuan or 769694 million dollars.[35] In 2003, the value of the GDP was 5104266 million yuan or 7598267 million dollars. Thus over this period the average annual compound growth rate experienced by the economy was 9.20 per cent. The total output in the period increased almost ten times. By all standards this is a very high growth rate. However, as stated above, a significant variation in the growth rate of GDP was observed, it is possible to analyse the whole period through different phases of business cycle. Annual growth rates for the entire period are depicted in Fig. 3.1.

The entire period can be divided into five phases using 10 per cent growth rate as criteria. In the entire period two phases experienced above 10 per cent growth rates while three experienced below 10 per cent growth rate. The last year of the period under consideration also had higher than 10 per cent growth rate.

The *first phase*, 1978-83, experienced an average growth rate of 7.67 per cent, 1.6 percentage points below the average for the entire period. Thus the initial phase of five years was a period of relatively lower growth rate. The *second phase*, 1984-88, had an average annual growth rate of 12.12 per cent. These five years represent a phase of very high growth rate almost 2.92 percentage points higher than the average for the period. The next two years, 1989-90, were years of very low growth rate, with an average 3.70 per cent annual growth. This was followed by another year, 1991, of relatively good growth, 8.42 per cent. On an average these three years represented the *third phase* of low and erratic growth for China. The *fourth phase*, 1992-96, represents a period of the highest growth in terms of GDP. In this phase the average annual growth of GDP

(Unit: Per cent)

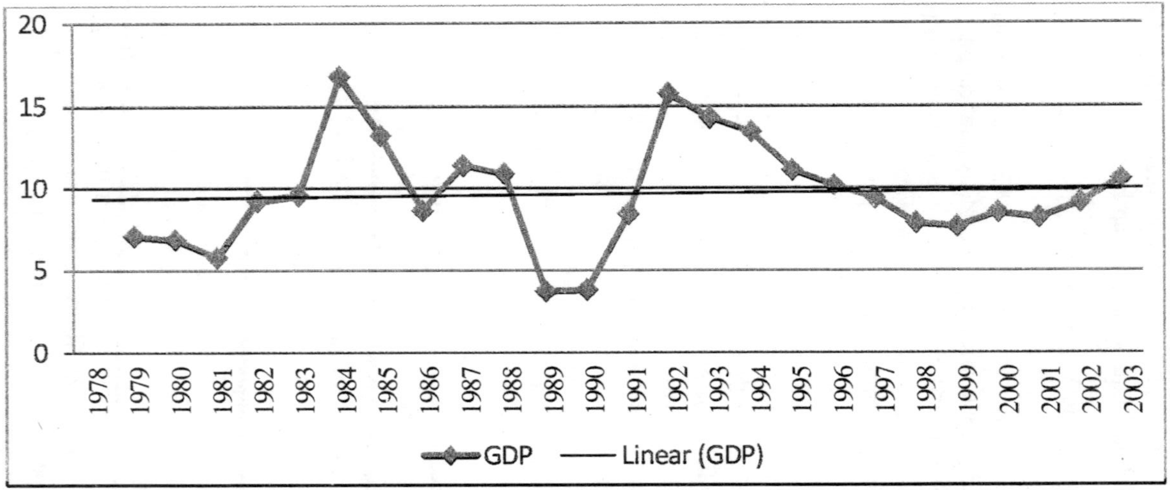

Fig. 3.1: Growth of GDP, 1978-2003.

Source: Developed from official statistics, see Appendix Chapter 3 Table 1 and Table 2.

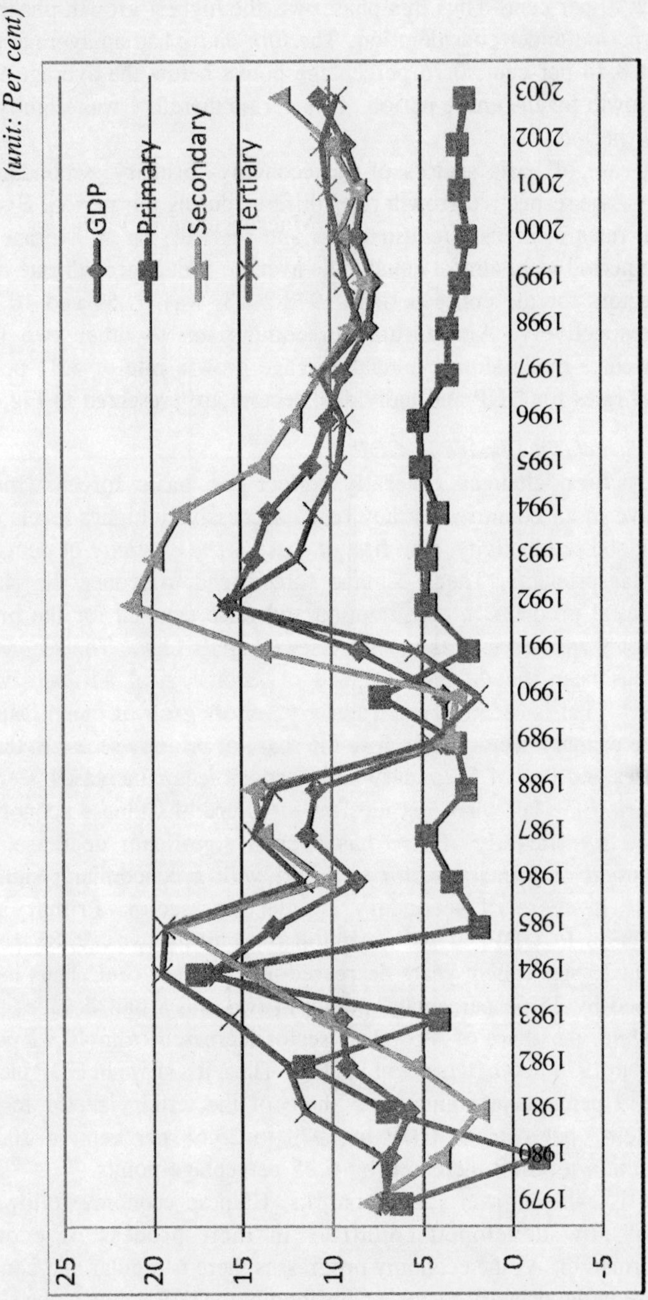

Fig. 3.2: Growth: GDP, Primary, Secondary and Tertiary Sectors, 1978-2003.

Source: Compiled and Developed from Official Statistics See Appendix Chapter 3 Table 1 and Table 2.

was 12.90 per cent. Thus this phase was the highest growth phase in the entire period under consideration. The *fifth phase* had an average growth rate of 8.44 per cent, 0.76 percentage points below the average 9.2 per cent growth for the entire period. This period therefore was slightly lower growth period.

In case of basic sectors of the economy—primary, secondary, and tertiary—the respective growth rates differed during this period. However, growth rates in industry/construction and services, on an average basis, for the period were almost equal. The average annual growth rate in these two sectors for the entire period, 1978-2003, was 10.69 and 10.24 per cent respectively. Agriculture, in comparison to other two sectors underwent a much slower annual average growth rate of 4.31 per cent. Growth rates for GDP and individual sectors are presented in Fig. 3.2.

3.4.2. Structural Change in GDP

Structural changes generally reflect two basic forces which are operative in all countries as they reach successively higher levels of real income and productivity. The first of these is the elasticity of demand for particular products. These demand forces tend to reduce the share of agricultural products in consumption and raise demand for the products of industry and services as income rises (Engel's Law). The second basic force has been the differential pace of technological advance between sectors.[36] That is secondary and tertiary sectors grow at much faster rate than the primary sector. Therefore the share of primary sector in the GDP decreases and that of Secondary and Tertiary sector increases.

During the last three decades the structure of Chinese economy has changed significantly. There has been a significant decrease in the contribution of primary sector to GDP, with a concomitant significant increase in share of secondary and tertiary sector. Primary sector contribution to GDP, at the inception of reforms, was 36.85 per cent which in 25 subsequent years decreased to 11.21 per cent. Thus its share decreased by 25.64 percentage points in two and a half decades. In the meanwhile, the share of secondary sector increased from 40.72 per cent of GDP in 1978 to 60.10 per cent in 2003. Thus, it's share in GDP increased by 19.39 percentage points. The share of the tertiary sector increased from 22.43 per cent of GDP in 1978 to 28.68 per cent in 2003. Its contribution to GDP increased by 6.25 percentage points.

As is evident from above analysis, Chinese economy followed the path of now developed countries in their process of economic transformation. As the economy progresses there is regular and consistent decrease in the primary sector's contribution to GDP while as the share of secondary and tertiary sector increases. However, in this historical process of transformation the share of secondary sector increases significantly in

(Unit: Per cent)

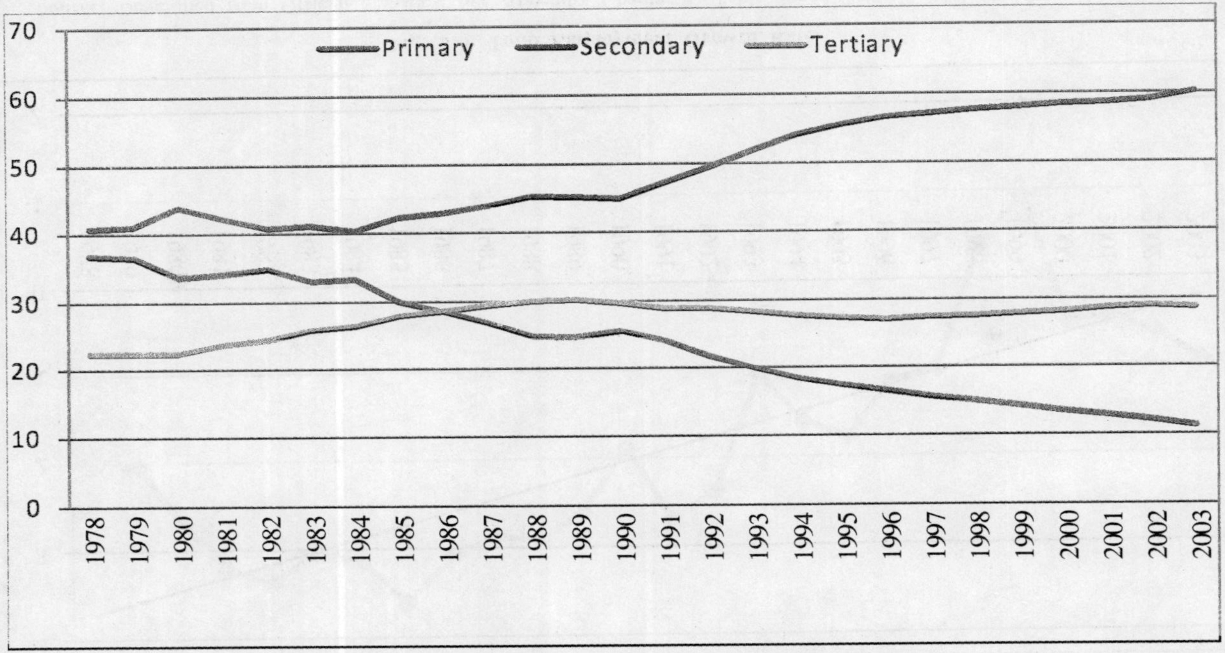

Fig. 3.3: Structural Change in Composition of GDP, 1978-2003.

Source: Compiled and Developed from official statistics See Appendix Chapter 3 Table 1 and Table 2.

(Unit: Per cent)

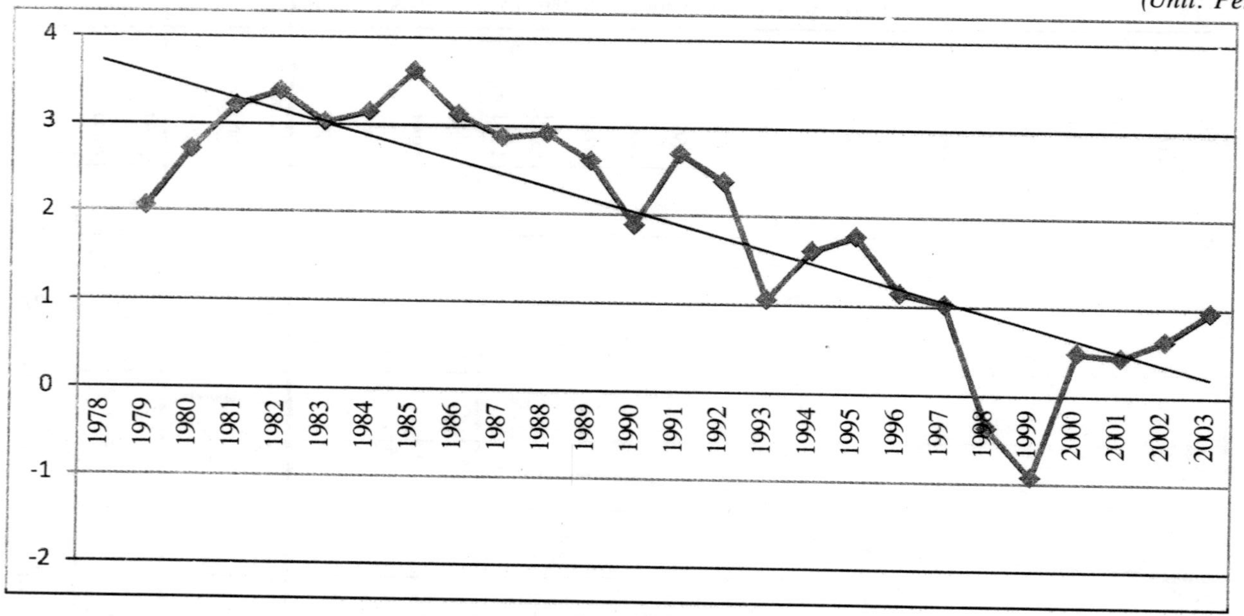

Fig. 3.4: Total Employment Growth Rate.

Source: Developed from Official Statistics, See Appendix Chapter 3, Table 3 and Table 4.

(Unit: Per cent)

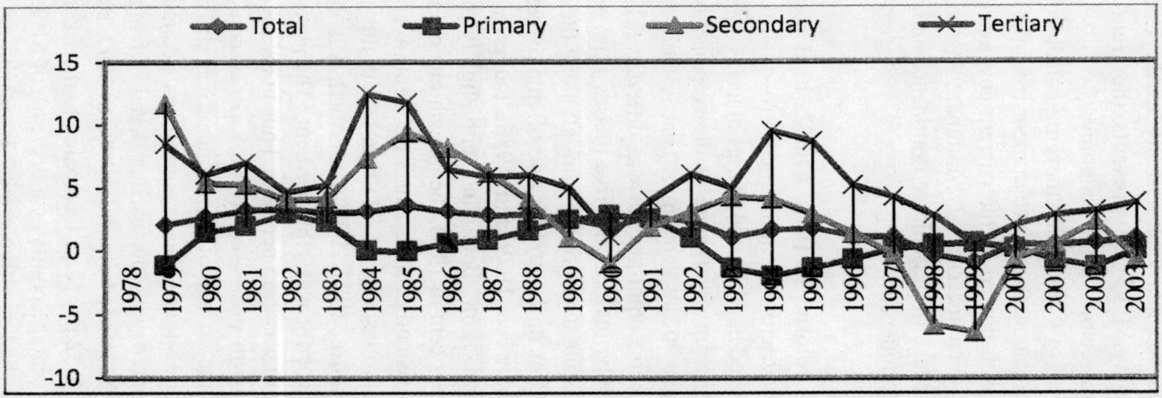

Fig. 3.5: Employment Growth: Total, Primary, Secondary and Tertiary.

Source: Compiled and developed from official statistics, see Appendix Chapter 3 Table 3 and Table 4.

beginning. As the economy further develops, the tertiary sector dominates the primary and secondary sectors. Thus the process of development proceeds from primary to secondary and finally to the tertiary sector dominance in the economy. Fig. 3.3 presents the trend of output contribution by three main sectors of the economy.

Looking at the statistics of China, the emerging conclusion is that its economy is in the intermediate state of development from the criterion of the general historical trends followed by the current developed countries. Its secondary sector has been increasingly dominant in the concerned period. It has passed the phase of agriculture dominance and is as yet to reach the service sector dominance.

3.4.3. Employment

After the inception of reforms in 1978, China's high output growth has not always corresponded with its employment growth. Like the GDP growth, the post-reform period has different phases in terms of employment growth. There was a significant divergence in the response of the three basic sectors to employment in the economy. That is their employment elasticity with respect to their output growth was different. The complete period for convenience can be divided into five phases from employment absorption perspective. Despite high growth rates all along the last twenty five years, these phases differ in the growth rate of employment.

In the *first phase*, between 1979 and 1986, the growth rate of employment was rather significant. Beginning with slightly more than 2 per cent in 1979 and 2.70 per cent in 1980, the growth rate of employment for next six years was consistently more than 3 per cent, averaging 3.24 per cent. Thus, employment elasticity of GDP growth in this period was very high. In the *second phase*, 1987-1991, the growth was more than 2 per cent apart from 1990 when it was 1.89 per cent. The average growth of employment for this phase was 2.55 per cent. Thus in the second half of the 1980s employment growth decreased by 0.68 percentage points, or 21.29 per cent. However, the growth of employment was still very good.

In the following periods there was a significant reduction in the employment growth compared with the earlier decade of high growth. Growth of employment in the *third phase*, from 1993 to 1997, substantially decreased to an average of 1.32 per cent. Compared to the second phase it was a decrease of 1.22 percentage points or a decrease of 51.76 per cent. The *fourth phase*, 1998-99, had negative growth rate, with an average of -0.65 per cent. This represents a decrease of 250 per cent in employment when compared to the third phase. In the *fifth phase* of four years, 2000-03, the employment scenario improved marginally and growth entered into positive figures but was not able to cross 1 per cent mark. The average growth of employment for the period was a mere 0.63 per cent. Annual growth rate of employment for the entire period is shown in Fig. 3.4.

3.4.5. Sectoral Composition of Employment

In contrast to its GDP structural change, the trends of change in employment between basic sectors for Chinese economy was rather awkward and economically unviable. While as there was a complete dominance of secondary sector in terms of GDP, the primary sector was the basic employer of China, surpassing secondary and tertiary sectors collectively. Nonetheless, there was a marked decrease in the employment burden of the primary sector in the subsequent 25 years.

In 1978, primary sector contributed 71.90 per cent, secondary sector 15.82 per cent and tertiary sector 12.27 per cent to the total employment in economy. In the next 25 years the three sectors experienced growth rates of 0.49, 2.73, and 5.32 per cent respectively. As a consequence, the share of the primary sector decreased consistently from 71.90 per cent to 51.13 per cent in 2003. In total primary sectors contribution decreased by 28.89 per cent or 20.77 percentage points. There was a significant increase in the contribution of tertiary sector the contribution of which increased from 12.27 to 28.96 per cent in the total employment. Tertiary sector's contribution increased by 136 per cent or by 16.69 percentage points. The highest growing sector of the Chinese economy, secondary sector, did not witness an increase in its employment share corresponding to its output growth. Its share increased from 15.82 per cent in 1978 to 19.90 per cent in 2003. Thus its share increased by 4 percentage points in the total employment.

One of the important weaknesses of the Chinese economy is the less share of employment by the manufacturing and construction sector. Therefore the burden of the employment is disproportionately borne by the primary sector. It must be emphasised that the secondary sector is more than 5.36 times larger in GDP terms and grows 2.51 times faster than the primary sector. Therefore, it needed to play a much stronger employment role in the economy. Fig. 3.6 shows the relative share of the basic sectors in total employment through the period.

3.4.6. Employment and Growth

The employment elasticity of GDP expansion in China has followed a progressively decreasing trend. The high response of growth to employment up to mid-1980s weakened progressively afterwards reaching a very low ebb in late 1990s. China's highest growth phase, from 1992 to 96, witnessed a substantial decrease in the growth rate of employment; from more than two per cent in the preceding phase to an average of 1.32 per cent. Employment growth has remained below one per cent after 1997. A linearised

(Unit: Per cent)

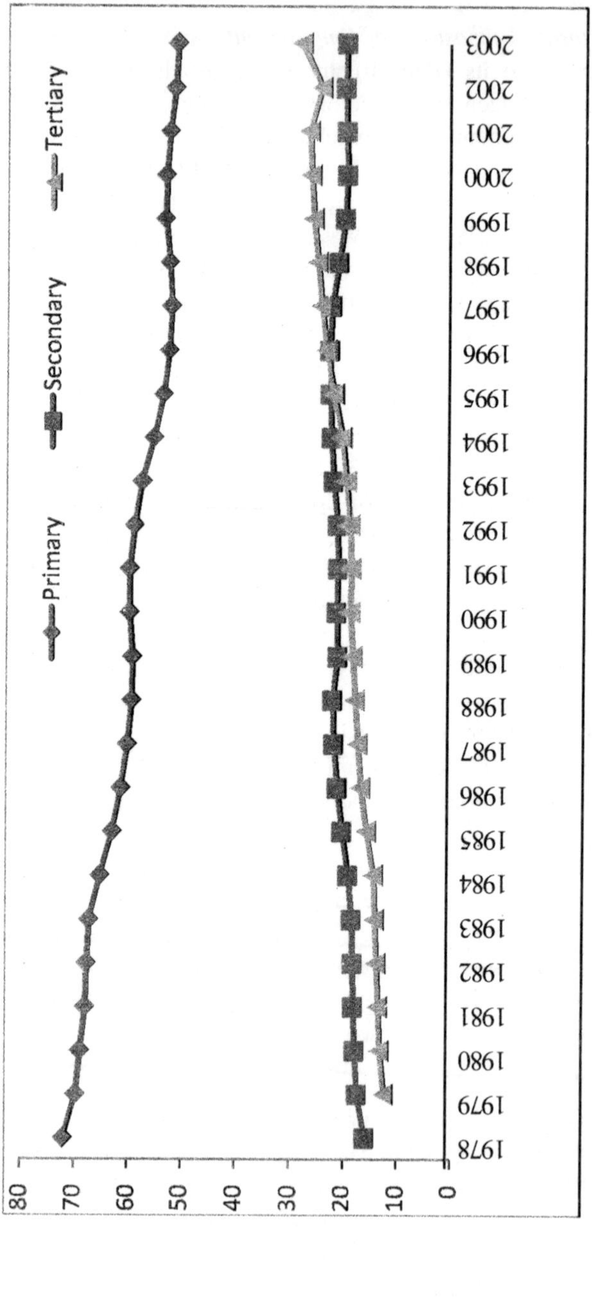

Fig. 3.6: Structural Change in Employment.

Source: Compiled and Developed from official statistics, see Appendix Chapter 3 Table 3 and Table 4.

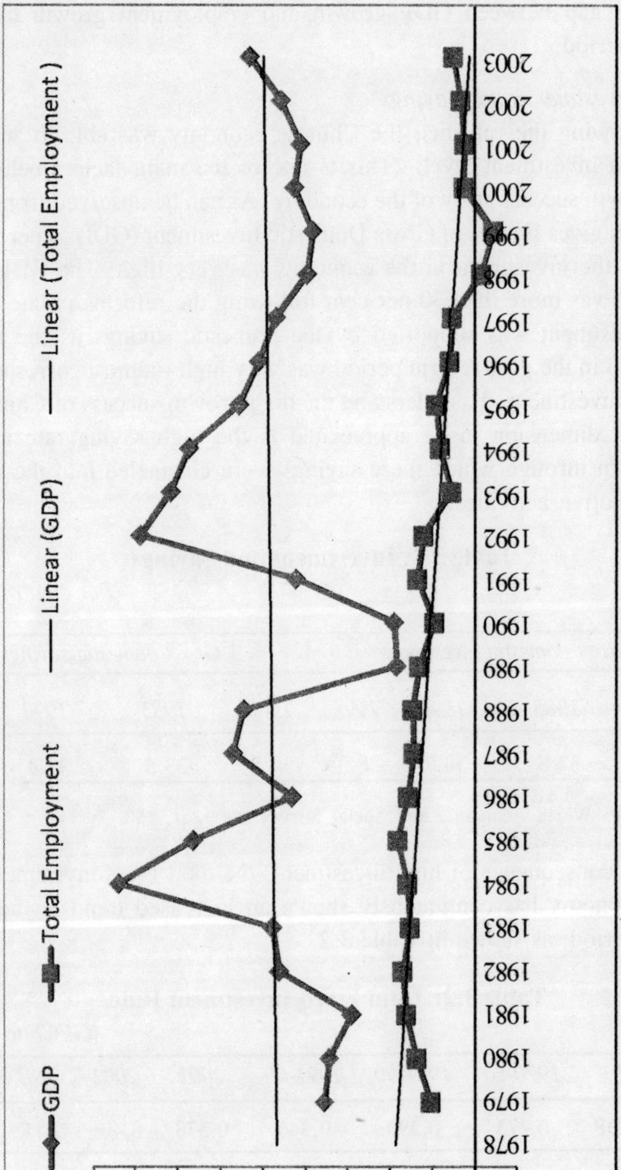

Fig. 3.7: Growth: GDP verses Total Employment.

Source: Compiled and Developed From Official Statistics, See Appendix Chapter 3 Table 5.

growth trend for the both is shown in Fig. 3.7 which reveals consistently widening gap between GDP growth and employment growth over the reform period.

3.4.7. Investment and Savings

Following the reforms, the Chinese economy was able to sustain a very high investment level. This is one of the main factors behind the high growth success story of the economy. As can be observed from Table 3.1 which gives figures of Gross Domestic Investment (GDI) as percentage of GDP, the investment in the economy was very high. The GDI of the economy was more than 30 per cent following the reforms in late 1970s. This investment was supported by the domestic savings as the rate of saving too in the post-reform period was very high—almost corresponding with the investment. To understand the high growth success of China, one important dimension to be appreciated is the high saving rate and the mechanism through which these savings were channeled into the market for productive activities.

Table 3.1: Investment and Savings

(Per cent of GDP)

Gross domestic investment				*Gross domestic savings*			
1980	*1985*	*1990*	*1998*	*1980*	*1985*	*1990*	*1998*
35.2	37.8	34.7	38.3	34.8	33.5	37.9	42.6

Source: World Economic and Social Survey 2000, p. 250.

As a consequence of high investment, the total fixed investment rate in the economy has continuously shown an increased trend in the post-reform period, as shown in Table 3.2.

Table 3.2: Total Fixed Investment Rate

(GFCF to GDP)

Period	*1970-80*	*1981-90*	*1991-00*	*2001*	*2002*	*2003*	*2004*
GFCF/GDP	0.273	0.290	0.346	0.378	0.401	0.442	0.449

Source: World Economic Situation and Prospects 2006, p. 158.

3.5. Primary Sector

3.5.1. Output

After sluggish growth following the Cultural Revolution, the reforms in the primary sector unleashing the latent energy of In the immediate

(*Unit: Per cent*)

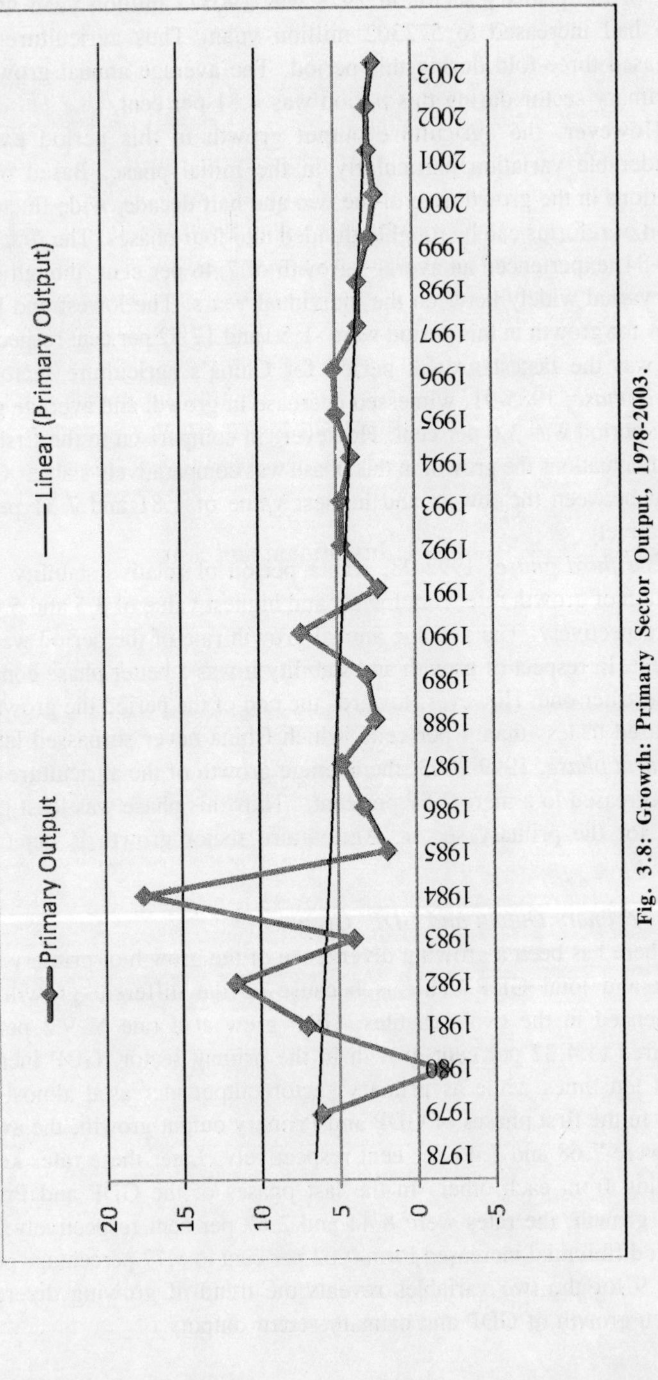

Fig. 3.8: Growth: Primary Sector Output, 1978-2003.

Source: Compiled and Developed From Official Statistics, See Appendix Chapter 3, Table 5.

post-reform period China's agriculture sector expanded robustly. Total GDP of the primary sector in 1978 was 190577 million yuan which in 2003 had increased to 572302 million yuan. Thus agriculture output increased three-fold during this period. The average annual growth rate of primary sector during this period was 4.31 per cent.

However, the agriculture output growth in this period exhibited considerable variation particularly in the initial phase. Based on such variations in the growth rate of the two and half decade, wide fluctuations period of reforms can be roughly divided into four phases. The *first phase*, 1979-84, experienced an average growth of 7.46 per cent, though growth rates varied widely between the individual years. The lowest and highest values for growth in this period were -1.50 and 17.52 per cent respectively. This was the fastest growth period for China's agriculture sector. The *second phase*, 1985-91, witnessed decrease in growth and average growth of the period was 3.6 per cent. However, in comparison to the first phase wide fluctuations the growth in this phase was comparatively stable. Growth varied between the lowest and highest value of 1.81 and 7.31 per cent respectively.

The *third phase*, 1992-98, was a period of relative stability with a variation of growth rate from lowest and highest value of 3.5 and 5.09 per cent respectively. The average annual growth rate of the period was 4.35 per cent. In respect of growth and stability it was a better phase compared to the earlier one. However, towards the end of the period the growth rate decreased to less than 4 per cent, which China never surpassed later. In the *fourth phase*, 1999-2003, the average growth of the agriculture sector had decreased to a mere 2.67 per cent. Thus this phase was least growth phase for the primary sector. Agriculture sector growth is depicted in Fig. 3.8.

3.5.2. Primary Output and GDP Growth

There has been a growing divergence of the growth of primary sector output and total GDP. This is because of the different growth rates experienced in the two variables. GDP grew at a rate of 9.2 per cent compared to 4.32 per cent growth in the primay sector. GDP increased almost ten times while as primary sector output increased almost three times. In the first phases of GDP and Primary output growth, the average rates were 7.68 and 7.46 per cent respectively. Later these rates kept on diverging from each other. In the last phases of the GDP and Primary output growth, the rates were 8.44 and 2.67 per cent respectively. Thus growth differential increased form 0.02 per cent to 5.77 percentage points. Fig. 3.9 for the two variables reveals the trend of growing divergence between growth of GDP and primary sector output.

(Unit: Per cent)

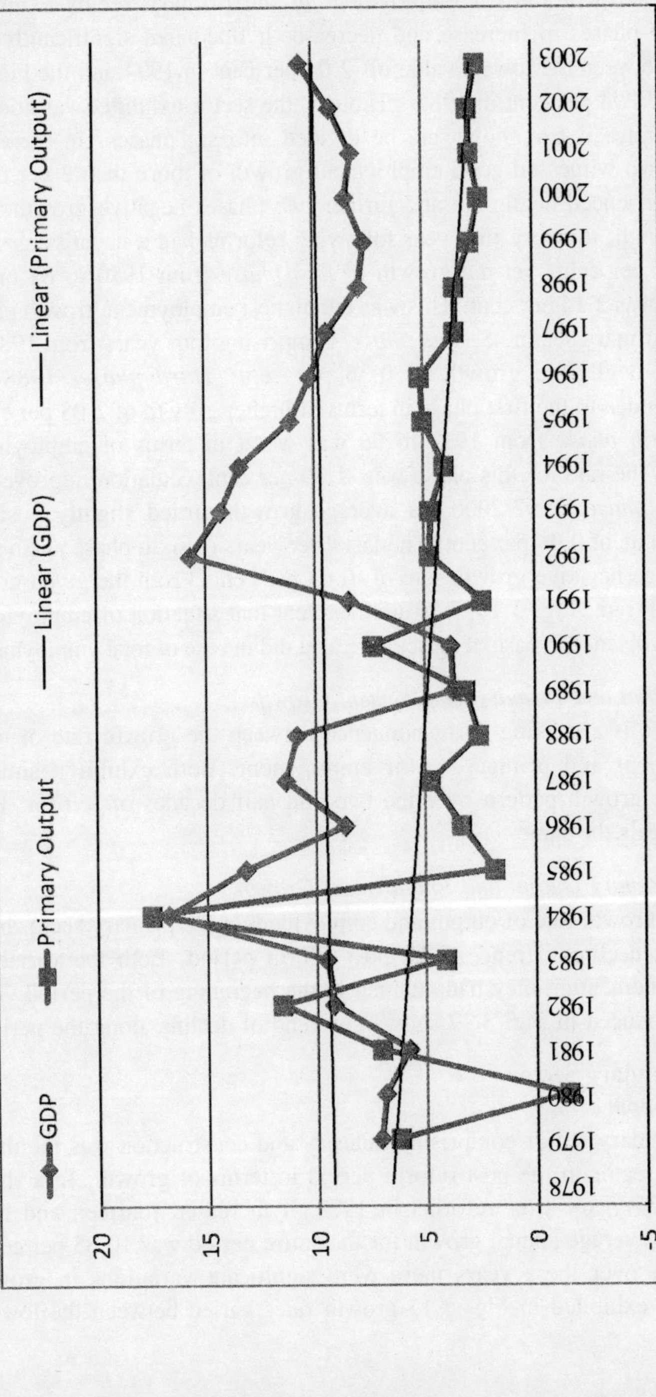

Fig. 3.9: Growth: Primary Sector GDP versus Total GDP.

Source: Compiled and Developed From Official Statistics, See Appendix Chapter 3 Table 2.

3.5.3. Employment

The growth rate of employment in the primary sector exhibited alternate phases of increase and decrease. It fluctuated significantly and varied between the lowest value of -2.04 per cent in 1994 and the highest value of 2.94 per cent in 1982. Though, the sector exhibited variation in growth rates it can, however, be divided into six phases. In these six phases two witnessed good employment growth of more than 2 per cent, two experienced negligible and further two phases negative growth.

Though, the very first year following reforms had a negative growth of -1.14 per cent, yet the growth of *first phase* from 1980 to 83 on an average was 2.14 per cent. This was the highest employment growth phase for the primary sector. *Second phase*, comprising four years from 1984 to 87, had negligible growth of 0.36 per cent. *Third phase*, 1988-92, corresponded to the first phase in terms of higher growth of 2.08 per cent. The *fourth phase* from 1993 to 96 was worst in terms of employment growth. The rate for this phase was -1.39 per cent. Situation improved in the *fifth phase*, 1997-2000, as average growth turned slightly positive with a value of 0.34 per cent. The last three years of sixth phase again saw an average negative growth rate of -0.68 per cent. From the given graph of growth rate, Fig. 3.10, it is quite evident that situation of employment growth worsened in case of agriculture as it did in case of total employment.

3.5.4. Total and Primary Employment Growth

There is a striking correspondence between the growth rate of total employment and primary sector employment. Both exhibit a similar declining growth pattern over the two and half decades of reform. Fig. 3.11 reveals the same.

3.5.5. Primary Output and Employment Growth

The growth rate of output and employment in the primary sector both exhibited declining trend in the post-reform period. Both the variables lost the momentum they had attained in the beginning of the period. The graph produced in Fig. 3.12 shows the trend of decline along the period.

3.6. Secondary Sector

3.6.1. Output

Secondary sector comprising industry and construction was the most dynamic sector in the post-reform period in terms of growth. In a short span of 25 years after reforms in 1978, it increased fourteen and half times. Its average annual growth for the entire period was 10.85 per cent. However, over these years there were significant variations in growth rates. As exhibited in Fig. 3.13 growth rates varied between the lowest

(Unit: Per cent)

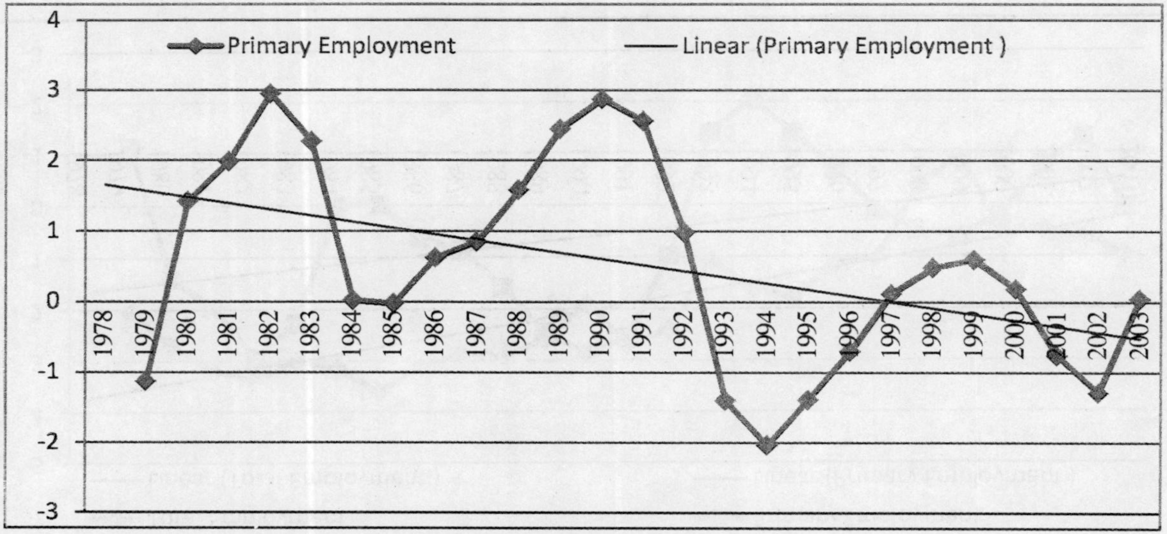

Fig. 3.10: Primary Employment Growth.

Source: Compiled and Developed from Official Statistics, See Appendix Chapter 3, Table 4 and Table 7.

(*Unit: Per cent*)

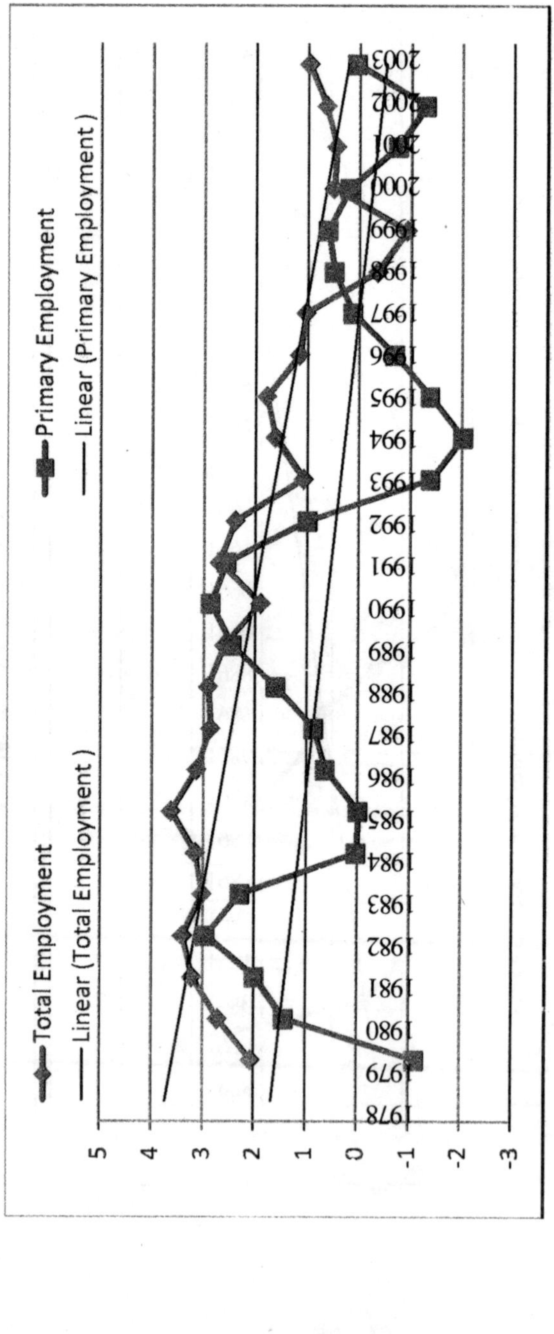

Fig. 3.11: Total and Primary Employment Growth.

Source: Compiled and Developed for Official Statistics, See Appendix Chapter 3, Table 4.

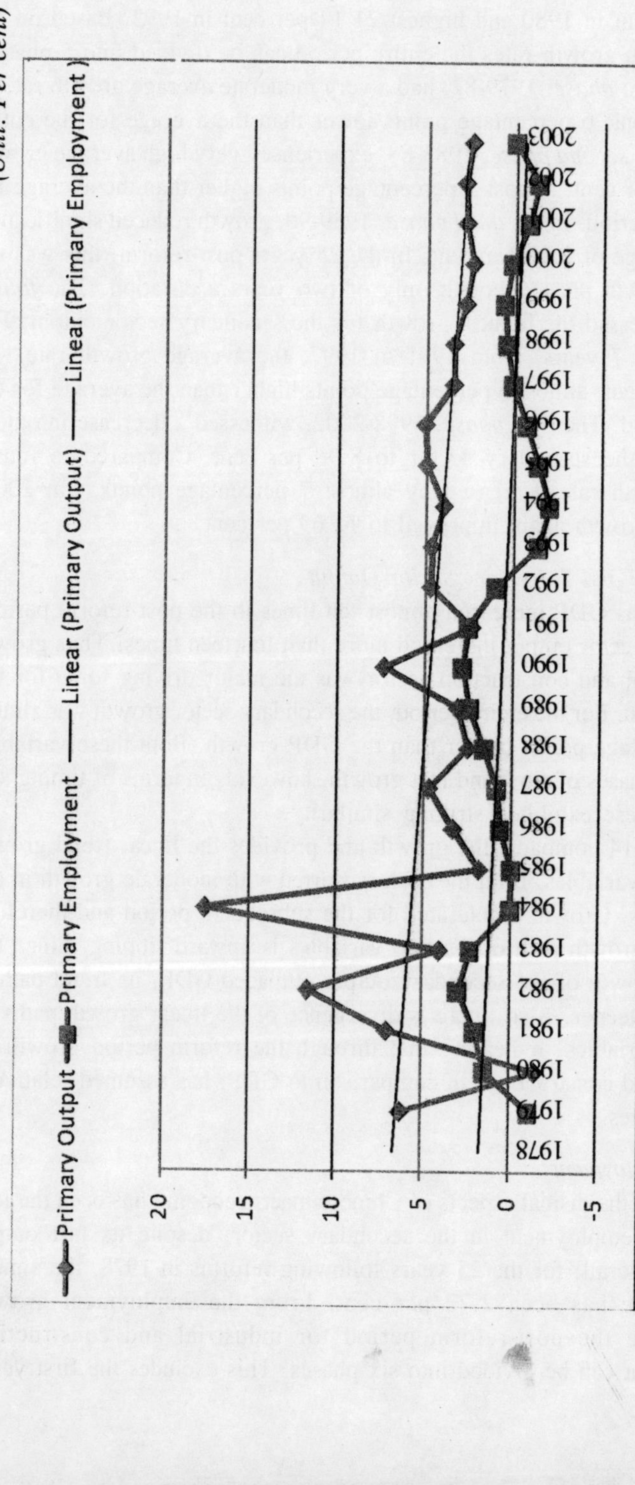

Fig. 3.12: Growth: Primary Output and Employment Growth.

Source: Compiled and Developed From Official Statistics, See Appendix Chapter 3 Table 5.

1.89 per cent in 1980 and highest 21.14 per cent in 1992. Based on the variations in growth rates the entire period can be divided into 5 phases.

The *first phase*, 1979-82, had a very moderate average growth rate of 4.85 per cent; 6 percentage points lower than the average for the entire period. The *second phase*, 1983-88, experienced very high average growth of 13.67 per cent, almost 3 percentage points higher than the average for the entire period. In the *third phase*, 1989-90, growth reduced significantly to an average of 3.28 per cent. In the 25 years post-reform, this was the lowest growth phase, though only of two years a duration. The *fourth phase* witnessed the highest growth for the secondary sector output. For duration of 7 years, from 1991 to 1997, the average growth rate was 15.69 per cent; almost 5 percentage points higher than the average for the entire period. The *fifth phase*, 1998-2002, witnessed a decrease in output growth of the secondary sector to 8.98 per cent. Compared to fourth phase growth rate decreased by almost 7 percentage points. In 2003, however, growth again improved to 12.69 per cent.

3.6.2. GDP and Secondary Sector Output

While as GDP increased almost ten times in the post-reform period, secondary sector output increased more than fourteen times. Thus growth of industrial and construction sector was the major driving force for the GDP growth. For the entire period, the secondary sector growth was almost two percentage points higher than the GDP growth. Both these variables followed phases of slow and fast growth, however, in terms of timing and duration these exhibited striking similarity.

Fig. 3.14 compares the growth and provides the linear trend growth of the two variables. Both the sectors started with moderate growth in the initial years. Growth accelerated for the subsequent period and therefore the linear growth path of the two variables is upward sloping. Since the average growth of the secondary output outpaced GDP, its trend path is relatively steeper. Also, there is divergence of the linear growth paths of the two variables, indicating that through the reform period growth of industry and construction, in comparison to GDP, has assumed relatively higher values.

3.6.3. Employment

One of the dismal aspects of Chinese macroeconomy has been the low growth of employment in the secondary sector, despite its fast output growth. Overall, for the 25 years following reforms in 1978, the annual growth rate has been 2.72 per cent. From the employment growth perspective the post-reform period for industrial and construction employment can be divided into six phases. This excludes the first year,

(Unit: Per cent)

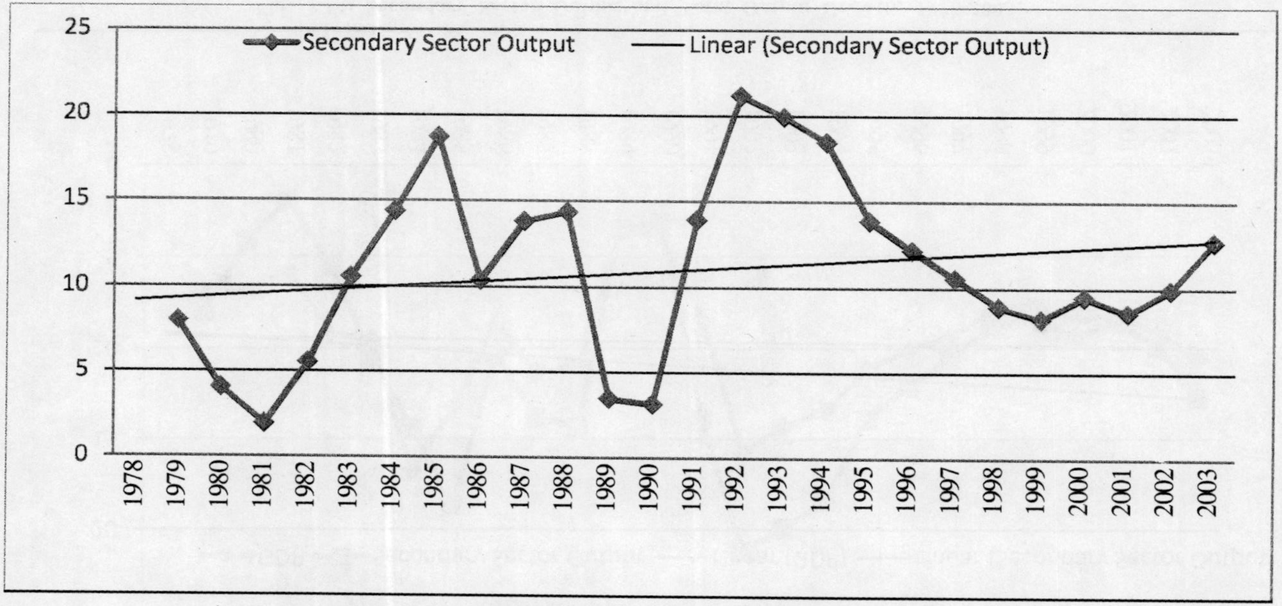

Fig. 3.13: Secondary Sector Output Growth, 1978-2003.

Source: Compiled and Developed from Official Statistics, see Appendix Chapter 3, Table 2. and Table 6.

(Unit: Per cent)

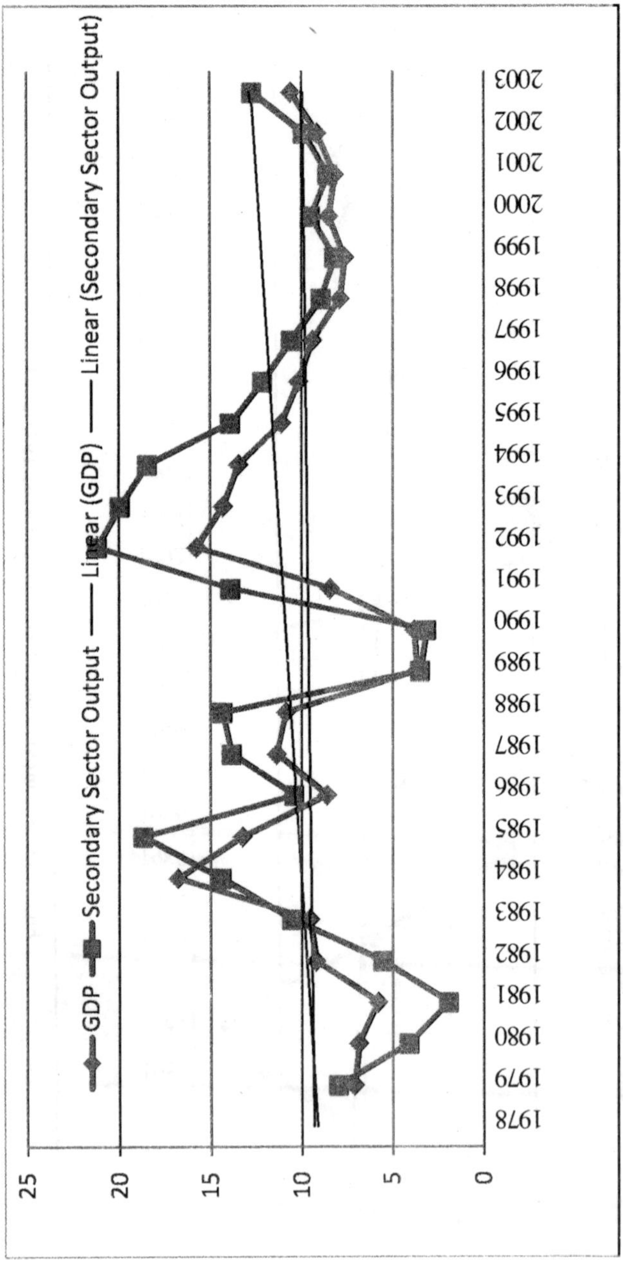

Fig. 3.14: Secondary Sector Output and Total Output Growth, 1978-2003.

Source: Compiled and Developed from Official Statistics, See Appendix Chapter 3, Table 2.

1979, when employment was highest, 11.65, for the entire period. The *first phase,* comprising four years from 1980 to 1983, experienced an average annual growth of 4.71 per cent in employment. *Second phase*, 1984-88, had the highest annual growth, seven per cent, for the entire period. Thus the first decade following initiation of reforms was very good from employment perspective in industry.

However, the *third phase*, 1989-91, showed the first signs of employment fatigue or saturation in the industry. Average growth for these three years was just 0.63 per cent. Thus this period represents the first employment slump in industry and construction. The *fourth phase*, comprising five years from 1992 to 1996, witnessed the revival of employment growth which attained a value of 3.14 per cent. However, growth rates of the first two phases were not attained. The *fifth phase*, 1997-2000, was a phase of employment reduction in absolute terms. The average annual growth was -3.36 per cent for these four years. This was the worst phase for the employment in industry and construction. In *sixth phase*, 2001-03, growth recovered from the negative slump, hovered around the average annual growth rate of less than one per cent. Thus the last seven years of reform period produced very negative growth trends in employment of industry and construction.

3.6.4. Total Employment and Secondary Sector Employment

Fig. 3.16 reproduces the Total and Secondary sector employment growth in the post-reform period. Both the variables show a decreasing trend over the post-reform period. On an average, growth rate of employment in secondary sector was higher than total employment till 1995-96. After 1996, this trend changed and average growth in total employment became higher than that of secondary sector. Thus the trend line of employment growth in secondary sector is steeper than the total employment.

3.6.5. Secondary Sector Output and Employment

The most striking contrast is between the output growth and employment growth of the secondary sector. Not only is there large difference between the growth of output, 10.85 per cent, and employment, 2.72, during the post-reform period as a whole. But there is an ever increasing divergence between the two variables through the period. This is depicted in Fig. 3.17.

The decline in employment absorption of industry can be attributed to increase in capital intensity in production process. Some of the reasons that account for such a trend which has substantial impact on the employment scenario of China include: (a) increased capacity of capital accumulation for business persons, (b) new machinery for erstwhile manual

(Unit: Per cent)

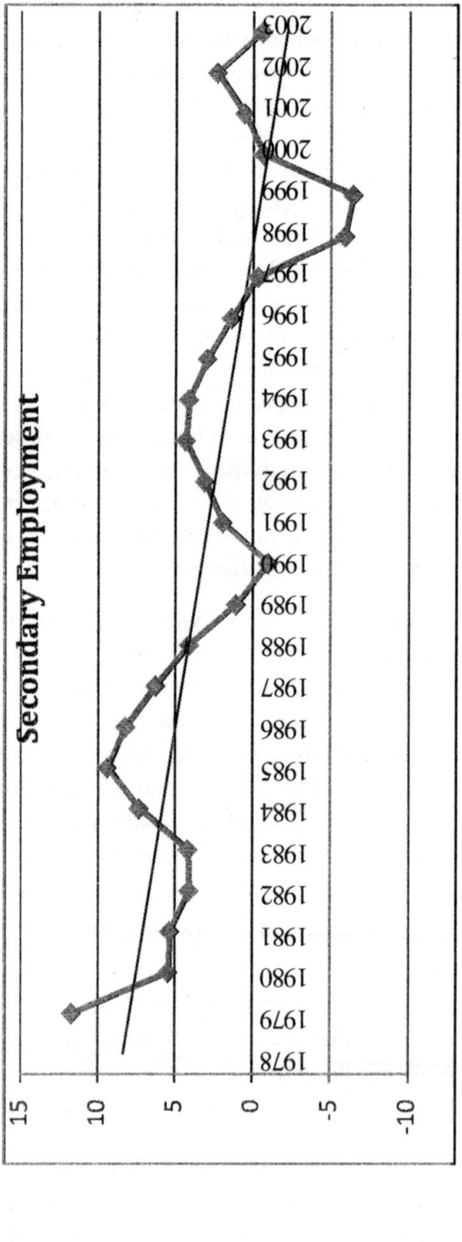

Fig. 3.15: Secondary Sector Employment Growth, 1978-2003.

Source: Compiled and Developed From Official Statistics, See Appendix Chapter 3, Table 4 and Table 7.

(Unit: Per cent)

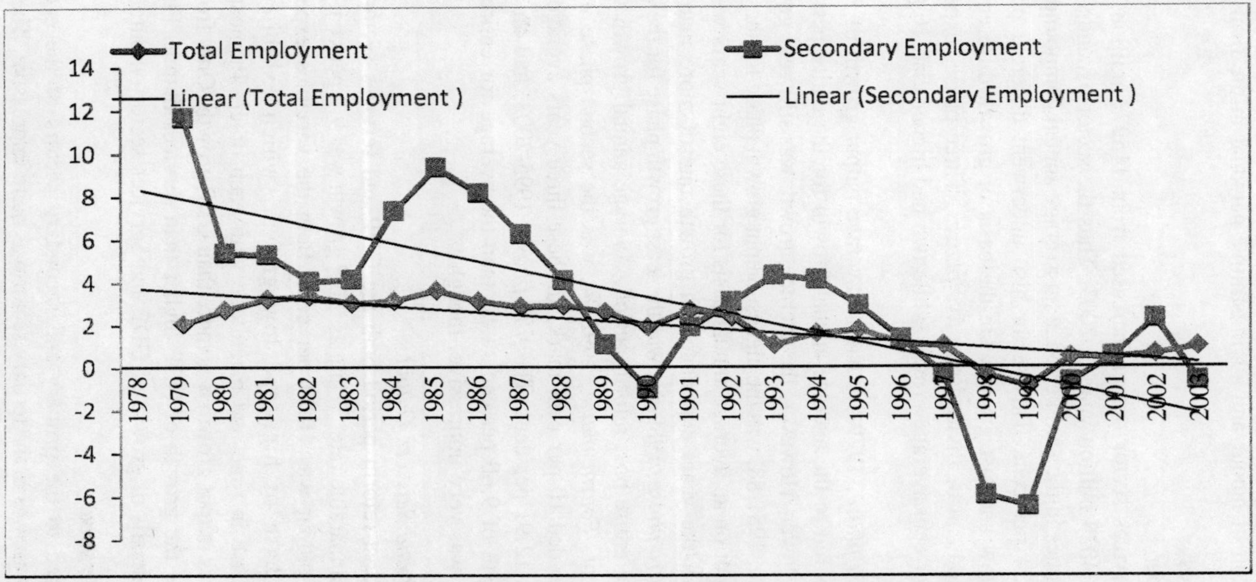

Fig. 3.16: Total and Secondary Sector Employment Growth, 1978-2003.

Source: Compiled and Developed from Official Statistics. See Appendix Chapter 3, Table 4.

jobs, (d) increase in FDI with larger capital content in manufacturing, and (d) decrease in the number of State Operated Enterprises with a thrust on rationalisation of labour and administrative personal in the firms.

3.7. Services

3.7.1. Output

The services sector output increased from 115972 million yuan in 1978 to 1464029 million yuan in 2003. Thus the sector expanded twelve and a half times in the said period at an average annual compound growth rate of 10.24 per cent. This sector also underwent different phases of relatively slow and fast growth. On the basis of growth differences, the reform period can be divided into *five phases.* Three phases experienced below 10 per cent average growth while two had higher than 10 per cent growth rate.

The *first phase*, 1979-80, had an average output growth of 7.09 per cent. Compared to the average annual growth for the entire period, this growth was lower. However, the average growth was still very good. The *second phase*, 1981-88, was the highest output growth phase for the services sector. Output on an average annual basis for these eight years was 14.69 per cent. All the years experienced a growth rate of more than 11 per cent. The *third phase*, 1989-91, was the least growth phase for the services sector in the entire post-reform period. Average annual growth was just 3.89 per cent. *Fourth phase*, 1992-94, was the second phase in which growth exceeded 10 per cent mark. In these three years average annual growth was 12.91 per cent. The *fifth phase,* 1995-2003, had an average annual growth of 9.60 per cent. Less than the average for entire period growth still was very impressive, though.

3.7.2. GDP and Services Output

In the post-reform period both the GDP and services sector output grew at a comparable rate. While as GDP growth was 9.2 per cent growth in services output was 10.24 per cent. Both the variables experienced alternate phase of high and low growth, which exhibited high correspondence in time and magnitude with each other. In most of the years services output growth was more than GDP growth. Only from 1993 to 1996 was the growth of GDP higher than services output. Fig. 3.18 depicts the details of growth of GDP and Services sector output.

3.7.3. Employment

Compared to the primary and secondary sectors of the economy, employment growth in the tertiary sector was quite impressive. The annual average compound growth rate for the entire period was 5.23 per cent. Based on the differences in growth rates, the entire period can be

(Unit: Per cent)

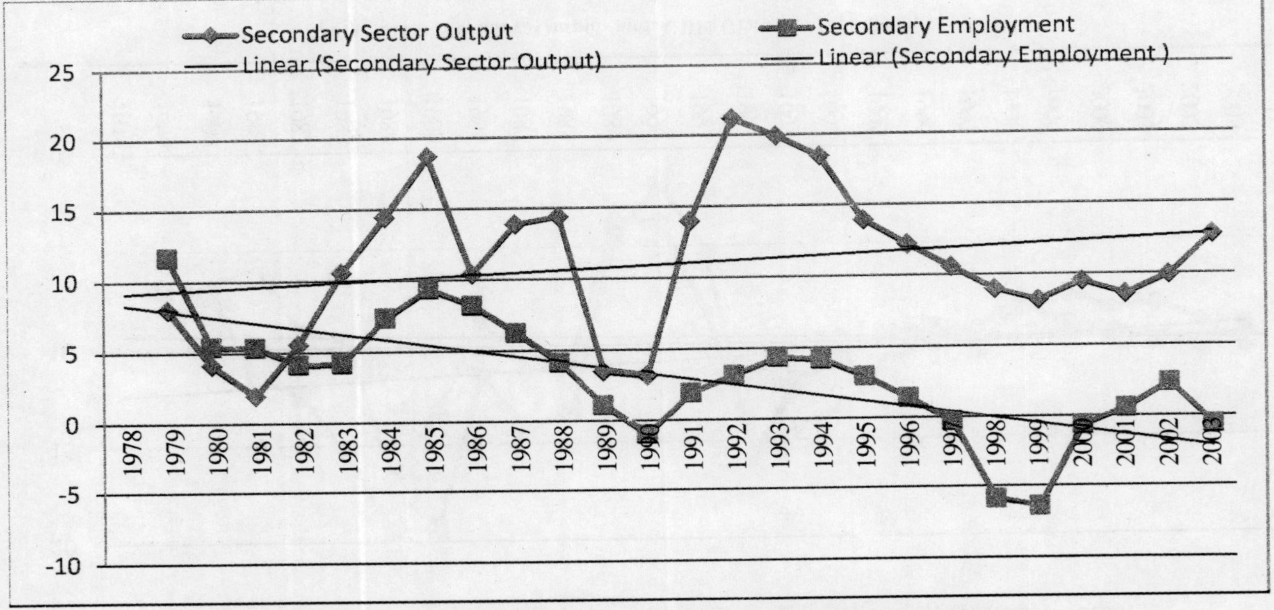

Fig. 3.17: Growth of Secondary Sector Output and Employment, 1978-2003.

Source: Compiled and Developed from Official Statistics, see Appendix Chapter 3, Table 5.

(Unit: Per cent)

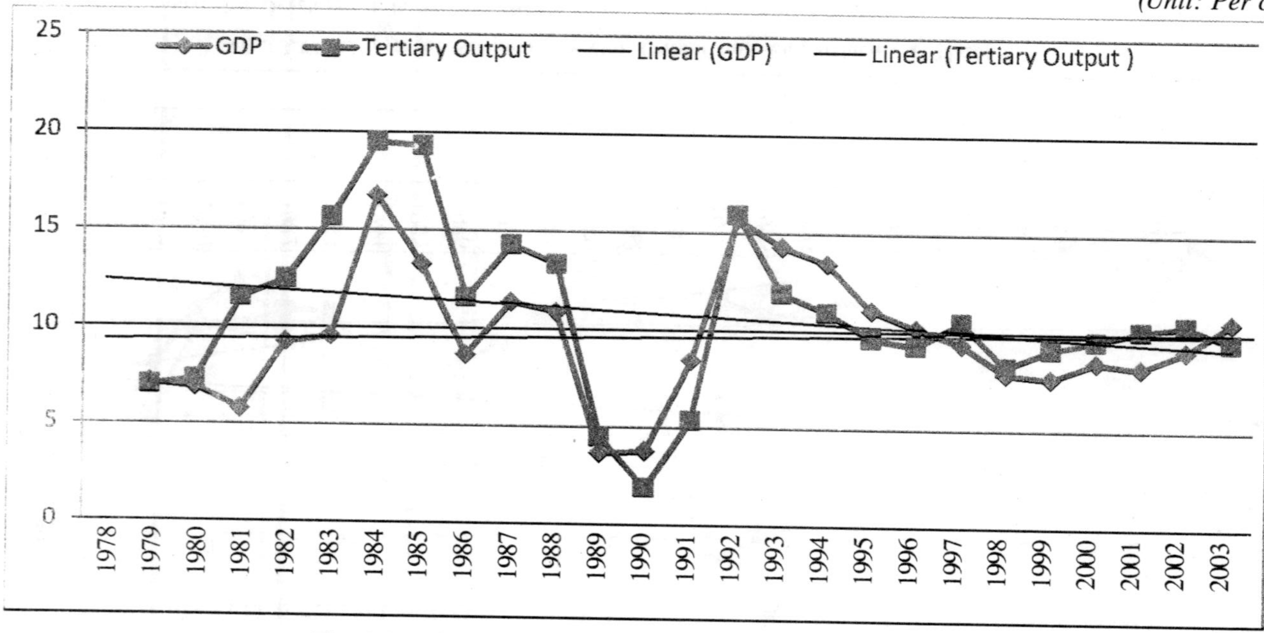

Fig. 3.18: Tertiary Output and GDP Growth, 1978-2003.

Source: Compiled and Developed from Official Statistics, see Appendix Chapter 3, Table 2.

(Unit: Per cent)

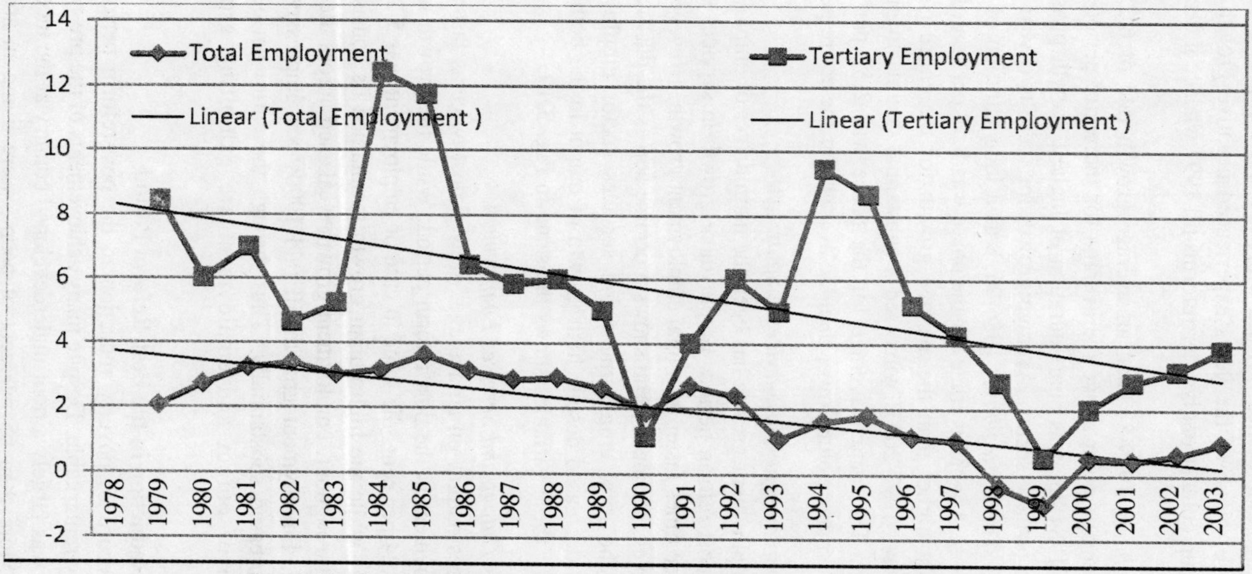

Fig. 3.19: Growth: Tertiary Sector and Total Employment 1978-2003.

Source: Compiled and Developed from Official Statistics, See Appendix Chapter 3, Table 4.

sub-divided into four phases, presented in Fig. 3.19. Three of these had more than average employment growth while the fourth experienced less than the average. None of the years experienced negative growth rate. Growth picked up quite strongly after reforms till 1997 whence it declined afterwards.

The *first phase*, 1979-83, had an average growth rate of 6.25 per cent, one percentage point above the average for the entire period. The *second phase*, 1984-85, was short duration of highest growth phase for employment in tertiary sector. Average growth for these two years was 12.07 per cent. The *third phase*, 1986-96, was a long duration of good and stable growth. Annual average for the phase was 5.57 per cent, half a percentage point higher than the average growth for the entire period. The *fourth phase*, 1997-2003, witnessed a substantial decline in growth of employment. The annual average for the phase was 2.52 per cent, nearly two percentage points lower than the average for the entire period.

3.7.4. Total Employment and Services Employment

Service employment growth has been the main driver of employment growth in the post-reform period. Employment growth in services sector was almost three times faster than total employment growth. However, for both the variables the linear trend shows a decline across the post-reform period. Both the total employment and services sector employment absorption has decreased despite high growth of output in the both. The graph drawn for these variables shows the same in Fig. 3.19.

3.7.5. Services Output and Services Employment

The services output, on an average, grew almost twice as fast as the services employment in the post reform period. While the growth rate of output was 10.24 per cent, the same in case of employment was 5.23 per cent. However, while the high output growth maintained its consistency and sustained throughout, employment growth weakened across the post-reform period. Employment growth till mid 1990s was impressive but afterwards decreased substantially. Thus through the entire period, the trend growth of output and employment are exhibiting growing divergence.

3.8. Poverty Reduction in the Post-Reform Period

China's record of poverty reduction in the post-reform period has been singularly remarkable. Despite many achievements of the pre-reform period, China was largely a poor underdeveloped country at the inception of reforms. More than 65 per cent of people were living in absolute poverty by one dollar criterion and 90 per cent were poor by two dollar a day standard. Out of one billion people, 634 million and 876 million

Table 3.3: Poverty Reduction in China: 1981-2004

	Percentage pop. living on < $1.08/ day	Number of people living on < $1.08/day (millions)	Percentage pop. living on < $2.15/day	Number of people living on < $2.15/day (millions)
1981	63.8	634	88.1	876
1990	33.0	374	72.2	819
1993	28.4	334	68.1	803
1996	17.4	211	53.3	650
1999	17.8	223	50.1	628
2002	13.8	177	40.9	524
2004	9.9	128	34.9	452
2015 (forecast)	2.6	37	14.1	196

Source: World Bank. 2007. Global Monitoring Report 2007 p. 65.

were absolutely poor by one and two dollar a day criteria respectively. After the inception of reforms in late 1970s, the magnitude of poverty has significantly reduced. The percentage of absolutely poor people, on one dollar a day criterion, decreased from 63.8 per cent in 1981 to 9.9 per cent in 2004. In absolute terms the number decreased from 634 million to 128 million during this period. In total 506 million people came out of absolute poverty. On the two dollar criterion, the percentage of poor people decreased from 88.1 per cent in 1981 to 34.9 per cent in 2004. Total number of people in absolute poverty from two dollar criterion decreased from 876 million in 1981 to 452 million in 2004. Table 3.3 presents these statistics.

3.9. Health

3.9.1. Health Expenditure

China's transition from pure state to relatively determined arrangement in the provision of health services in the post-reform period has been remarkable. While 80 per cent of the health expenditure in 1980 was non-personal, after a lag of two and a half decade the same was only 50 per cent. The non-personal expenditure takes the forms of government and social spending. In 1980 the respective expenditures of government, social and personal spending was 36.2 per cent, 42.6 per cent, and 21.2 per cent respectively. The respective values in 2006 have substantially altered to 18.1 per cent, 32.6 per cent, and 49.3 per cent respectively. Thus the personal spending having least value at the inception of reforms has assumed the largest value in 2006. Health expenditure on health services is shown in Table 3.4.

3.9.2. Improvement in Health Indicators

In the post reform period, in most of the health indicators significant improvement was made. Infant mortality decreased from 85 per thousand in 1970 to 23 per thousand in 2005. Under-five mortality rate decreased from 120 to 20 per thousand in the same period. Thus the basic health indicators were substantially improved upon in this period. According to the State of World's Children 2008, (UNICEF-2007), infant mortality rate decreased from 36 to 20 per thousand from 1990 to 2006. In the same time duration, under-five mortality rate decreased from 45 to 24 per thousand. The statistics presented in Table 3.5 show the improvements from 1970s onwards.

However, it is also maintained that progress in health related indicators despite improvement is too slow in the post-reform period. Because of the shift from state to market, implications for health indicators were adverse in the sense that improvements were markedly slow. Despite being fastest

Table 3.4: Expenditures on Health Services by Source

(1980-2006)

	1980	*1990*	*2000*	*2006*
Total expenses on health (billion Yuan)	14.3	74.7	458.7	984.3
Government spending	5.2	18.7	71	177.9
Social spending	6.1	29.3	117.2	321.1
Personal spending	3.0	26.7	270.5	485.4
Structure of total expenses (per cent)	100	100	100	100
Government spending	36.2	25.1	15.5	18.1
Social spending	42.6	39.2	25.5	32.6
Personal spending	21.2	35.7	59.0	49.3
Percentage of total expenses in GDP	3.17	4.03	4.6	4.7
Per-capita total expenses (Yuan)	14.5	65.4	361.9	828
Urban		158.8	828.6	1,145.1
Rural		38.8	209.4	442.4

Sources: UNDP-China. China Human Development Report 2007/08 p. 48.

Table 3.5: Health Indicators

Life Expectancy at birth		*Infant Mortality Rate (per 1000 live births)*		*Under-Five Mortality Rate (/1000, live Births)*	
1970-75	2000-2005	1970	2005	1970	2005
63.2	72.0	85	23	120	27

Source: Human Development Report 2007-08 p. 262.

growing economy of the world for last three decades health indicators did not show the same trend. The correspondence between economic growth and health indicators has been rather weak. This is particularly evident from the average life expectancy statistics for the post-reform period. In 1978, life expectancy at birth was almost 67 years. After three decades life expectance is about 72 years. Thus in the period of immense economic expansion, such improvement is rather unimpressive. By contrast, the average life expectancy had improved from 35 years in 1949 to 67 in 1978, which is an improvement of 32 years.

Table 3.6: Longevity in the Post-reform Period

Year	*1981*	*1990*	*2000*	*2005*
Average life expectancy	67.9	68.6	71.0	72.4

Source: China Human Development Report 2007/08 pp. 6-7.

3.9.3. Health Infrastructure

The health service infrastructure showed good improvement in the post-reform period. Table 3.7 presents the statistics. Total number of hospitals increased more than twice from 9,293 to 19,246 in 2006. Number of clinics increased from 94,395 to 212,243 in the same period; an increase of 2.25 times. Child care centers increased from 2,571 in 1978 to 3,003 in 2006; an increase of 16.8 per cent. Number of agencies for special diseases increased from 887 to 1,402. Disease control centers increased from 2,989 to 3,548 in the same period.

However, there was also decrease in certain health service infrastructural facilities. These notably include the *township health centers* and *village health clinics*. Total number of township health centers in 1978 was 55,018 which reduced to 40,791 in 2006. Thus a decrease of 14,227 township health centers was recorded in the post-reform period. Similarly the number of villages with health clinics as a proportion of total villages decreased from 97.9 per cent to 85.8 per cent in the same period. The impact of the reduction of these two essential health facilities had a very adverse effect over the health indicators. This was not in terms

Table 3.7: Types of Health Agencies

(1978-2006)

	Hospitals	*Clinics*	*Child care centres*	*Agencies for special diseases*	*Disease control centres*	*Township health centres*	*Villages with health clinics*
1978	9,293	94,395	2,571	887	2,989	55,018	97.9
1993	15,436	115,161	3,115	1,872	3,729	45,024	89.1
1998	16,001	229,349	3,191	1,889	3,746	50,613	89.5
2003	17,764	204,468	3,033	1,749	3,584	45,204	77.6
2005	18,703	207,457	3,021	1,502	3,585	41,694	85.8
2006	19,246	212,243	3,003	1,402	3,548	40,791	--

*The percentage of incorporated villages with health clinics in 1978 refers to the ratio of villages with part-time paramedical workers to the total number of villages, which at the time were known as production brigades.

Source: 2007 China Health Statistical Yearbook China Human Development Report 2007/08 p. 49.

Table 3.8: Number of Health Workers

(1978-2006)

	Total health workers	*Doctors*	*Nurses*	*Pharmacists*	*Inspectors*	*Management staff*
1978	2,463,931	1,033,018	406,649	266,570	98,806	298,104
1993	4,117,067	1,831,665	1,056,096	413,025	183,657	432,903
1998	4,423,721	1,999,521	1,218,836	423,644	200,846	435,507
2003	4,306,471	1,867,957	1,265,959	357,378	209,616	318,692
2005	4,460,187	1,938,272	1,349,589	349,533	211,495	312,826
2006	4,624,140	1,994,854	1,426,339	353,565	218,771	323,705

Source: *2007 China Health Statistical Yearbook China* Human Development Report 2007/08 p. 49.

of retardation of health indicators but in terms of the slow down in the pace of improvement of the health indicators, notably life expectancy.

The workforce serving in the health sector of Chinese economy exhibited increasing trends in totality as well as in the individual catagories. As shown in the Table 3.8, total number of health workers increased from 2.46 million in 1978 to 4.62 million in 2006. Number of doctors increased from one million to two million in the same period. Increasing trends were also observed in the number of nurses, pharmacists, inspectors, and management staff. The exact figures for the same are shown in the table.

3.10. Education

3.10.1. Introduction

In the post-reform period China's progress in improving educational parameters were quite significant when compared to most other developing countries. There were quantitative as well as qualitative improvements in the education structure of the economy. The basic literacy parameters improved significantly. Enrollments at all the tires of education improved. There is a continual structural transformation from primary to tertiary and skill oriented education. At the same time the gender composition has also shown significant improvement. Furthermore, the inflow and outflow of students has increased substantially.

3.10.2. Literacy and Education

Though China's achievements in literacy in the pre-reform period were quite impressive, however, the accomplishments of post-reform period were also very significant. China improved its literacy profile by a significant margin within a period of three decades following reforms in 1978. In 1990, the adult literacy rate was already 77.8 per cent which increased to 93.5 per cent in 2007. Literacy rate for the youth (15-24 years) was 94.3 in 1990 which improved to 99.3 in 2007. These statistics are presented in Table 3.9.

Table 3.9: Literacy

Literacy rates		*1990*	*2007*
	Male + Female	77.8	93.5
Adult (15+)	Male	87.0	96.5
	Female	68.1	90.0
	Male + Female	94.3	99.3
Youth (15-24)	Male	97.0	99.4
	Female	91.5	99.1

Source: UNESCO 2007, www.unesco.org.

3.10.3. Structure of Education

As China's demographic and developmental profile changed, the structure of education also underwent gradual transformation in terms of enrollment and proportionate teachers at different levels of education.

In 1978 the percentage of total enrolment in primary schools was 68.5 per cent which reduced to 52.8 per cent in 2004. Thus an overall decrease of 16 percentage points was experienced in primary enrollment as a proportion of total enrollment. In the same period the enrollment in secondary education increased from 31.1 per cent to 40.9 per cent. Thus secondary education recorded a growth of almost 10 percentage points in total enrollment. Colleges and university made an improvement from 0.4 per cent to 6.3 per cent in the total enrollment, from 1978 to 2004. According to these statistics, presented in Table 3.10, overall percentage enrollment of primary school students in the total enrollment is decreasing while as that of secondary, college and university students is increasing. Thus more people make up to higher study which is a sign of development.

Table 3.10: Structure of Student Enrollment

(Unit: Per cent)

	1978	*1989*	*1997*	*2004*
College and university	0.4	1.2	1.5	6.3
Secondary school students	31.1	28.7	32.8	40.9
Primary school students	68.5	70.1	65.7	52.8

Source: China statistical census, 2007. www.allcountries.org/China statistics.

The trend of increasing role of higher education is also evident from the structure of teacher employment. The proportion of teachers in primary education is declining while that of secondary and tertiary education is increasing. In 1978 the proportion of full time teachers to total teachers in primary education was 60 which reduced to 50.5 per cent in 2004. In the same time span, this proportion for secondary education increased from 37.6 to 41.8 per cent while as that of tertiary education teacher percentage increased from 2.4 to 7.7 per cent. The statistics for the same are presented in Table 3.11.

3.11. Energy Sector

One of the critical indicators of economic activity in a country is the consumption and production of energy. The post-reform period witnessed consistent growth of both the demand and production of energy. However,

Table 3.11: Full Time Teachers by Type

(Unit: Per cent of total)

	1978	*1989*	*1997*	*2004*
College and university	2.4	4.2	3.9	7.7
Secondary school	37.6	36.6	40.3	41.8
Primary school	60.0	59.2	55.8	50.5

Source: China statistical census, 2007. www.allcountries.org/China statistics.

the growth of demand exceeded the domestic supply in 1997 when first time net exports worth -11 Mtoe were realised. Thus in 1997 China became a net importer of energy. Till then it maintained a positive energy surplus. The energy deficit of China which it fulfills through imports reached 45 Mtoe in 2003.

The overall growth rate of the energy production in the economy from 1980 to 2003 was 3.52 per cent. The largest energy production sector in the economy was coal, which also accounts for the increasing contribution by China to global pollution. Contribution of coal to total energy production in 2003 was 66.6 per cent. Biomass and waste contributed 15.91 per cent; the second largest energy production sector in the economy. 12.28 per cent of total energy production was through oil which was the third largest energy production sector. Natural gas, hydro-electricity and nuclear sectors contributed 2.61 per cent, 1.74 per cent and 0.8 per cent of the total energy production in the country respectively.

The growth rate of energy consumption in the given period was 3.82 per cent, i.e., 0.3 percentage points larger than the production. As the gap between production and consumption increased through time China incurred deficits which are made up by import of oil from resource oil exporting countries. However, as production of coal is the largest element of the energy sector, so it is in case of consumption. Coal contributed 60.6 per cent of total energy consumption. This is followed by oil which contributes 19 per cent of the overall production. The contribution of oil in total energy production is only 169 Mtoe but its consumption is 270 Mtoe (2003). Therefore, 101 Mtoe of oil have been imported from rest of the world. This deficit is partly corrected by the export of coal by China worth 55 Mtoe in 2003 so as to leave the total deficit equal to 45 Mtoe.

Contribution of biomass and waste in total consumption is 15.41 per cent, while as that of natural gas, hydroelectricity, and nuclear energy is 2.46 per cent, 1.68 per cent, and 0.77 per cent respectively. All these figures are collectively shown in Table 3.12.

Table 3.12: Energy Balance in China, 1980-2003

Year	*Production and Stock Change (Mtoe)*[#] *Coal*	*Oil*	*Natural gas*	*Hydro*	*Biomass and Waste*	*Nuclear*	*Total*
1980	316	107	12	5	180	0	620
1985	405	130	13	8	189	0	745
1990	545	136	16	11	200	0	908
1995	691	149	19	16	206	3	1084
2000	698	151	24	19	214	4	1115
2003	917	169	36	24	219	11	1376
Growth[†] 1980-2003	4.74	2.00	4.89	7.05	0.85		3.52
Contribution by each sector (%) 2003	66.64	12.28	2.61	1.74	15.91	0.80	100.00

(Contd.)

(Contd. Table 3.12)

		Consumption (Mtoe)					
Year	Coal	Oil	Natural gas	Hydro	Biomass and Waste	Nuclear	Total
1980	313	89	12	5	180	0	599
1985	401	93	13	8	189	0	704
1990	535	110	16	11	200	0	872
1995	673	158	19	16	206	3	1075
2000	664	222	26	19	214	4	1149
2003	862	270	35	24	219	11	1421
Growth 1980-2003	4.50	4.94	4.76	7.05	0.85		3.82
Contribution by each sector (Per cent) 2003	60.66	19.00	2.46	1.68	15.41	0.77	10.00
	Year	1980	1985	1990	1995	2000	2003
Energy Balance or Net Export (Mtoe)		21	41	36	9	-34	-45

#million tones of oil equivalents; †annual average compound growth rates derived from given data; derived from the given data.

Source: International Energy Agency, 2005, cited in *Dancing with Giants: China, India and the Global Economy*, World Bank (2007), p. 136.

References

1. Qian, Yingyi. 1999. The Process of China's Market Transition (1978-98): The Evolutionary, Historical, and Comparative Perspectives. Stanford University p. 4.
2. Justin Yifp Lin, Fang Cai Zhou Li. 1994. *China's Economic Reforms: Pointers for other economies in Transition*? Policy Research Working Paper. World Bank p. 19.
3. *Ibid.* p. 20.
4. *Ibid.* p. 20.
5. World Bank. 1996. *World Development Report, 1996: From Plan to Market.* World Bank/Oxford University Press, p. 24.
6. Chow, Gregory C. 1987. Development of a More Market-Oriented Economy in China. *Science, New Series,* Vol. 235, No. 4786 (Jan. 16, 1987), p. 296.
7. Qian, Yingyi. 1999. *op. cit.* p. 5.
8. *Ibid.* pp.7-8.
9. Maddison, Angus. 2007. *Chinese Economic Performance in the Long Run.* OECD, p. 74.
10. Qian, Yingyi. 1999. *op. cit.* p. 9.
11. *Ibid.* p.10.
12. Gelb, Alan, et, al. 1993. Can Communist Economies Transform Incrementally? The Experience of China NBER Macroeconomics Annual, Vol. 8 (1993), p. 98.
13. Qian, Yingyi. 1999. *op. cit.* p. 21.
14. *Ibid.* p. 22.
15. *Ibid.* p. 17.
16. *Ibid.* p. 7.
17. *Ibid.* p. 7.
18. *Ibid.* p. 98.
19. Qian, Yingyi. 1999. *op. cit.* p. 19.
20. Maddison, Angus. 2007. *op. cit.* p. 89.
21. *Ibid.* p. 91.
22. Qian, Yingyi. 1999. *op. cit.* p. 20.
23. *Ibid.* 20.
24. United Nations. 2003. China, a current perspective: updated common country assessment. UN Country Team in China, Beijing, p. 19.
25. *Ibid.* p. 19.
26. *Ibid.* p. 20.
27. Qian, Yingyi. 1999. *op. cit.* p. 18.
28. United Nations. 2003. *op. cit.* p. 20.
29. Shanghai flash. 2005. Short history of reforms concerning Chinese state owned enterprises. Issue no. 2 February 2005.

30. George J. Gilboy and Benjamin L. Read. 2008. Political and Social Reform in China: Alive and Walking. *The Washington Quarterly,* Summer 2008 p.155.
31. Maddison, Angus. 2007. *op. cit.* p. 86.
32. Qian, Yingyi. 1999. *op. cit.* p. 6.
33. *Ibid.* p. 11.
34. Gautam Jaggi, *et. al.* 1996. China's Economic Reforms: Chronology and Statistics Institute for International Economics Working Paper 96-5, p. 25.
35. Yuan at 1987 prices and dollars at 1990 international dollars.
36. Maddison, *op. cit.* p. 69.

4

Rural Transformation

4.1 Introduction

In developing countries, more people live in rural than in urban area. Due to limits to urbanization, it is highly unlikely that most of these can migrate to cities for meaningful economic alternative. Therefore, the basic challenge faced by the developing countries is transformation of the rural sector from subsistence or low income to higher income one. That is, the process of economic development should be such that the economic status of rural sector itself is raised, without an indirect reliance on the growth of the urban sector. Since the economic and social indicators of development fair systematically unfavourable in rural areas, there will be a direct and larger impact on the overall development of an economy.

Thus, reforms have to be directed toward the rural sector of the economy to unleash the latent potential therein and make a direct impact on the rural poverty in its diverse forms. One of the empirical investigations that lend credit to this view is the experience of China in the post-reform period. In the process of reform and sustained growth what happened to the rural sector of the Chinese economy is of paramount significance. According to World Urbanisation Prospectus, 2007, almost 75 per cent of people in China in 1980 were living in rural areas, which by 2007 decreased to 58 per cent.

The current part of the study analyses the impact of the reforms on the rural economy of China from diverse perspectives. Important among these dimensions is the broader dimensions of the level and the change in the role of the agriculture sector in the livelihood of the rural population. Also important is the change in the economic status of the people and the evolving composition of the rural society in income terms. One of the most important dimensions related with the welfare state of the rural society is the level of poverty and the change therein during the course of the process of the trickle down effects of a sustained high growth process the Chinese economy has experienced.

While analysing the impact of the reforms, important determinants of the state of well being—which directly or indirectly have bearing on the livelihood and other development indicators of the rural society—have been thoroughly discussed within the scope of the present study. Most of the indicators, either from qualitative or quantitative perspectives, have shown satisfactory improvement in the aftermath of the reform. Notable among these are; reduction in poverty, increase in per capita income, decrease in illiteracy, increase in the production of the agriculture sector, enhanced asset base of the rural society, and growth of the rural non-farm sector.

However, some important determinants and indicators of development, which notably include insecure land-use rights and rising inequality, are as yet to be addressed with adequate seriousness. This has not only obvious detrimental socio-political consequences but significantly inhibits the economic potential and incentives of the rural sector.

4.2 Institutional Change in the Historical Perspective

The economic transformation of the rural economy proceeded from an institutional change of far reaching consequences. Towards the closing phase of the pre-reform period, first the stagnation and later the negative growth experienced in the agriculture sector output had a direct bearing on the well being of the rural society. This is quite obvious because countryside depended critically on this sector. The pressure on the government to guarantee economic performance as well as the change in the guard at the central government level—with less conservative ideological persuasions—led to a departure from previous policies. The system was fundamentally relaxed to allow room for those policies which rendered results.

As a result, peasants in Yongjia County in the region of Wenzhou, Zhejiang, and in Fengyang County, Anhui, seeking to end their food shortages, implemented a policy of contracting collective land to families. This was at a time when all land and labour resources in China were held by hundreds of thousands of people's communes.[1] Thus, the institutional change, called ***household responsibility system,*** was initiated that gave the households the right to use land for profit after fulfilling certain quota requirements.

The first step of the reform replaced the commune-based agricultural production system with a family-based production system. This weakened the communes; however, other functions such as marketing crops, public services, etc. were still organised by the collectives. In September 1980, the government completely disbanded the communes when it ordered total de-collectivisation of all aspects of agricultural production and marketing.[2]

To prevent a political backlash or resurgence of a new cultural revolution, three measures were conceived. To begin with, the production responsibility system was implemented within the existing framework of communes. This prevented an abrupt move to a completely new institutional arrangement. Secondly, the responsibility system was not a monolithic technical and administrative programme, but had enough flexibility to adjust to the varying conditions and practices across the geographic extent of China. Thus responsibility system could vary in different regions to suit the local conditions. Finally, before implementing the system elsewhere, popular consent was ensured in the areas where the system was implemented on experimental basis.

On the whole, the reforms occurred in two reasonably distinct phases. The first phase focused on decentralising the system of agricultural production, while the second phase emphasised liberalising factor and output markets. .. . During the initial phase of the reforms, the state raised its procurement prices for agricultural products and reopened rural markets for farmers to trade produce from their private plots. After two years of experiments, in 1981 the government began to decentralise agricultural production from the commune system to individual farm households.[3]

In 1985 the uniform grain procurement system had been changed to contract purchasing. Beyond the contract, purchases negotiated with the government changed to market purchases. Of 132 agricultural products that had been subject to state procurement, only silk thread, medical materials, and tobacco stayed that way, whereas transactions and price setting for the rest were through the market.[4] The number of commodities subject to state procurement programs declined from 38 in 1985 to only nine in 1991. In 1993, the grain market was further liberalised, and the grain rationing system that had been in existence for 40 years was abolished.[5]

4.3 Agricultural Sector

The transformation of primary sector can be analysed from different dimensions. Before analysing the data pertaining to the transformation of the primary sector of the Chinese economy, specification of the essential parameters and a theoretical consideration of the same are indispensable. This furnishes the essential background for the analytical treatment of the variables that form parts of the following discussion on the subject. Among the central variables, deemed to be essential in the context of and within the present study, include: institutional change, output and employment share, technical change, productivity increase, market orientation, and change in composition of output and employment.

One of the fundamental requirements for development and transformation of any sector of economy is the institutional arrangement that determines the right to own, use and dispose off or sell the inputs and output of the sector. An arrangement which restricts the factor, product and labour market of any sector essentially restricts the role of profit incentive of the producers and suppliers. This inhibits the incentive mechanism of the economy resulting into stagnation. Therefore, a change in the institutional arrangements that guarantees the rights of the private actors in the economy to retain the outcome of their hard-work and risk endurance provides much needed incentives for the growth and investment in the sector. One of the basic factors determining transformation of the primary sector (or any sector for that matter) is the change in the institutional arrangement or property rights regime of the economy.

As a general rule, with development in the economy, share of the primary sector in output and employment progressively decreases. However, the magnitude of output in the sector itself witnesses improvement. Though the share of agriculture in total output decreases the output in the primary sector itself increases. Thus the reduction in output and employment share is in relation to increasing share of secondary and tertiary sectors which have more scope to grow—due to important peculiarities of supply and demand factors—than agriculture. The successful transformation of economy to higher stages of development requires every sector to grow significantly through time. Primary sector output also requires to expand robustly to ensure growth of the overall economy. Therefore, for a case of successful transformation of an economy, share of the primary sector decreases, but its productivity should improve quite significantly.

Successful primary sector transformation requires technical changes in agriculture which include improvement in irrigation, fertiliser and pesticide application, seed quality and quantity, as well as mechanisation. This increases the supply potential of the sector by improving its productivity. The level of technical change, therefore, is one of the parameters of transformation of the primary sector. Since, the aim of technical improvement and mechanisation is to increase the productivity of the primary sector; therefore, productivity increase itself is one of the indicators of the transformation of the rural economy.

One more dimension to analyse agriculture transformation is the process of commercialisation, which is representative of market orientation. Transition from planning to market leads the profit incentive (the *invisible hand*) to maximise the production of most profitable products. It warrants the efficient use of resources as well as the production of optimal basket of commodities. Through increased income of the producers, like farmers, commercialisation has a very strong impact on the demand side of the sector. Thus, the level of commercialisation is itself a parameter of transformation of the sector.

Yet another dimension, to look at the primary sector transformation, is in terms of the change in the composition of the output. A move from farming towards non-farm activities like animal husbandry, fisheries, and forestry is diversification of the primary sector with positive implication from output, employment and income perspective.

All these changes thus represent transformation of agriculture in positive direction. Nonetheless, the exact magnitude of positive change(s) to qualify a successful transformation is fraught with significant theoretical and practical limitations. The determination of the threshold degree of change for transformation, in any of these factors, or in their collective index, despite having some importance, is unviable because of its limitations. Such an exercise itself is not only beyond the scope of the present study but is not indispensably required to analyse the transformation of the primary sector of Chinese economy.

Therefore, change in the magnitude of the basic parameters of the primary sector, deemed to follow trajectory of now more developed countries, is itself taken equivalent to transformation, without specification of the required magnitudes for the same. In other words, the change that improves the prospects of population directly or through an indirect mechanism and brings or helps them to come out of poverty and deprivation are taken as changes that represent transformation of the sector. The analysis is without specification of the level of transformation that the economy has attained after the reform period. Therefore, the judgment of extent of transformation of the primary sector, despite based on quantitative data, is qualitative in the sense that the required qualifying quantity of change is unspecified.

In the post-reform period, China's primary sector underwent important changes with many positive impacts on its rural population. The reforms unleashed a myriad of forces which changed the composition and output of different variables in the primary sector.

4.3.1. Output and Employment Share

Following the reforms in late 1970s, output of the primary sector experienced three-fold increase. Primary sector average annual compound growth rate for two and half decade was 4.31 per cent. When, compared with secondary and tertiary sector growth rates and output increases, during the same period, such an increase seems rather meager. However, given the inherent limitation of primary sector from the perspective of diversification, economies of scale, technological improvement, market availability, life duration of the products and geographical peculiarity of

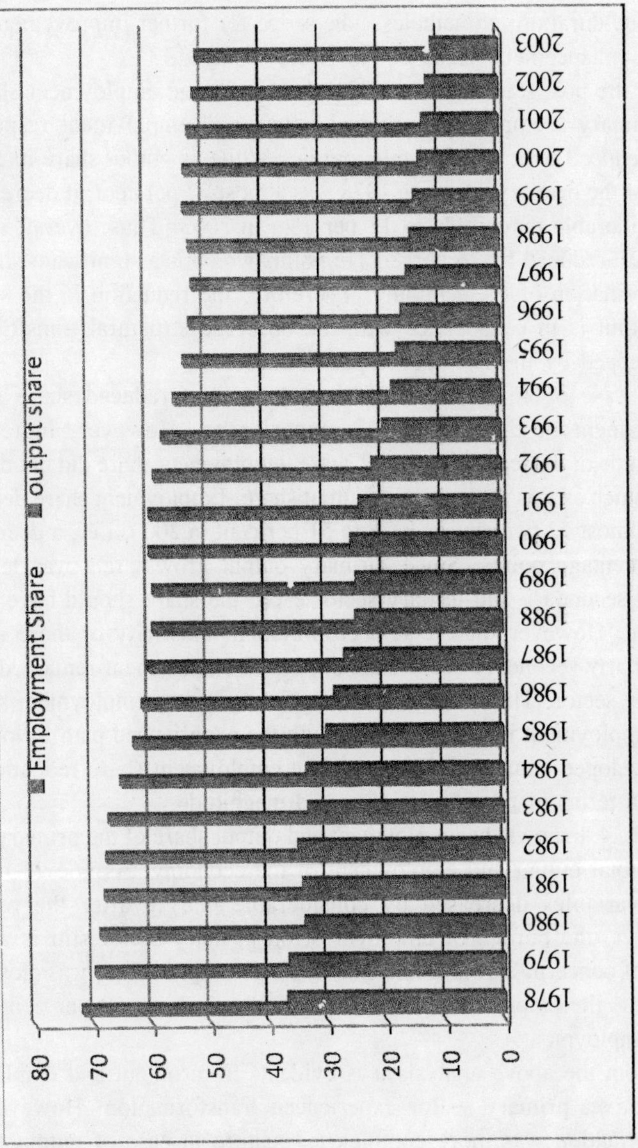

Fig. 4.1: Employment and Output Shares of Primary Sector

Source: Compiled and Developed from Official Statistics: see Tables 2 and 4, Appendix Chapter 3.

the country; such an increase seems rather significant. This change in the output was made possible by increase in the productivity in agriculture—because arable land did not increase by any significant margin—during the same duration. Nonetheless, the scope for further improvement in the output enhancement needs not to be downplayed.

In the post-reform period both the output and employment shares of the primary sector in the national output and employment respectively have reduced by a considerable margin. While as output share in national GDP of the primary sector in 1978 was almost 37 per cent, it decreased by a considerable magnitude to 11 per cent in 2003. Thus, overall share in the GDP reduced by 26 percentage points which is a significant structural transformation of the economy. Therefore, the reduction in the share of the output is in consonance with the observed structural transformation experienced by the now developed countries.

In case of employment, the same trend of reduced share in total employment of the economy is experienced. However, in terms of magnitude of decrease in the total share, employment share did not decrease by as much as was the case with output share. Employment share decreased from almost 72 per cent in 1978 to 51 per cent in 2003, i.e., a decrease of 21 percentage points. Since, primary output growth rate was less than half of secondary and tertiary sector each; the share should have further reduced. However, due to less **employment elasticity** of these sectors, particularly secondary sector, the burden of employment remained on the primary sector. The reduction of the primary sector employment share in total employment is in consonance with the experienced path followed by the developed countries. However, the employment share reduction falls short in terms of required or expected magnitude.

Fig. 4.1 shows the employment and output share of the primary sector in the total output and employment of the economy. As is evident, both these variables decreased by considerable margin after the reforms. However, the burden of employment on primary sector still is a major cause of concern. Towards the end, while as output shares was close to 10 per cent, the employment share still remained above 50 per cent of the total employment.

From the above analysis it is evident, from output and employment perspective, primary sector experienced transformation. However, this transformation was more complete or mature in case of output than in case of employment. For a more mature and meaningful transformation of the primary sector, the employment burden on the primary sector has to be significantly reduced. This demands a substantial increase in the employment elasticity of output of the secondary and tertiary sectors. In particular the secondary sector is required to rescue the primary sector from its employment hangover of the pre-reform period. This is because it has lagged much behind in the employment creation for the economy, though its output share is very high.

4.3.2. Primary Output: the Sub-Sectoral Perspective

After the inception of reform, output of the primary sector experienced a substantial increase. The gross output of primary sector with disaggregated data into its sub-sectors is presented in the Table 4.1. At current prices,

Box 1: Inflation—Growth Correlation

Inflation, Demand and Supply: the Case of Chinese Primary Sector. From the given data the level of inflation in the primary sector can be measured. The effective indicator for the same is **GDP Deflator,** which measures the relation (ratio) between the nominal and real GDP. The formula that we employ is:

GDP Deflator = Nominal GDP growth / Real GDP growth

GDP Deflator = 13.34 / 4.32 = 3.08 Overall GDP Deflator in primary sector was 3.08, which measures the effect of inflation on the primary output. That is for every unit increase of Real Output in primary sector, Nominal GDP of the sector increased by 3.08 units. Therefore, the rate of inflation in the sector was 3.08 per cent in the concerned period, from 1978 to 2004. Such a level of inflation can be considered quite moderate from the consumers' standpoint. It does not substantially influence the purchasing capacity of the consumer, particularly in a fast growing economy where income is consistently increasing. However, a certain level of inflation is also significant from the perspective of the producers. Increase in prices represents increase in the demand of the products. If the above data is analysed from the perspective of the correspondence of the nominal and real growth rates of sub-sectors, the relation between nominal and real growth is quite strong. A high nominal growth is followed by a relatively high growth on the real side. This can be interpreted as: **Given supply, high nominal growth rate means increase in demand of the products, resulting in higher prices and therefore higher levels of profitability. This induces the producers to produce more which leads to high real growth rate.** Therefore, the real growth rates of fishery and animal husbandry were more as compared to farming and forestry. Inflation influences an economy from diverse angles. High rate of inflation strips the consumers of their purchasing power and below poverty. It can also be detrimental for investment by making returns uncertain; because higher the level of inflation beyond a benchmark, higher the magnitude of fluctuations in it. On the other hand lower the level of inflation below a benchmark, lower the incentive for investors or producers. This may bring stagnation in the economy. Thus both the incentive and disincentive effects require a proper balance. A moderate rate of inflation therefore is necessary to safeguard the interests of producers and consumers in the long run.

Table 4.1: Gross Output Value of Farming, Forestry, Animal Husbandry and Fishery and Related Indices

Year	*Gross Output Value of Farming, Forestry, Animal Husbandry and Fishery (100 million yuan)*					*Indices of Gross Output of Farming, Forestry, Animal Husbandry and Fishery (preceding year=100)*				
	Total	*Farming*	*Forestry*	*Animal Husbandry*	*Fishery*	*Total*	*Farming*	*Forestry*	*Animal Husbandry*	*Fishery*
1978	1397.0	1117.5	48.1	209.3	22.1					
1980	1922.6	1454.1	81.4	354.2	32.9	101.4	99.7	112.2	107.0	107.7
1985	3619.5	2506.4	188.7	798.3	126.1	103.4	99.8	104.5	117.2	118.9
1989	6534.7	4100.6	284.9	1800.4	348.8	103.1	102.4	100.4	105.5	107.2
1990	7662.1	4954.3	330.3	1967.0	410.6	107.6	108.0	103.1	107.0	110.0
1991	8157.0	5146.4	367.9	2159.2	483.5	103.7	100.9	108.0	108.8	107.6
1992	9084.7	5588.0	422.6	2460.5	613.5	106.4	104.2	107.7	108.8	115.3
1993	10995.5	6605.1	494.0	3014.4	882.0	107.8	105.2	108.0	110.8	118.4
1994	15750.5	9169.2	611.1	4672.0	1298.2	108.6	103.2	108.9	116.7	120.0
1995	20340.9	11884.6	709.9	6045.0	1701.3	110.9	107.9	105.0	114.8	119.4

(Contd.)

(Contd. Table 4.1)

Year	Gross Output Value of Farming, Forestry, Animal Husbandry and Fishery (100 million yuan)					Indices of Gross Output of Farming, Forestry, Animal Husbandry and Fishery (preceding year=100)				
	Total	Farming	Forestry	Animal Husbandry	Fishery	Total	Farming	Forestry	Animal Husbandry	Fishery
1996	22353.7	13539.8	778.0	6015.5	2020.4	109.4	107.8	105.7	111.4	114.0
1997	23788.4	13852.5	817.8	6835.4	2282.7	106.7	104.5	103.3	110.1	111.5
1998	24541.9	14241.9	851.3	7025.8	2422.9	106.0	104.9	102.9	107.4	108.8
1999	24519.1	14106.2	886.3	6997.6	2529.0	104.7	104.3	103.2	104.6	107.2
2000	24915.8	13873.6	936.5	7393.1	2712.6	103.6	101.4	105.4	106.3	106.5
2001	26179.6	14462.8	938.8	7963.1	2815.0	104.2	103.6	99.3	106.3	103.9
2002	27390.8	14931.5	1033.5	8454.6	2971.1	104.9	103.9	107.1	106.0	106.1
2003	29691.8	14870.1	1239.9	9538.8	3137.6	103.9	100.5	106.9	107.3	105.3
2004	36239.0	18138.4	1327.1	12173.8	3605.6	107.5	108.5	102.0	107.2	106.0
Growth* 1978-2004	13.34	11.31	13.60	16.91	21.64	4.32	2.94	3.9	6.8	8.0

*Growth rates calculated from the given data.

Data in value terms in this table are calculated at current prices, while the indices are calculated at comparable prices.

Source: Developed from data by China Statistical Census, 2007.www.allcountries.org/China statistics.

the total gross value output of the primary sector increased at an average compound growth rate of 13.34 per cent annually for the period 1980-2004. However, looking at the indices of gross output of primary sector, the growth rate was 4.32 per cent. In real terms growth was least in case of farming, i.e., 2.94 per cent, followed by forestry with a growth rate of 3.9 per cent. While as the highest growth was observed in case of fishery, 8.0 per cent, followed by animal husbandry with a growth rate of 6.8 per cent.

4.3.3. Structural Change in Agricultural Output

As the economy advances to the higher stages of development, a change in the composition within the output of the primary sector occurs. In Fig. 4.2 variations in the composition of different sub-sectors within the primary sector are shown. Since, fishery and animal husbandry grew at much faster rate than farming and forestry, such a change in composition is natural. While emphasising the change in the composition, the fact that all sub-sectors grew in absolute sense must not be overlooked. Therefore, the shift in the composition occurs as a result of the differences in the relative growth rates of the sub-sectors.

The structural transformation and diversification within the primary sector is depicted by decrease in the share of farming and forestry and increase in other primary sector activities in gross output of agriculture. In 1978 the share of farming in the agriculture was 80.0 per cent which decreased to 50 per cent in 2004. Share of animal husbandry increased from 15 per cent to 33.6 per cent during the same period. Fishery's share in the agriculture out put increased from 1.6 per cent in 1978 to 9.9 per cent in 2004, while as the share of forestry increased from 3.4 per cent to 3.7 per cent during the same period. Thus, there was a significant reduction in the relative importance of farming in the agriculture with a concomitant increase in significance of animal husbandry and fishery.

The above statistical facts confer a substantial role to animal husbandry and fishery in transforming the primary sector of the economy. High growth rates in these sub-sectors warranted relatively good growth of the main sector. Their collective share increased from less than 17 per cent in 1978 to more than 43 per cent in 2004, which is a substantial structural change within this sector. Thus, collectively output of both these sub-sectors was just 7 percentage points less than farming. If their growth momentum sustained, in near future, collectively these could replace farming as the major output contributor in the primary sector. Even, animal husbandry, with constant high rate of growth, can replace farming as the main source of the primary output. Looking at Chinese experience, livestock development should be an important policy consideration for developing countries.

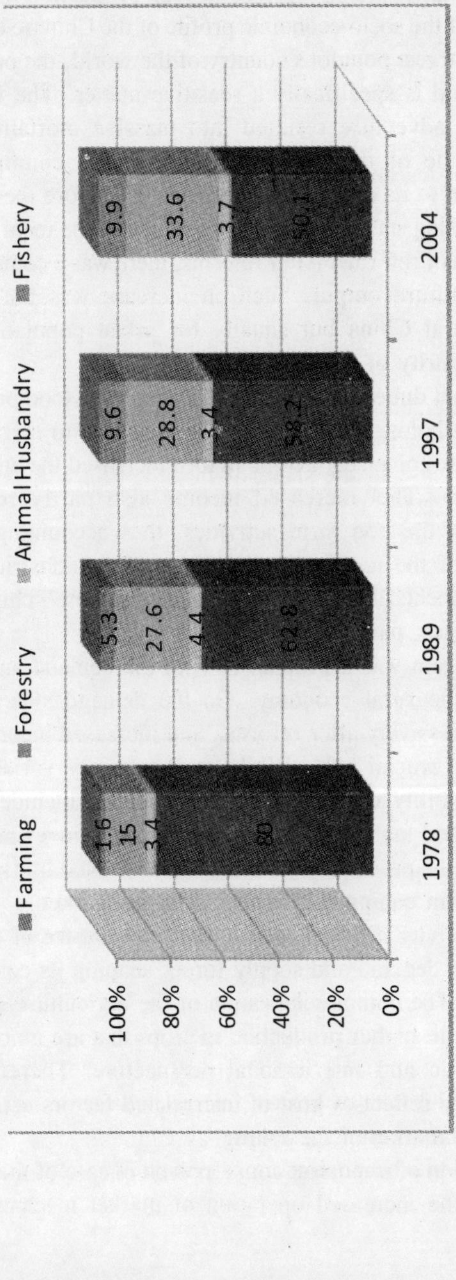

Fig. 4.2: Structure of Gross Output Value of Agriculture.

Source: Developed from data by China Statistical Census, 2007. www.allcountries. org/China_statistics.

4.3.4. Major Crops: Growth and Implications

Following the reforms, production of crops increased. This was the result of increased productivity experienced in the agricultural sector. As a consequence, per capita output as well as per capita agricultural labour output increased measurably. The increase in crop production had effects on many dimensions of the socio-economic profile of the Chinese economy.

China being the largest populous country of the world, the production and availability of food is specifically a sensitive matter. The failure of Great Leap Forward adventure resulted into massive mortality in the country. Therefore one of the major concerns of the country is the availability of the food to its population. Immediately before the reforms, agriculture was witnessing stagnation and this was one of the main concerns leading to the initiation of reforms. After reforms, there was a commendable increase in the agriculture output. Such an increase was not only an imperative for the rural China but equally for urban population. This increased the food security of the country.

The other important dimension in which the increased food production affected the rural population was increase in income due to marketing of surplus production. The enhanced income in turn increased the entitlement basket of the farmers. This increased income also partly represents additional demand for the non farm activities, thus accounting for the demand and growth of the non-farm as well as other industries of the economy. The complementarities of different industries were in high action because of these changes, particularly in rural China.

The productivity gain was a product of both the demand and supply factors operating in the rural economy. On the demand side enlarged markets, opened progressively after reforms, and increased income of the people played a very crucial role. While as the supply variables that strengthened the possibility of higher crop production, included higher "land-right security" and higher profitability turned into investment. The other factors affecting the productivity include the improved transportation facilities and better farm equipments available in the market.

Growth in productivity differed according to the **nature of the crop and soil** as well as the demand and supply forces shaping its equilibrium price and investment. The commercialisation of the agriculture generally increases the incentive to higher production in crops that are more market oriented from domestic and international perspective. Therefore, the increase in productivity reflects a host of interrelated factors acting upon the factor and product market of the crops.

One more dimension of important consideration in case of the China's experience has been the increased operation of market mechanism and reduced role of the government in setting the production targets for the farmers. As the state monopoly over the grain production progressively decreased, product composition became more efficient in the Paretan sense[6]. The product-mix now is more determined by the cost and benefit consideration from the market perspective and a shift in production occurred from a low profit combination to a higher one. Though the conditions of perfect competition are very restrictive to be operationalised in the real world, yet the case of primary products is relatively stronger as compared to other sectors of the economy.

4.3.5. Productivity Growth

The productivity of major farm crops in the post-reform period increased measurably. The best productivity increase performers, as shown by the statistics in Table 4.2, have been sesame, beet-roots, rapeseeds, cotton, and peanuts with an average annual productivity growth of 5.21, 3.27, 3.26, 2.97 and 2.85 per cent respectively. A moderate increase of 1.62, 1.32 and 0.18 per cent occurred in cereals, sugarcane, and flue cured tobacco respectively. Only in case of jute and ambary hemp there was a negative productivity growth, -1.04 per cent, recorded. Thus, in most of the farm crops of commercial importance productivity has increased in contrast to the stagnation faced in the late 1970s which led to the subsequent reforms.

4.3.6. Per Capita Output

Among the indicators of agriculture transformation, per capita farm output is a very relevant indicator. This is particularly in terms of the potential range of the effects on the larger masses as productivity increases. It is true that productivity improvement leads to a very positive and subtle change in any sector of the economy. However, there may be a simultaneous change in the population as well which may nullify the positive gains, at per capita level, of increase in productivity. Thus, any net positive gains of productivity in a population increasing situation demands that productivity should not only increase but should increase more than the population of the economy. Therefore, high per capita output increase in the major farm crops is very vital for successful transformation of an economy.

In case of China, there were large productivity gains even in per capita terms after the reforms in late 1970s. The crops for which time series data is available at the per capita level include: grain; cotton; oil-bearing crops; pork, beef and mutton; aquatic products; and milk.

Among all the crops the per capita absolute output is highest in case of grain, as shown in Table 4.3. However, the same has the least

Table 4.2: Yield of Major Farm Crops Per Hectare (kg/hectare)

Year	Cereals	Cotton	Peanuts	Rape-seeds	Sesame	Jute and Ambary Hemp	Sugar-cane	Beet-roots	Flue-cured Tobacco
1980		550	1539	838	333	3497	47562	14242	1806
1985		807	2008	1248	657	4154	53430	15913	1927
1989		728	1820	1089	467	2310	50856	16243	1600
1990		807	2191	1264	702	2421	57106	21668	1683
1991	4206	868	2188	1212	640	1902	58345	20791	1709
1992	4342	660	2000	1281	692	2233	58606	22832	1687
1993	4557	750	2492	1309	747	2449	59012	20124	1654
1994	4500	785	2564	1296	794	2020	57671	17936	1491
1995	4659	879	2687	1416	908	2534	58136	20132	1584
1996	4894	890	2804	1366	969	2491	56470	24150	1750

(Contd.)

(Contd. Table 4.2)

Year	*Cereals*	*Cotton*	*Peanuts*	*Rape-seeds*	*Sesame*	*Jute and Ambary Hemp*	*Sugar-cane*	*Beet-roots*	*Flue-cured Tobacco*
1997	4822	1025	2592	1479	919	2649	60158	24475	1809
1998	4953	1009	2943	1272	1042	2677	59550	24805	1740
1999	4945	1028	2961	1469	1066	2538	57338	25334	1797
2000	4753	1093	2973	1519	1034	2516	57626	24518	1763
2001	4800	1107	2888	1597	1061	2046	60625	26807	1732
2002	4885	1175	3011	1477	1180	2868	64663	30232	1792
2003	4873	951	2654	1582	863	2462	64023	24925	1768
2004	5187	1111	3022	1813	1128	2719	65199	30829	1889
Yield Growth 1978-2004	1.62	2.97	2.85	3.26	5.21	-1.04	1.32	3.27	0.18

Source: China Statistical Census, 2007. www.allcountries.org/China_statistics.

Table 4.3: Output of Major Farm Crops' Per Capita

kg

Year	*Grain*	*Cotton*	*Oil-bearing Corps*	*Pork, Beef and Mutton*	*Total Aquatic Products*	*Milk*
1980	327	2.8	7.8		4.6	1.2
1985	361	3.9	15.0		6.7	2.4
1989	364	3.4	11.6		10.3	3.4
1990	393	4.0	14.2		10.9	3.7
1995	387	4.0	18 7		20.9	4.6
1997	402	3.7	17.5	34.6	29.3	5.4
2000	366	3.5	23.4	38.3	33.9	6.6
2001	356	4.2	22.5	39.5	34.4	8.1
2002	357	3.8	22.6	40.8	35.6	10.2
2003	334	3.8	21.8	42.7	36.5	13.6
2004	362	4.9	23.7	44.6	37.8	17.4
Growth 1980-2004	0.42	2.35	4.73	1.06	9.17	11.78

Source: China Statistical Census, 2007. www.allcountries.org/China_statistics.

per capita growth after the reforms. The per capita increase of grain in the period has been from 327 kg in 1980 to 362 kg in 2004. The average annual compound growth, therefore, has been 0.42 per cent only. In case of cotton the growth per capita has been 2.35 per cent. It increased from 2.8 kg in 1980 to 4.9 kg in 2004. Oil-bearing crops experienced a per capita growth of 2.35 per cent after the reforms. In absolute terms, this category experienced a three fold increase from 7.8 kg in 1980 to 23.7 per cent in 2004. Growth in pork, beef and mutton has been relatively slow. The collective growth experienced was only 1.06 per cent for the period 1978 to 2004. In absolute terms the total increase was from 34.6 kg to 44.6 kg.

4.3.7. Per Capita Agriculture Labour Output

With the process of development the need for food supply increases as more people are engaged in secondary and tertiary sectors of the economy. One of the convenient measures to estimate the potential supply of food grains is the increase in food production per agricultural labourer. This on the one hand represents the surplus of food to be supplied to the other industries and on the other exhibits the increase of income to the farmers in real terms. Such an increased supply can both be translated into better health, higher incomes and improved living standards. Both of these bring a significant improvement in the human development of the beneficiaries. The income dimension here is particularly important in the background of reforms because the production of food crops is determined by the market forces which generate profits for the producers.

Thus, an increase of output measured in terms of per capita labour force engaged in the sector itself can be taken as an appropriate measure of transformation of the sector. This can be used to measure some of the effects not included into the former two indicators of increased production.

While analysing this measure of transformation, China pictures fairly well. The items for which statistics have been made available by the Statistical Bureau include: grain; cotton; oil-bearing crops; pork, beef and mutton; total aquatic products; and milk. As revealed by Table 4.4, the per capita agricultural labour production of grain in 1985 was 1222 kg which increased to 1518 kg in 2004. Thus the annual compound growth of the same was 1.14 per cent. However, grains have been a relatively well cultivated and well explored item in agriculture. Therefore, the scope of improvement in the same is less as compared to other farm crops which are relatively less explored and subjected to less technological experimentation. In case of cotton the annual compound growth has been 2.23 per cent. It increased from 13.4 kg per agricultural labourer in 1985 to 20.4 kg in 2004. Oil-bearing crops experienced a growth rate of

3.57 per cent in the same period increasing from 50.8 kg per agricultural labourer in 1985 to 99.1 kg in 2004. Therefore, for this item the production per capita agricultural labourer doubled in the said period.

The data available for pork, beef and mutton is from 1997 to 2004; (Table 4.4). According to it, the per capita agricultural labourer output increased from 131.4 kg in 1997 to 186.8 in 2004. The annual average compound growth rate was 5.15 per cent. Total aquatic products experienced a growth rate of 10.76 per cent in the period 1985 to 2004. Total per capita agricultural labour production increased from 22.7 kg to 158.5 kg. Thus, this item experienced a seven fold increase in the concerned period. The highest growth in terms of per capita agricultural labourer out put has been due to comparatively higher growth in milk production. The absolute increase was from 8.1 kg in 1985 to 73.1 kg in 2004. Milk production per agricultural labour thus increased nine fold in this period.

Analysing the six items, for which statistics are available, in just 19 years, the production has fairly increased on per agricultural laborer basis. Therefore, farm production has changed over the reform period.

4.3.8. Increased Commercialisation of Primary Sector

An increase in per agricultural labour output only shows the potential supply or income from the produce. The actual income can be obtained only by the level of commercialisation of the primary sector which allows the translation of the surplus production into income. While as the increase in the productivity of output is necessary condition for the improved economic status of the agricultural labourer, it is not the sufficient condition. For the actual improvement in the economic stature of the primary sector, one important condition is the commercialisation of the sector. This allows the fulfillment of the profit incentive for the farmers which results into increased income, right combination of farm products, larger private investments, diversification and decentralised technological upgradation of the primary sector.

When one compares the growth of sales of main agricultural products of rural households, the dominant trend is an overall increase in the sales. However, the magnitude of this growth varies between different agricultural products. This reveals the elasticity or flexibility of supply and demand side of the products. Certain crops have the possibility of increased production as these can be sown in relatively varying climatic and soil conditions whereas others do not. The output per hectare may respond differently to the same quantity and quality of inputs used. Thus, there is a **geographical and soil dimension** to the supply side of the crops. Similarly, demand patterns also determine the equilibrium production and sales of crops. It may be possible to produce a crop in

Table 4.4: Output of Major Farm Crops Per Agriculture Labourer

(kg)

Year	*Grain*	*Cotton*	*Oil-bearing Corps*	*Pork, Beef and Mutton*	*Total Aquatic Products*	*Milk*
1985	1222	13.4	50.8		22.7	8.1
1989	1276	11.9	40.5		36.0	11.9
1990	1357	13.4	47.9		36.7	12.6
1995	1435	14.7	69.2		77.4	17.7
1997	1528	14.2	66.7	131.4	111.3	18.6
2000	1407	13.4	89.9	147.3	130.2	25.2
2001	1387	16.3	87.8	154.0	134.3	31.4
2002	1419	15.3	89.9	162.3	141.7	40.3
2003	1362	15.4	88.9	174.1	148.8	55.2
2004	1518	20.4	99.1	186.8	158.5	73.1
Growth 1985-2004	1.14	2.23	3.57	5.15	10.76	12.27

Source: China Statistical Census, 2007. www.allcountries.org/China_statistics.

Table 4.5: Sales of Main Agricultural Products of Rural Households—1

(Unit Kg/Person)

Year	*Grain*	*Cotton*	*Oil-bearing crops*	*Fiber crops*	*Sugar crops*	*Tobacco*	*Vegetables*	*Fruits*
1985	123.49	4.13	14.37	2.80	57.87	2.25	53.76	6.78
1990	180.24	4.31	12.87	1.56	70.64	2.67	65.07	13.17
1991	179.44	5.54	13.22	1.32	74.46	3.17	68.70	15.74
1992	165.89	4.16	11.27	1.18	86.80	3.58	75.58	16.92
1993	159.35	3.26	10.48	0.86	82.87	3.19	77.73	19.60
1994	188.53	4.01	10.68	0.50	62.22	2.02	72.68	22.64
1995	179.20	4.31	12.02	0.73	56.66	2.21	79.96	24.28
1996	203.47	3.90	11.64	0.83	68.65	3.07	97.00	29.78
1997	228.01	5.12	11.13	0.57	75.82	4.45	106.22	36.21
1998	227.53	5.10	12.39	0.41	81.69	2.33	108.72	38.51

(Contd.)

(Contd. Table 4.5)

Year	Grain	Cotton	Oil-bearing crops	Fiber crops	Sugar crops	Tobacco	Vegetables	Fruits
1999	243.34	4.43	15.59	0.28	86.30	2.42	111.66	43.17
2000	264.74	5.59	18.43	0.47	76.36	2.73	132.07	46.43
2001	268.04	7.05	18.31	0.44	62.42	2.42	132.94	48.21
2002	281.15	6.94	18.47	0.64	93.59	2.59	143.77	49.06
2003	294.40	16.77	19.22	0.71	101.12	2.62	147.58	48.83
2004	287.25	19.19	18.88	0.53	91.57	2.47	151.57	57.48
2005	375.79	22.06	20.09	0.69	84.74	3.69	167.93	61.62
2006	394.64	23.79	17.79	0.43	87.33	3.83	172.98	59.49
2007	394.06	24.92	17.24	0.39	117.63	3.45	169.99	66.79
Growth 1985-2007	5.41	8.51	0.83	-8.57	3.27	1.96	5.37	10.95

much larger quantities successfully but the demand constraint may not allow the same.

Thus, the change in sales in agricultural products is determined by many factors affecting demand and supply sides, thereby determine profitability. However, an increased level of commercialisation results into proper market orientation of the sector in terms of production, prices, investment, and product-mix, as well as it results into higher income of the producers.

The level of commercialisation in terms of the sales of the agricultural products has been significant, significant, the scope of which was determined largely by the nature of earlier economy. However, right policies afterwards ensured both the demand and supply improvement resulting in its sustained increase.

Sales in grains increased at an annual compound growth rate of 5.41 per cent from 1985 to 2007, as shown in Table 4.5. It increased from 123.49 kg per person in 1985 to 394 kg per person in 2007. In case of cotton, oil-bearing crops, sugar crops, tobacco, vegetables and fruits, the growth rates were 8.51 per cent, 0.83 per cent, 3.27 per cent, 1.96 per cent, 5.3 per cent, and 10.95 per cent respectively. Only in case of fiber crops, the growth rate of sales was considerably negative, at -8.57 per cent.

Sales of pork, beef, mutton, milk, poultry, poultry egg, and aquatic products increased at an annual average compound growth rate of 2.42 per cent, 7.87 per cent, 8.29 per cent, 12.86 per cent, 7.42 per cent, and 8.19 per cent respectively. The absolute figures as well as corresponding growth rates for the entire period are shown in Table 4.6.

4.3.9. Growth of Rural-Non Farm Sector

In the post-reform period, rural economy witnessed unprecedented growth in the non-, both from employment and output perspectives. Rural non-farm output as percentage of national GDP increased from 4 per cent in 1978 to 28.20 per cent in 1997. Thus, non-farm output growth played a significant role in the expansion of the total output of the economy following reforms. Furthermore, the share of rural employment to this sector increased more than four fold in this period, from 7 per cent of total rural employment in 1978 to 29 per cent in 1997. Thus, elasticity of employment of the sector was significant. In absolute terms, total employment of the rural non-farm sector increased from 2243 thousand in 1978 to 13527 thousand in 1997. Real wages in the sector also increased more than three-fold in the said period. These figures are presented in Table 4.7.

One of the major factors influencing both the income and employment dimensions of the rural sector in China has been the non-farm sector of rural economy. This sector was largely responsible for transformation of

Table 4.6 : Sales of Main Agricultural Products of Rural Households—2

Unit kg/Person

Year	*Pork*	*Beef*	*Mutton*	*Milk*	*Poultry*	*Poultry egg*	*Aquatic products*
1985	16.27	0.57	0.52	1.02	1.00	2.21	1.74
1990	17.84	0.71	0.55	1.68	1.45	1.89	2.05
1991	20.07	0.90	0.76	1.91	2.18	2.65	2.92
1992	21.17	0.86	0.72	1.85	2.23	2.90	3.21
1993	23.80	1.02	0.86	1.76	2.41	2.89	3.10
1994	23.31	1.11	0.93	1.81	2.30	3.35	2.97
1995	24.17	1.15	0.96	1.90	2.42	3.54	2.94
1996	25.73	1.68	2.01	2.55	2.45	2.58	3.27
1997	26.08	1.76	2.33	2.76	2.99	3.76	4.50
1998	23.04	1.67	1.04	2.60	2.42	3.57	4.31

(Contd.)

(Contd. Table 4.6)

Year	*Pork*	*Beef*	*Mutton*	*Milk*	*Poultry*	*Poultry egg*	*Aquatic products*
1999	28.41	1.85	1.86	3.00	3.41	4.07	6.20
2000	30.19	2.40	2.06	2.67	4.60	6.32	5.82
2001	30.86	2.76	2.31	3.65	5.03	5.96	6.53
2002	32.30	2.73	2.50	4.87	6.01	6.54	8.04
2003	29.49	2.71	2.87	7.29	6.67	7.06	7.47
2004	26.62	2.49	2.94	7.67	6.87	6.39	7.28
2005	32.19	2.87	3.26	11.27	9.62	10.52	8.54
2006	34.44	3.07	3.12	13.27	8.86	10.96	8.94
2007	27.55	3.02	3.00	14.62	10.21	10.69	9.85
Growth 1985-2007	2.42	7.87	8.29	12.86	11.13	7.42	8.19

Source: China Yearbook 2008: Rural Household Survey. Department of Rural Surveys, National Bureau of Statistics, p. 18.

Table 4.7: Development of the Rural Non-farm Sector, 1978-1997

Year	*Employment (000's)*	*Employment as a percentage of total rural employment*	*Rural non-farm GDP (index)*	*Rural non-farm GDP as a percentage of national GDP*	*Rural nonfarm annual wage (1990 yuan)*
1978	2243	7.00	100	4.00	640
1980	1956	6.00	133	4.30	763
1985	6715	18.00	370	6.70	1141
1990	8673	21.00	938	10.40	1322
1995	12708	28.00	4662	25.50	2001
1997	13527	29.00	6007	28.20	2286

Source: Official statistics calculated by Shenggen Fan, Linxiu Zhang, Xiaobo Zhang. 2002. Growth, Inequality, and Poverty in Rural China: The Role of Public Investments. International Food Policy Research Institute Washington, D.C. p. 9.

the rural sector from many perspectives. In terms of income, much of the initial reduction in poverty in rural sector can be attributed to its success. From 1980 to 1985 the employment of the sector as a proportion of total employment increased three fold. Real wages increased almost twofold. From 1985 to 1995, employment as a proportion of total rural employment increased from 18 per cent to 28 per cent. At the same time, output as a proportion of national GDP increased from 6.7 per cent to 25 per cent. Thus there was a four fold increase in its contribution to national output in just one decade. The result of this whole process was enormous reduction in poverty, diversification of rural production system, increase in employment, and reduced dependence on farm activity.

4.3.10. Technical Transformation of Agriculture

After the reforms, China's agriculture also underwent technological transformation. Use of fertilisers, irrigation and tractor-ploughing as well as other mechanisation process received boost. The fertiliser application, per hectare, increased from 36 kg in 1975 to 280.62 kg in 2002. Similarly, irrigated area as a proportion of arable land increased from 43 per cent to 55 per cent in the same period. Tractor ploughed land increased from 33 per cent in 1975 to 60 per cent as a proportion of arable land. Statistics for these are presented in Table 4.8.

4.3.11. Government Expenditure on Agriculture

As agriculture assumed market contours in the post-reform period, government engagement seemed to slack. Such a process can be natural as the engagements with other sectors become progressively more vital. However, this can be only feasible if the potential of agriculture stands broadly exploited and scope for its proper improvement exists. As shown by the statistics presented in Table 4.9, government expenditure as a percentage of total expenditure decreased from 13.43 per cent in 1978 to 8.28 per cent in 2004. It attained its lowest value of 7.12 per cent in 2003.

However, the total expenditure experienced an overall growth of 11.15 per cent in this period. The categories of this total expenditure include: expenditure for supporting rural production, expenditure for capital construction, science and technology promotion funds, and rural relief funds.

Among these categories the maximum growth was in expenditure for supporting rural production, which had an average growth rate of 18.73 per cent. This was followed by rural relief funds, science and technology funds and expenditure for capital construction which had growth rates of 15.05 per cent, 15.04 per cent and 14.27 per cent respectively. In terms of total share, the largest was that of rural production (71.83 per cent), followed by capital construction (23 per cent), relief funds (3.64 per cent), and science and technology (0.56 per cent).

Table 4.8: Fertiliser Use, Irrigation and Mechanisation Indices

Year	*Grain yield (kg/ha)*	*Fertiliser Application (kg/ha)*	*Irrigated area/arable land*	*Tractor-plough arable/arable land*
1975	2355	36.00	0.43	0.33
1980	2745	87.00	0.45	0.41
1985	3480	123.60	0.45	0.36
1989	3690	160.86	0.47	0.45
1992	4342	196.63	0.51	0.54
2002	4885	280.62	0.55	0.60

Sources: Official statistics compiled by Shujie Yao. 2005. Economic growth, income distribution and poverty reduction in contemporary China. Rutledge Curzon, Taylor and Francis Group London p. 67.

Table 4.9: Government Expenditure for Agriculture ('00' million yuan)

Year	*Total*	*Growth annual average compound*[*]	*Expenditure for supporting rural production*	*Expenditure for capital construction*	*Science and technology promotion funds*	*Rural relief funds*	*Percentage to total government expenditure*
1978	150.66		76.95	51.14	1.06	6.88	13.43
1980	149.95	-0.23	82.12	48.59	1.31	7.26	12.20
1985	153.62	0.48	101.04	37.73	1.95	12.90	7.66
1989	265.94	14.70	197.12	50.64	2.48	15.70	9.42
1990	307.84	15.75	221.76	66.71	3.11	16.26	9.98
1991	347.57	12.90	243.55	75.49	2.93	25.60	10.26
1992	376.02	8.18	269.04	85.00	3.00	18.98	10.05
1993	440.45	17.13	323.42	95.00	3.00	19.03	9.49
1994	532.98	21.10	399.70	107.00	3.00	23.28	9.20
1995	574.93	7.87	430.22	110.00	3.00	31.71	8.43

(Contd.)

(Contd. Table 4.9)

Year	Total	Growth annual average compound*	Expenditure for supporting rural production	Expenditure for capital construction	Science and technology promotion funds	Rural relief funds	Percentage to total government expenditure
1996	700.43	21.82	510.07	141.51	4.94	43.91	8.82
1997	766.39	9.41	560.77	159.78	5.48	40.36	8.30
1998	1154.76	50.67	626.02	460.70	9.14	58.90	10.69
1999	1085.76	-5.80	677.46	357.00	9.13	42.17	8.23
2000	1231.54	13.42	766.89	414.46	9.78	40.41	7.75
2001	1456.73	18.28	917.96	480.81	10.28	47.68	7.71
2002	1580.76	8.51	1102.70	423.80	9.88	44.38	7.17
2003	1754.45	10.98	1134.86	527.36	12.43	79.80	7.12
2004	2357.89	34.39	1693.79	565.01	13.22	85.87	8.28
1978-2004		11.15	18.73	14.27	15.04	15.05	

*calculated from previous (Total Expenditure) column.

Source: China Statistical Census, 2007 www.allcountries.org/China_statistics.

4.4. Income

Income is one of the most crucial determinants as well indicator of development. Its possession entitles a person the use of different goods and services which determine his capacity to satisfy the basic and other necessities. Its growth over a period of time reveals the change in the living standard of a society.

4.4.1. Income Growth

In case of China's rural economy, the net per capita income after the reforms reported a considerable increase. While as the net per capita income in 1978 was only 133 yuan, the same in 2007 was 4140 yuan. The annual compound growth of per capita income in the period was 12.5 per cent. The statistics for the same are given in Table 4.10.

The main factor in reducing rural poverty in China was the increase in per capita income. Such an increase was a product of multitude of factors among which changed property rights regime, introduction of markets, foreign orientation of local production, proper incentives, development of infrastructure are immediate ones to mention.

4.4.2. Changing Income Structure of Rural Society

One of the important parameters of economic transformation of a society is the change in per capita income. A successful economic transformation requires a progressive improvement of a society as a whole from a low per capita state to a higher one. One way to look at the same phenomenon is to find the number of households under different ranges of per capita income across time. This will reveal the change in the relative

Table 4.10: Net Per Capita Income of Rural Residents

Year	*Net Income*	*Annual Compound growth*
1978	133.57	
1980	191.33	19.68
1985	397.60	15.75
1990	686.31	11.53
1995	1577.74	18.11
2000	2253.42	7.38
2005	3254.93	7.63
2007	4140.36	12.78
1978-2007	133.57-4140.36	12.57

Source: China Yearbook 2008: Rural Household Survey. Department of Rural Surveys, National Bureau of Statistics, p. 28.

Table 4.11: Percentage of Rural Households Grouped by Per Capita Annual Net Income

Item	*1990*	*1995*	*2000*	*2003*	*2004*
Percentage of Households Grouped by Per Capita Annual Net Income (per cent)					
100 Yuan and below	0.30	0.21	0.31	0.49	0.40
100-200 Yuan	1.78	0.36	0.20	0.18	0.13
200-300 Yuan	6.56	0.78	0.43	0.31	0.21
300-400 Yuan	12.04	1.47	0.69	0.52	0.31
400-500 Yuan	14.37	2.30	1.01	0.78	0.53
500-600 Yuan	13.94	3.37	1.37	1.19	0.85
600-800 Yuan	20.80	9.54	4.44	3.25	2.43
800-1000 Yuan	12.49	11.63	5.72	4.87	3.64
1000-1200 Yuan		11.83	6.75	5.52	4.04

(Contd.)

(Contd. Table 4.11)

Item	*1990*	*1995*	*2000*	*2003*	*2004*
Percentage of Households Grouped by Per Capita Annual Net Income (per cent)					
1200-1300 Yuan	12.25	5.38	3.75	2.97	2.51
1300-1500 Yuan		9.74	7.42	6.39	5.11
1500-1700 Yuan	3.48	7.92	7.48	6.45	5.69
1700-2000 Yuan		9.39	10.45	9.39	8.57
2000-2500 Yuan		10.29	14.54	13.79	13.69
2500-3000 Yuan		5.89	10.29	10.81	11.76
3000-3500 Yuan		3.49	7.11	8.02	8.85
3500-4000 Yuan	1.99	1.95	4.76	5.84	7.09
4000-4500 Yuan		1.34	3.44	4.20	5.25
4500-5000 Yuan		0.86	2.40	3.16	3.92
5000 Yuan and over		2.26	7.45	11.85	15.02

Source: China Statistical Census, 2007. www.allcountries.org/China_statistics.

composition of households under different ranges of income and the magnitude of this change reveals the extent of transformation that the society has undergone from strictly economic perspective.

Comparing the data for different ranges of per capita income after 1990, rural society has undergone substantial change. As shown in Table 4.11, in 1990, most of the rural households (92.45 per cent) were falling under the range of 200 to 1300 yuan. Progressively, this range assumed higher end values and in 1995 there was a tendency for common rural household (81.61 per cent) to live in 600 to 3000 yuan range. In 2000, the lower end of the range further increased to 800 yuan while the upper end to 4000 yuan in which 78.27 per cent of households would fall. In 2004, 84.95 per cent of the households were in the range of 1300 to 5000 yaun per capita.

Thus, the range in which 92.45 per cent of the rural household would fall in 1990 only had 15.05 per cent of the rural households in 2004. In 1990, only 5.47 per cent of the rural households enjoyed a per capita income more than 1300 yuan; the same per capita income range was enjoyed by 84.95 per cent in 2004. Therefore, compared to its 1990 position of per capita income structure of rural households, there was a significant improvement in just one and a half decade.

The statistics developed from above data and presented in Table 4.12 bring home the transformation of rural China from per capita income perspective. The changing proportion of rural households income per capita represents the tendency of the society to move to higher living standards. In 1990, 35 per cent of the rural households were having per capita income below 500 yuan. In 2004, this proportion had reduced to a mere 1.58 per cent. Similarly, 47 per cent of the rural households had a per capita income ranging from 500 to 1000 yuan while as the proportion of households under this income range in 2004 was just 4.04 per cent. In the same period the proportion of rural households in 1000 to 2000 yuan range increased from 15.73 per cent to 25.92 per cent, while proportion in 2000 to 3000 yuan range increased from almost zero per cent to 25.45 per cent. The income range of 3000-4000 yuan was only attained by two per cent households in 1990 while as the proportion of rural households in this range increased to 16 per cent by 2004. Similarly, the proportion of households under 4000-5000 yuan range increased from zero per cent in 1990 to 9.17 per cent. While as, none of the rural households enjoyed a per capita income of more than 5000 yuan in 1990, 15 per cent of rural households had it in 2004.

Table 4.12: Changing Economic Status of Rural China

Year	*< 500*	*500-1000*	*1000-2000*	*2000-3000*	*3000-4000*	*4000-5000*	*> 5000*
1990	35.05	47.23	15.73		1.99		
1995	5.12	24.54	44.26	16.18	5.44	2.2	2.26
2000	2.64	4.53	35.85	24.83	11.87	5.84	7.45
2003	2.28	5.52	30.72	24.6	13.86	7.36	11.85
2004	1.58	4.04	25.92	25.45	15.94	9.17	15.02

Source: Developed from Table 13.

Table 4.13: Composition of Net Income of Rural Households by Source.

(Unit: Per cent)

Year	*Net Income*	*Wage income*	*Household business income*	*Property income*	*Transfer income*
1978	100.00	66.08	26.79		7.13
1980	100.00	55.60	32.69		11.71
1985	100.00	18.15	74.44		7.41
1990	100.00	20.22	75.76		4.22
1995	100.00	22.42	71.35	2.60	3.63
2000	100.00	31.17	63.34	2.00	3.50
2005	100.00	36.08	56.67	2.72	4.53
2007	100.00	38.55	52.98	3.10	5.37

Source: China Yearbook 2008: Rural Household Survey. Department of Rural Surveys, National Bureau of Statistics, p. 28.

Thus, the progressive march towards higher slabs of per capita income in rural China was considerable. This obviously affected the other dimensions of well being of the rural society.

4.4.3. Composition of Income

A disaggregation of income of rural households over time reveals the sources, types as well as sectoral contribution. Such a change indicates the changes in the economic activities and relative importance of sectors of the rural economy. As the process of transformation proceeds, the dependence on farms, wages, and income in kind decreases. At the same time, non-farm income, businesses and cash income are institutionalised in the rural sector of the economy. Chinese experience in the change of income composition is a representative case of such transformation in just a short duration of time. This transformation is part of the larger economic restructuring of the rural economy in the wake of significant reforms.

4.4.4. By Source

Besides increase in the Net Income of rural residents after the reforms, there was an equally important structural change in its composition as documented in Table 4.13. While as at the time of reform the net income largely comprised the wage income followed by the household business income, the trend was reversed during the last three decades. The proportion of wages in Net Income of rural residents decreased from 66.08 per cent in 1978 to 38.55 per cent in 2007. During the same period the proportion of household business income increased from 26.79 per cent to 52.98 per cent. An increase of property income in the Net Income was also recorded from 2.60 per cent in 1995 to 3.10 per cent in 2007. Furthermore, there was a reduction in the proportion of transfer income in the net income from 7.13 per cent in 1978 to 5.37 per cent in 2007.

Table 4.14: Composition of Net Income of Rural Households by Income Type

(Unit: Per cent)

Year	*Net income*	*Cash net income*	*Net income in kind*
1978	100.00	41.92	58.08
1980	100.00	49.32	50.68
1985	100.00	63.10	36.90
1990	100.00	64.07	35.93
1995	100.00	62.56	37.44
2000	100.00	73.16	26.84
2005	100.00	84.13	15.87
2007	100.00	85.15	14.85

Source: China Yearbook 2008: Rural Household Survey. Department of Rural Surveys, National Bureau of Statistics, p. 29.

Table 4.15: Household Business Income of Rural Households by Source (Sector)

Year	Household Business Income yuan/ person	Household Business Income by Sectors Absolute Amount			Household Business Income by Sectors Percentage of Total		
		Primary industry	Secondary industry	Tertiary industry	Primary industry	Secondary industry	Tertiary industry
1978	54.01	50.81		3.20	94.08		5.92
1980	87.44	78.87		8.57	90.20		9.80
1985	445.25	400.56	12.25	32.44	89.96	2.75	7.29
1990	815.79	735.57	25.88	54.34	90.17	3.17	6.66
1995	1877.42	1652.31	65.44	159.67	88.01	3.49	8.50
2000	2251.28	1810.65	133.71	306.92	80.43	5.94	13.63
2005	3164.43	2621.29	167.06	376.08	82.84	5.28	11.88
2007	3776.70	3122.01	210.35	444.34	82.66	5.57	11.77
Growth 1978-2007	15.77	15.25	13.79	18.54			

Source: China Yearbook 2008: Rural Household Survey. Department of Rural Surveys, National Bureau of Statistics, p. 23.

4.4.5. By Type

Another important factor which indicates the progressive commercialisation, monetisation as well as privatisation of the rural economy is the cash-kind composition of the net income of the rural households. It represents a departure of the rural sector from token to cash arrangement. At the time of the reforms, the proportion of the income in kind to net income was 58.08 per cent. In 2007, the same was only 14.85 per cent. The proportion of cash income in the net income increased from 41.92 per cent in 1978 to 85.15 per cent in 2007. This continuous change in the composition is depicted by the statistics presented in Table 4.14.

4.4.6. By Sector

One of the important peculiarities of China's rural transformation is that even when income and assets increased considerably after the reforms the source of income has largely remained the same, i.e. the primary sector. China's rural change has been effected largely by the developments in the primary sector. The change of source of income, from predominantly wage-income to business-income, is affected by growth of the primary sector itself.

As revealed by Table 4.15, the growth of the household business income was largely a result of expansion of the primary sector of the economy. By comparison the contribution of secondary and tertiary sectors to income growth along the period was moderate. Therefore even by 2007, 82 per cent of the household business income emerged within the primary sector. The household business income increased at 15.77 per cent annual compound growth rate during the period 1978 to 2004. The growth rate of primary, secondary and tertiary sector business incomes was 15.25 per cent, 13.79 per cent and 18.54 per cent respectively. Primary sector's contribution to household business income decreased from 94.08 per cent in 1978 to 82.66 per cent in 2007. During the same time, contribution of the secondary sector increased from 2.75 per cent to 5.57 per cent, while as the contribution of the tertiary sector increased from 5.92 per cent to 11.77 per cent.

4.5. Household Expenditure

One of the dimensions quite significantly related with the level or change of development and well being of any society is the magnitude and composition of expenditure. This shows the actual economic engagement of the people on the demand side. In contrast to income which shows potential state of entitlements attainable thereby, expenditure reveals where the income is actually spent and thus reveals the actual state of well being.

4.5.1. Total Expenditure

Total expenditure of the rural households is divided into six main categories: household business, productive fixed assets, taxes and fee, living, property and transfer expenditure. This is as per the official classification, presented in Table 4.16 with corresponding time series trends. In the three decades following reforms, the overall growth rate of total household expenditure was 13.34 per cent. Thus, there was an appreciable increase in the expenditure of the rural households' per capita expenditure during this period.

On the basis of annual growth rates of total expenditure within these three decades, the entire period can be divided into two sub-periods. Before 1995, the growth rate of expenditure was quite significant with an overall growth rate of 15.74 per cent. After 1995, overall growth rate of household expenditure decreased to 7.57 per cent. In fact, the lowest phase of expenditure growth was from 1995 to 2000. This trend corresponds to the fact that growth of net income also declined in the post-1995 period for rural households. As the income failed to increase by pre-1995 rates, the effects were considerably felt on the expenditure side of the rural economy.

Household business expenditure experienced a growth rate of 16.75 per cent during 1978 to 2007. Living expenditure grew at a rate of 12.14 per cent while as the growth rate of transfer expenditure was 17.52 per cent in the period.

In terms of the composition of the rural household expenditure, a measurable change occurred after the reforms. Expenditure structure was altered in favour of household businesses, while as the share of the living expenditure decreased considerably. This indicates the increasing share devoted to non-perishable or durable items. It also implies an increasing share to investment than to consumption because household business expenditure is investment which produces income.

The composition or structure of expenditure reveals an increasing trend in case of business expenditure, taxes and fee and transfer expenditure. The proportion of living expenditure, productive fixed assets and property expenditure experienced a decreasing trend, however. As shown in Table 4.17, household business expenditure increased from 12.36 per cent of the total expenditure in 1978 to 27.89 per cent in 2007. Thus, it increased by 15 percentage points in the total expenditure basket of the rural households. This represents an important development in the economic status of the rural society wherein the dependence on household businesses witnesses a strong growth in the post-reform period. The contribution of rural households in taxes and fee also witnessed a relative increase in the structure of the rural expenditure. In case of transfer expenditure also an

Table 4.16: Total Expenditure of Rural Households

(Unit: Yuan/Person)

Year	*Total expenditure*	*Annual average compound growth**	*Household business*	*Productive fixed assets*	*Taxes and fee*	*Living*	*Property*	*Transfer*
1978	135.82		16.79		0.24	116.06		2.73
1980	196.23	20.19	25.32		0.28	162.21		8.42
1985	485.51	19.86	121.39	18.70	18.43	317.42		9.57
1990	903.47	13.22	241.09	20.29	38.66	584.63		18.80
1995	2138.33	18.80	621.71	62.33	88.65	1310.36		55.28
2000	2652.42	4.40	695.97	63.90	95.52	1670.13	19.74	148.86
2005	4126.92	9.24	1189.70	131.14	13.08	2555.40	21.97	215.63
2007	5137.68	11.57	1432.69	147.17	11.93	3223.85	26.77	295.26
Growth 1978-2007	13.34	13.34	16.57	9.83	14.41	12.14	4.44	17.52

Source: China Yearbook 2008: Rural Household Survey. Department of Rural Surveys, National Bureau of Statistics, p. 33 *growth rates worked from the total expenditure column.

Table 4.17: Composition of Total Expenditure of Rural Households

(unit: Per cemt)

Year	Total expenditure	Household business	Productive fixed assets	Taxes and fee	Living expenditure	Property expenditure	Transfer expenditure
1978	100.00	12.36		0.18	85.45		2.01
1980	100.00	12.90		0.14	82.66		4.29
1985	100.00	25.00	3.85	3.80	65.38		1.97
1990	100.00	26.88	2.25	4.28	64.71		2.08
1995	100.00	29.07	2.91	4.15	61.28		2.59
2000	100.00	24.67	2.41	3.60	62.97	0.74	5.61
2005	100.00	28.83	3.18	0.32	61.92	0.53	5.22
2007	100.00	27.89	2.86	0.23	62.75	0.52	5.75

Source: China Yearbook 2008: Rural Household Survey. Department of Rural Surveys, National Bureau of Statistics, p. 33.

Table 4.18: Composition of Living Expenditure of Rural Households

(Unit: Per cent)

Items	*1978*	*1980*	*1985*	*1990*	*1995*	*2000*	*2005*	*2007*
Food	67.71	61.77	57.79	58.80	58.62	49.13	45.48	43.08
Clothing	12.70	12.32	9.69	7.77	6.85	5.57	5.81	6.00
Residence	10.30	13.85	18.23	17.34	13.91	15.47	14.49	17.80
Household Facilities, Articles and Services		2.55	5.10	5.29	5.23	4.52	4.36	4.63
Transport, Post and Telecommunication		0.36	1.76	1.44	2.58	5.58	9.59	10.19
Cultural, Educational, Recreational Articles and Services		5.09	3.89	5.37	7.81	11.18	11.56	9.48
Medicine and Health Care		2.11	2.42	3.25	3.24	5.24	6.58	6.52
Other Commodities and Services	9.30	1.95	1.12	0.74	1.76	3.14	2.13	2.30
Total Living Expenditure	100	100	100	100	100	100	100	100

Source: China Yearbook 2008: Rural Household Survey. Department of Rural Surveys, National Bureau of Statistics, p. 37.

increase in the proportion of the total expenditure occurred. From 2.10 per cent of the total rural household expenditure in 1978 its proportion increased to 5.75 per cent in 2007.

During the same period there was a substantial decrease in the proportion of living expenditure in the basket of rural expenditure. It decreased from 85.45 per cent of total expenditure in 1978 to 62.75 per cent in 2007. Thus, in the total expenditure living expenditure experienced a decrease of around 24 per cent. This represents a departure from the state of consumption dependence to a state of asset building. However, in the same period there was decrease in the expenditure in productive fixed assets. Nonetheless, the proportion of income spent on this item was quite insignificant. Therefore, such a decrease does not represent a substantial change in the asset holding of rural population. Also, as the income increases the need for productive assets does not increase proportionately. On the contrary, the expenditure would be extended to other activities that were earlier uncovered. As a result the relative importance in the expenditure on productive assets decreases.

4.5.2. Living Expenditure

The rural household living expenditure not only decreased as proportion of the total expenditure but has had a change in its own composition. After the reforms it has diversified and included many items which were altogether absent or marginally present at the inception of the reforms. Looking at the statistics of the composition of expenditure, given in Table 4.18, the main items of living expenditure in 1978 were food, clothing, residence, and some other commodities and services. However, many items became important in the consumption basket of rural households subsequently. This includes: household facilities, articles and services; transport, post and communication; cultural, educational, recreational articles and services, and; medicine and health care expenditure.

Such a shift in the pattern of living expenditure had significant impact on the quality and standard of life. It depicts the trend towards enlargement of choices and entitlements to the rural households. While as the main items in the consumption basket in 1978 were food, clothing and residence, other items including transport, education, recreation, medicine and health care attained good level of significance during the post-reform period.

4.6. Consumption

Within the category of food items consumed by rural households at per capita level, there was some change which again is indicative of the changing pattern of China's post reform economy. While as the consumption of grain and vegetables decreased by very good proportion,

Table 4.19: Consumption of Major Food Items of Rural Households—1

Year	*Grain*	*Edible oil*	*Vegetable*	*Fruit and related products*	*Pork, beef and mutton*	*Milk and dairy products*
1978	247.83	1.97	141.50		5.75	
1980	257.16	2.48	127.21		7.74	
1985	257.45	4.04	131.13	3.40	10.97	0.80
1990	262.08	5.17	134.00	5.89	11.34	1.10
1991	255.58	5.65	126.97	6.79	12.15	1.30
1992	250.50	5.85	129.12	7.54	11.83	1.50
1993	251.81	5.66	107.43	13.02	11.68	0.90
1994	257.57	5.66	107.86	12.58	11.00	0.70
1995	256.07	5.80	104.62	13.01	11.29	0.60
1996	256.19	6.07	106.26	15.63	12.90	0.80
1997	250.67	6.16	107.21	17.77	12.72	1.00

(Contd.)

(Contd. Table 4.19)

Year	*Grain*	*Edible oil*	*Vegetable*	*Fruit and related products*	*Pork, beef and mutton*	*Milk and dairy products*
1998	248.90	6.13	108.96	19.24	13.20	0.90
1999	247.45	6.17	108.89	18.35	13.87	1.00
2000	250.23	7.06	106.74	18.31	14.41	1.10
2001	238.62	7.03	109.30	20.33	14.50	1.20
2002	236.50	7.53	110.55	18.77	14.87	1.20
2003	222.44	6.27	107.40	17.54	15.04	1.70
2004	218.30	5.29	106.61	16.97	14.76	2.00
2005	208.85	6.01	102.28	17.18	17.09	2.86
2006	205.62	5.84	100.53	19.09	17.03	3.15
2007	199.48	5.96	98.99	19.43	14.88	3.52
Growth 1978-07	-0.74	3.89	-1.22	8.24	3.33	6.96

Source: Table. 4.20.

Table 4.20: Consumption of Major Food Items of Rural Households—2

Year	*Poultry*	*Egg and Related Products*	*Aquatic Products*	*Sugar*	*Liquor*
1978	0.25	0.79	0.84	0.73	1.22
1980	0.66	1.21	1.10	1.06	1.89
1985	1.03	2.05	1.64	1.46	4.37
1990	1.25	2.41	2.13	1.50	6.14
1991	1.34	2.73	2.21	1.40	6.38
1992	1.49	2.85	2.25	1.54	6.56
1993	1.62	2.88	2.76	1.43	6.53
1994	1.63	3.03	2.96	1.34	6.03
1995	1.83	3.22	3.36	1.28	6.53
1996	1.93	3.35	3.68	1.37	7.11

(Contd.)

(*Contd. Table 4.20*)

Year	*Poultry*	*Egg and Related Products*	*Aquatic Products*	*Sugar*	*Liquor*
1997	2.36	4.08	3.75	1.35	7.13
1998	2.33	4.11	3.66	1.40	6.98
1999	2.48	4.28	3.82	1.46	6.98
2000	2.81	4.77	3.92	1.28	7.02
2001	2.87	4.72	4.12	1.43	7.10
2002	2.91	4.66	4.36	1.64	7.50
2003	3.20	4.81	4.65	1.24	7.67
2004	3.13	4.59	4.49	1.11	7.84
2005	3.67	4.71	4.94	1.13	9.59
2006	3.51	5.00	5.01	1.09	9.97
2007	3.86	4.72	5.36	1.07	10.18
Growth 1978-2007	9.89	6.35	6.59	1.32	7.59

Source: China Yearbook 2008: Rural Household Survey. Department of Rural Surveys, National Bureau of Statistics, p. 19 (Unit: kg/person)

the consumption of almost all other major food items increased. The details of food consumption are given in Table 4.19 and Table 4.20. Grain consumption decreased at an annual compound growth rate of -0.74 while as vegetable consumption decreased at a rate of -1.22 per cent annually. Both of the items were, however, the highest consumed items in the food basket of rural households.

The growth rates of consumption in other major items were: edible oil, 3.89 per cent; fruit and related products, 8.24 per cent; pork, beef, and mutton, 3.33 per cent; milk and dairy products, 6.96 per cent; poultry, 9.89 per cent; egg and related products, 6.35 per cent; aquatic products, 6.59 per cent; sugar 1.32 per cent; liquor, 7.59 per cent.

Thus, one can find a gradual departure from grain and vegetables to a more diversified food basket in the post-reform period, in spite of the fact that grain and vegetables are still the staple items. Fruits, milk and dairy products, poultry and eggs, as well as aquatic products assumed enhanced importance in case of rural China food consumption.

4.7. Assets

One of the basic approaches towards poverty reduction is the increase of assets which can become a regular source of employment and income for poor. This contrasts with the **wage approach** to poverty reduction which largely results into temporary phases of income generation without inbuilt sustainability. Asset base of a person determines income earning strength as well as the scope of self employment. At the same time, possession of assets increases production by providing different productive services. Furthermore, increased asset base in the form of durables increases different services to households. This further enhances their state of well being.

4.7.1. Productive Assets

In the aftermath of reforms, the assets involved in the productive activities of rural households increased perceptibly. These assets include trucks, large and medium tractors, mini and walking tractors, motorised thrashing machines, pumps for agriculture, draught animals and commodity animals.

Table 4.21 provides the time series statistics of the major productive assets owned by rural households. From 1985 to 2007, the number of trucks per hundred household increased from 0.25 to 1.91, recording an annual growth rate of 9.68 per cent. Large and medium tractors increased from 0.35 per hundred households to 2.85 per hundred households. Mini and walking tractors increased from 2.71 per hundred households to 19.10 per hundred households. Motorised thrashing machine experienced a growth rate of 7.69 per cent during the same period. Pumps for agriculture

Table 4.21: Number of Major Productive Assets Owned

(Set/100 Households)

Year	Truck	Large and medium tractor	Mini and walking tractors	Motorized threshing machine	Pump for agriculture	Draught animal	Commodity animal
1985	0.25	0.35	2.71	1.91	1.69	57.15	32.12
1990	0.28	0.45	5.30	3.55	3.86	57.27	30.91
1991	0.24	0.51	6.61	3.85	4.73	53.93	28.73
1992	0.28	0.55	7.25	4.16	5.48	52.95	30.07
1993	0.33	0.64	8.40	5.30	8.54	59.98	53.15
1994	0.40	0.79	8.77	5.15	7.90	58.79	56.70
1995	0.51	0.77	9.93	6.33	9.07	55.99	50.72
1996	0.78	0.99	12.46	6.87	10.97	54.99	56.26
1997	0.82	1.39	14.26	7.41	12.12	55.58	52.72
1998	1.01	1.22	14.34	8.58	13.73	48.39	52.20

(Contd.)

(Contd. Table 4.21)

Year	Truck	Large and medium tractor	Mini and walking tractors	Motorized threshing machine	Pump for agriculture	Draught animal	Commodity animal
1999	1.09	1.44	16.28	8.35	14.02	45.02	54.08
2000	1.32	1.41	16.72	9.59	17.73	41.75	41.56
2001	1.20	1.50	17.41	9.28	19.92	39.67	54.65
2002	1.29	1.53	18.48	9.62	21.53	39.38	56.43
2003	1.40	1.79	18.93	10.06	21.12	35.52	58.62
2004	1.40	2.20	18.80	10.10	22.06	34.83	51.83
2005	1.76	2.13	20.24	8.69	21.03	29.33	60.28
2006	1.83	2.39	21.06	9.44	22.12	28.75	61.76
2007	1.91	2.85	19.10	9.76	23.35	27.50	63.59
Growth* 1985-2007	9.68	10.00	9.28	7.69	12.67	-3.27	3.15

*Annual compound growth rate worked from the data contained in the table.

Source: China Yearbook 2008: Rural Household Survey. Department of Rural Surveys, National Bureau of Statistics, p. 17.

Table 4.22: Main Durable Goods Owned

(Unit set/100 household)

Item	*1978*	*1980*	*1985*	*1990*	*1995*	*2000*	*2005*	*2007*	*Growth* 1978-2007*
Bicycle	30.75	36.87	80.64	118.33	147.02	120.48	98.37	97.74	4.06
Coloured TV set			0.80	4.72	16.92	48.74	84.08	94.38	17.88
Mobile phone						4.32	50.20	77.84	51.14
Telephone						26.38	58.37	68.36	14.57
Motorcycle				0.89	4.91	21.94	40.70	48.52	26.51
Washing machine			1.90	9.12	16.90	28.58	40.20	45.94	15.58
Refrigerator			0.06	1.22	5.15	12.31	20.10	26.12	31.80
Black and white TV set		0.39	10.94	39.72	63.81	52.97	21.77	12.14	13.58
Air conditioner					0.18	1.32	6.40	8.54	37.97
Camera				0.70	1.42	3.12	4.05	4.30	11.26
Computer						0.47	2.10	3.68	34.17

*Annual compound growth rate worked from the data given.

Source: China Yearbook 2008: Rural Household Survey. Department of Rural Surveys, National Bureau of Statistics, p. 21.

increased at an annual rate of 12.67 per cent. Commodity animals increased from 32.12 per hundred households to 63.59 per hundred households. Only in case of draught animals a decreasing trend was observed. This is because of the mechanisation reduced the scope for use of animals in agriculture.

The increase of these productive assets also indicated the level of mechanisation in the Chinese agriculture. Generally, and up to a threshold, the higher the level of mechanisation, larger will be the level of productivity. However, the higher level of mechanisation may also have adverse employment consequences as it reduces the number of people required on farm.

4.7.2. Durable Assets

After the reforms the durable assets of rural households showed both quantitative and qualitative improvement. From qualitative standpoint, new items were introduced into the basket of households which now comprise most of the assets possessed by these households. However, the quantity of these assets also increased gradually, at varying pace for different commodities, in the post-reform period. The composition and trends with regard to the items of durable basket of the consumers is shown in Table 4.22. The important durable assets in the rural household basket include: bicycle, motorcycle, washing machine, refrigerator, air conditioner, television set, camera, computer, telephone, and mobile phone. Among these only bicycle was possessed in some measurable magnitude by rural households at the beginning of the reforms. Thus out of 11 elements of rural durable basket 10 were almost missing or present in insignificant quantity at the inception of reforms.

The three items which were not present in the rural durable basket at the inception of reforms but are now (2007) owned more than 50 sets per 100 households include: coloured TV, 94.38 per cent; mobile phone, 77.84 per cent; telephone, 68.36 per cent. Another three items not owned or owned in insignificant magnitude but are now more than 25 but less than 50 sets per 100 rural households include: motorcycle, 48.52 per cent; washing machine, 45 per cent; refrigerator, 26.12 per cent. Rest of the four items owned at less than 25 sets per 100 households are: black and white TV, 12.14 per cent; air conditioner, 8.54 per cent; camera, 4.30 per cent and; computer, 3.68 per cent.

From the above analysis, it is very clear that the durable asset basket of the rural households in China has changed significantly from both qualitative as well as quantitative dimensions.

4.8. Rural Poverty

The central feature of any meaningful development effort is to bring the masses from a state of deprivation to a state of **well being**. Even with high growth, the process of successful economic transformation is incomplete without the masses being direct beneficiaries of that growth. Therefore, one central variable in development indices is the poverty from economic perspective. This is also known as **income poverty**. The level of poverty below the agreed upon income standard, at national or international level, called **poverty line,** is known as **absolute poverty.** This level of income is supposed to be the least level of subsistence income, or that which is indispensable for existence. It is meant to represent a specific minimum level of income needed to satisfy the basic physical needs of food, clothing, and shelter in order to ensure continued survival.[7]

One of the systematic trends in the global poverty profile is its rural bias. Rural residents in almost all countries are poorer than their urban counterparts. Main determinants of this larger magnitude of rural poverty include larger population share, less policy efforts to transform the rural sector (urban-bias′ in economic policies), lack of political will to bring institutional changes necessary for higher incentives and rural participation, as well as relative difficulty of catering to larger country side. Nonetheless, any meaningful effort at development demands a strong rural orientation in policy formulation so as to target poverty in an effective way. Thus, any attempt at successful economic transformation has necessarily to focus on poverty, which in turn means focusing on the reduction of rural poverty.

Decline in Poverty

The most outstanding achievement of China in the post-reform period has been poverty reduction. Table 4.23 provides the poverty statistics of rural China, after the reforms. As per the national poverty line, the poverty head-count ratio in 1978 was 30.7 per cent. Within a period of three decades this ratio decreased to a mere 1.6 per cent. The number of below poverty line people in 1978 was 250 million. The same decreased to a mere 14.79 million in 2007.. Thus, in three decades almost 235 million people came out of absolute poverty. The average rate of poverty reduction was 9.3 per cent. Poverty in 1978 was 17 times that of poverty in 2007. In the same duration the poverty line was upgraded from 100 yuan in 1978 to 785 yuan in 2007. Thus, by 2007, poverty line was upgraded by almost eight times of its value in 1978.

Such a rapid pace of poverty reduction has had enormous implication for the rural society as well as the overall economy of China. In itself, reduction of poverty is a significant achievement, because it eliminates or at least significantly reduces the state of deprivation of citizens. By this standard this is an objective of development which represents the demand side of the poverty reduction. It is always a priority objective of economic planning to reduce poverty and the failure to achieve the same is the failure of planning itself.

Table 4.23: Absolute Poverty of Rural Households, 1978—2007

Year	*Poverty line (yuan /person)*	*Poverty head-count index (per cent)*	*Number of poor persons (10 thousand persons)*	*Poverty Growth rate** *(annual compound) (per cent)*
1978	100	30.7	25000	
1980	130	26.8	22000	-06.19
1981	142	18.5	15200	-30.90
1982	164	17.5	14500	-04.60
1983	179	16.2	13500	-06.89
1984	200	15.1	12800	-05.18
1985	206	14.8	12500	-02.34
1986	213	15.5	13100	04.80
1987	227	14.3	12200	-06.87
1988	236	11.1	9600	-21.31
1989	259	11.6	10200	06.25
1990	300	9.4	8500	-16.66
1991	304	10.4	9400	10.58

(Contd.)

(Contd. Table 4.23)

Year	Poverty line (yuan /person)	Poverty head-count index (per cent)	Number of poor persons (10 thousand persons)	Poverty Growth rate* (annual compound) (per cent)
1992	317	8.8	8000	-14.89
1994	440	7.7	7000	-12.50
1995	530	7.1	6540	-06.57
1997	640	5.4	4962	-24.12
1998	635	4.6	4210	-15.15
1999	625	3.7	3412	-18.95
2000	625	3.5	3209	-05.94
2001	630	3.2	2927	-08.78
2002	627	3.0	2820	-03.65
2003	637	3.1	2900	02.83
2004	668	2.8	2610	-10.00
2005	683	2.5	2365	-09.38
2006	693	2.3	2148	-09.17
2007	785	1.6	1479	-31.14
1978-2007	100-785	30.7-1.6	25000 1479	-09.30

*Annual compound growth rate worked from the previous column.

Source: China Yearbook 2008: Rural Household Survey. Department of Rural Surveys, National Bureau of Statistics, p. 4.

On the other hand, enhanced standard of living furnishes necessary inputs for the populace to be active and productive participants in the economy. This further increases the prospects of better standards and strengthens the national economy. More income usually means better education, health, housing, food, etc., which are necessary ingredients for a productive and progressive workforce. Thus, higher income or reduction of poverty strengthens the supply side of the economy. Such a trend has been quite evident in the Chinese case.

Also, higher income means higher purchasing power and thus larger expenditure. Increased demand in the economy results in higher output or acts as a growth propeller. Further, increase in income diversifies the demand of the citizens which gives impetus to the growth of marginal industries. This obviously leads to diversification and structural changes in economy.

4.9. Rural Employment

While as growth of GDP is quite essential for increase in national output and welfare, it is not the sufficient condition for the well being of the society. For the increased output to be distributed with reasonable degree of equity among the members of a society, the basic market mechanism is that it should increase the demand for their services. In other words, market should ensure that common people become contributors in the growth process.

What happened to the employment scenario of the rural economy of China is significantly correlated with the development state of rural China. Or what failed to happen in this dimension is among the basic determinants of the failure of the rural China to proceed to a higher development state. Both commission and omission had significant impact on the state of welfare of average Chinese rural person.

In the following discussion we analyse the growth of employment in the rural economy as well as the structural change it underwent after the reforms. Structural change in rural employment can be looked into from two different perspectives. The first is the change in the composition of total employment in terms of rural-urban contributions or share. At a still deeper level, we specifically analyse the rural employment in terms of its composition and change therein, which forms the second dimension of our structural analysis.

4.9.1. Employment: Total, Urban and Rural

In the post-reform period the growth rate of rural employment was just 1.8 per cent. Compared to the growth rate of the national output this is significantly low. In comparison to the total employment growth rate of the economy, i.e., 2.44 per cent, in the post-reform period, rural

Table 4.24: Employment: Total, Urban and Rural

(10,000 persons)

Year	*Total*	*Urban Area*	*Rural Area*	*Proportion of rural in total (per cent)*
1978	40152	9514	30638	76.30
1980	42361	10525	31836	75.15
1985	49873	12808	37065	74.31
1989	55329	14390	40939	73.99
1990	64749	17041	47708	73.68
1991	65491	17465	48026	73.33
1992	66152	17861	48291	73.00
1993	66808	18262	48546	72.66
1994	67455	18653	48802	72.34
1995	68065	19040	49025	72.02

(Contd.)

(Contd. Table 4.24)

Year	*Total*	*Urban Area*	*Rural Area*	*Proportion of rural in total (per cent)*
1996	68950	19922	49028	71.10
1997	69820	20781	49039	70.23
1998	70637	21616	49021	69.40
1999	71394	22412	48982	68.60
2000	72085	23151	48934	67.88
2001	73025	23940	49085	67.21
2002	73740	24780	48960	66.40
2003	74432	25639	48793	65.55
2004	75200	26476	48724	64.80
Growth 1978-2004	2.44	4.01	1.80	-0.62

Source: China Statistical Census, 2007. www.allcountries.org/China_statistics.

employment growth was again lagging. In strict contrast to this, the rate of urban employment growth was four per cent, more than twice that of the rural employment. Thus, looking in isolation the employment scenario of the rural economy was not that impressive as other indicators of development. Employment statistics are presented in Table 4.24.

However, two factors make even this employment growth look not so gloomy. One is the relatively small growth of population compared to its existing size. Since the population growth declined because of government intervention and endogenous reasons related to economic development. Therefore, almost two per cent average annual employment growth rate is relatively less discomfiting.

The other factor is the relatively higher growth of cities due to urbanisation and migration. Due to the process of urbanisation, around forty per cent of the Chinese people live in urban areas currently. Since the growth of the urban areas is higher, therefore, urban employment growth will also be higher. This, however, does not justify the low rate of growth in rural employment given the fact that employment elasticity in case of agriculture has been falling over the years of reform, as has been discussed in the preceding chapter.

From the composition perspective of the employment, a decreased share of the rural sector in the total employment is expected as cities grow, manufacturing and services sector become increasingly important and primary sector ceases to be the main activity of the economy. The share of the rural employment in the total employment of the economy decreased from 76 per cent in 1978 to 65 per cent in 2004.

4.9.2. Structure of Rural Employment

The structure of rural employment comprises six broad categories, as shown in Table 4.25: The first category which includes employment in farming, forestry, animal husbandry and fishery, corresponds to employment in the agricultural sector. Almost all the employment in rural China at the time of reforms belonged to this category. However, in the post-reform period this category experienced the lowest rate of employment growth. Employment in this category increased from 284.55 million persons in 1978 to 305.96 million in 2004. The average annual compound growth rate for the period is 0.28 per cent. The second category is rural employment in industry. Employment in this category increased from 9.16 million persons in 1980 to 54.38 million people in 2004, recording an annual average growth rate of 7.70 per cent. Employment in construction increased at an annual rate of 5.93 per cent from 11.3 million in 1985 to 33.80 million persons in 2004. Employment in transport, storage, post and communication—the fourth category—increased from

Table 4.25: Rural Labourers at the Year-end*

(10 000 persons)

	Farming, Forestry, Animal Husbandry and Fishery	*Industry*	*Construction*	*Transport Storage, Post and Communication Services*	*Wholesale, Retail Trade and Catering Services*	*Other Nonagricultural Trades*
1978	28455.6					
1980	29808.4	916.3				
1985	30351.5	2741.0	1130.1	434.1	462.6	1945.8
1989	32440.5	3255.6	1501.8	614.2	652.4	2474.3
1990	33336.4	3228.7	1522.8	635.3	693.2	2593.1
1991	34186.3	3267.9	1533.8	655.0	722.8	2726.7
1992	34037.0	3468.2	1658.8	706.3	813.7	3117.6
1993	33258.2	3659.0	1886.8	799.9	948.8	3703.1
1994	32690.3	3849.5	2057.3	908.3	1084.3	4064.5
1995	32334.5	3970.7	2203.6	983.0	1170.4	4379.7

(Contd.)

(Contd. Table 4.25)

	Farming, Forestry, Animal Husbandry and Fishery	Industry	Construction	Transport Storage, Post and Communication Services	Wholesale, Retail Trade and Catering Services	Other Nonagricultural Trades
1996	32260.4	4018.5	2304.3	1027.6	1261.5	4415.7
1997	32677.9	4031.3	2373.7	1059.0	1386.8	4705.6
1998	32626.4	3928.6	2453.5	1087.9	1461.9	4874.0
1999	32911.8	3953.0	2531.9	1115.8	1584.6	4799.3
2000	32797.5	4108.6	2691.7	1170.6	1751.8	5441.9
2001	32451.0	4296.0	2797.4	1205.4	1864.5	5614.6
2002	31990.6	4505.6	2959.0	1259.1	1996.8	5815.8
2003	31259.6	4937.1	3201.1	1328.2	2059.2	6185.9
2004	30596.0	5438.9	3380.5	1475.9	2701.6	6102.4
Growth in the Period	0.28	7.70	5.93	6.65	9.73	6.20

*The number of labourers by sector in this table is classified by main economic activity. For example, those engaged primarily in agriculture and secondarily in commerce are classified as the labourers under farming, forestry, animal husbandry and fishery.

Source: China Statistical Census, 2007. www.allcountries.org/China_statistics.

Table 4.26: Structure of Rural Employment

Year	Total	Farming, Forestry, Animal Husbandry and Fishery	Industry	Construction	Transport Storage, Post and Communication Services	Wholesale, Retail Trade and Catering Services	Other Non-agricultural Trades
1978	28455	28455.6					
	(100.00)	100.00					
1980	30724	29808	916.3				
	(100.00)	(97.01)	(2.98)				
1985	37063	30351	2741	1130	434	462	1945
	(100.00)	(81.900	(7.40)	(3.04)	(1.17)	(1.24)	(5.24)
1989	40936	32440	3255	1501	614	652	2474
	(100.00)	(79.24)	(7.95)	(3.66)	(1.50)	(1.60)	(6.04)
1990	42007	33336	3228	1522	635	693	2593
	(100.00)	(79.35)	(7.68)	(3.62)	(1.51)	(1.64)	(6.17)
1995	45039	32334	3970	2203	983	1170	4379
	(100.00)	(71.70)	(8.81)	(4.89)	(2.18)	(2.60)	(9.72)
2000	47958	32797	4108	2691	1170	1751	5441
	(100.00)	(68.38)	(8.56)	(5.61)	(2.44)	(3.65)	(11.34)
2004	49692	30596	5438	3380	1475	2701	6102
	100.00	(61.57)	(10.94)	(6.80)	(2.96)	(5.43)	(12.27)

Source: Compiled from Table 25. (Unit: 10,000 absolute above and per cent in brackets).

4.34 million in 1985 to 14.75 million in 2004; thus recording a growth rate of 6.65 per cent. The fifth category comprising wholesale, retail trade and catering services increased at an annual growth rate of 9.73 per cent; from 4.62 million persons in 1985 to 27.01 million in 2004. The last category which includes other nonagricultural trades experienced a growth rate of 6.20 per cent. Its employment increased from 19.45 million persons in 1985 to 61.02 persons in 2004.

As is worked out in the above table, the highest growth rate was experienced in the fifth category—wholesale, retail trade, and catering services. The lowest growth rate was recorded in the first category. Thus different sub-sectors of rural employment experienced different growth rates. These differing growth rates resulted into change in the structural composition of the rural employment. The structure of rural employment and changes in it during the post-reform period are depicted in Table 4.26 below.

While as in 1978 almost all the employment in rural China was contributed by the primary sector, its contribution was reduced to 61.57 per cent by 2004. From 1980, the contribution of industry increased from three per cent to 11 per cent. Contribution of construction increased from three per cent in 1985 to almost 7 per cent in 2004. Thus contribution of secondary sector (industry plus construction) increased from almost negligible level in 1978 to almost 18 per cent in the twenty six years following reforms. Contribution of the tertiary sector (last three categories in Table 4.26) also increased from negligible level to 7.65 per cent in 1985 and further to 20.66 per cent in 2004.

Therefore, in the total rural employment, contribution of the primary sector decreased while as the contribution of the secondary and tertiary sector increased significantly.

4.10. Education and Literacy

4.10.1. Decrease in Illiteracy

Although China's literacy record of the pre-reform period was quite impressive, yet at the time of reform more than 30 per cent of the rural population was illiterate. After the reforms the growth in literacy in rural China has been quite significant. The proportion of illiterate or semi-illiterate people in rural China decreased from 27.87 per cent in 1985 to 6.65 per cent in 2006. Thus 21 percentage points reduction occurred in these 22 years. Given the sheer size of the population, the record of illiteracy reduction was significant.

4.10.2. Composition of Rural Education

Apart from the reduction in the magnitude of illiteracy, the structure of education for rural households also underwent a positive change. The proportion of rural population in the higher levels of education increased

Table 4.27: Education Level of Labourers of Rural Households

(unit: Per cent)

Year	Illiterate or semi-illiterate	Primary school	Junior middle school	Senior middle school	Special secondary school	College and higher
1985	27.87	37.13	27.69	6.96	0.29	0.06
1990	20.73	38.86	32.84	6.96	0.51	0.10
1991	16.91	39.54	35.23	7.60	0.59	0.13
1992	16.20	39.05	36.21	7.82	0.60	0.12
1993	15.29	38.21	37.43	8.20	0.70	0.17
1994	14.68	37.19	38.59	8.51	0.82	0.21
1995	13.47	36.62	40.10	8.61	0.96	0.24
1996	11.23	35.52	42.83	8.91	1.20	0.31
1997	10.10	35.11	44.31	8.91	1.24	0.33
1998	9.56	34.48	44.98	9.15	1.46	0.37

(Contd.)

(*Contd. Table 4.27*)

Year	*Illiterate or semi-illiterate*	*Primary school*	*Junior middle school*	*Senior middle school*	*Special secondary school*	*College and higher*
1999	8.96	33.66	46.05	9.37	1.57	0.39
2000	8.09	32.22	48.07	9.31	1.83	0.48
2001	7.87	31.14	48.89	9.65	1.94	0.51
2002	7.59	30.63	49.33	9.81	2.09	0.56
2003	7.39	29.94	50.24	9.68	2.11	0.64
2004	7.46	29.20	50.38	10.05	2.13	0.77
2005	6.87	27.23	52.22	10.25	2.37	1.06
2006	6.65	26.37	52.81	10.52	2.40	1.25
2007	6.34	25.76	52.91	11.01	2.54	1.45

Source: China Yearbook 2008: Rural Household Survey. Department of Rural Surveys, National Bureau of Statistics, p. 15.

in the said period. In 1985, the proportion of total enrollment in primary school education level was 37.13 per cent. The same in 2007 was 25.76 per cent. The largest increase in the proportion of total enrollment was recorded in the junior middle school. Its proportion increased from 27.69 per cent in 1985 to 52.91 per cent in 2007. An increase from 6.96 per cent in 1985 to 11.01 in 2007 was also recorded in senior middle school. Special secondary school proportion increased from 0.29 per cent in 1985 to 2.54 per cent in 2007. In case of college and higher education, the proportion increased from 0.06 per cent in 1985 to 1.45 per cent in 2007. Thus, proportion of primary school in total education recorded a decrease of almost 12 percentage points. While as the junior middle school, senior middle school special secondary school and college and higher level of education recorded an increase of approximately 25, 4, 2.25, and 1.4 percentage points respectively. These variables, related with education level of labourers, are presented in Table 4.27.

4.11. Infrastructure

One of the basic inputs in the production system of an economy is infrastructure. It is a sort of universal input which brings an all-round improvement in the productivity of an economy. Infrastructure, being a public good, demands public intervention for its provision. The following table presents statistics of public expenditure on infrastructure in rural economy of China in five basic infrastructure catagories of the economy. These are: research and development; irrigation; education; roads; power; and communication.

The annual growth rate of real expenditure in case of Research and Development (R & D) from 1978 to 1997 was 3.42 per cent. It increased from 1145 million yuan to 2170 million yuan during this period. Expenditure on irrigation increased form 8556 million yuan in 1978 to 234515 million yuan in 1997. The annual growth rate of expenditure was 5.44 per cent. Expenditure on education grew at a rate of 9.33 per cent; increasing from 7524 million yuan in 1978 to 41024 in 1997. Expenditure on roads increased at an annual rate of 15.59 per cent; increasing from 682 million yuan in 1978 to 10700 million yuan in 1997. Expenditure on power increased from 1046 million yuan in 1978 to 14147 million yuan in 1997; an annual growth rate of 14.69 per cent. Highest growth in expenditure occurred in case of telecommunication. The annual growth rate in this sector of rural economy was 19.88 per cent.

In 1978, the composition of public expenditure on infrastructure in rural China was like this: R & D, 5.94 per cent; irrigation, 44.4 per cent; education, 39.09 per cent; roads, 3.54 per cent; power, 5.43 per cent and; communication, 1.54 per cent. After reforms there was a continuous change

Table 4.28: Public Spending in Rural China, 1978-97

(millions of 1990 yuan)

Year	*Total[†] expenditure*	*R&D*	*Irrigation*	*Education*	*Roads*	*Power*	*Communication*
1978	19,253	1,145	8556	7526	682	1046	298
1979	22,410	1,319	9856	9198	733	1044	260
1980	21,330	1295	7457	10,660	693	988	237
1981	19,383	1212	5188	11289	381	1073	240
1982	21,287	1221	5700	12454	416	1237	259
1983	23,794	1516	6160	13815	449	1551	303
1984	26,607	1765	5803	16208	481	1943	407
1985	30,247	1764	5183	19025	1253	2565	457
1986	35,251	1770	5510	22359	1381	3642	589
1987	41,225	1644	6154	26432	1626	4522	847
1988	41,909	1833	5862	26988	1916	4482	828
1989	37,548	1754	5744	22917	2082	4151	900

(Contd.)

(Contd. Table 4.28)

Year	*Total*† *expenditure*	*R&D*	*Irrigation*	*Education*	*Roads*	*Power*	*Communication*
1990	42,400	1625	7164	25006	2559	4968	1078
1991	50,134	1790	9820	28530	2973	5607	1414
1992	62,814	2143	13739	32261	5200	7110	2361
1993	72,064	2230	14344	38059	3795	8633	5003
1994	72,443	2291	13600	34695	4938	8910	8009
1995	74,888	2267	15417	34139	5673	9597	7795
1996	86,760	2348	15136	38636	7956	15195	7489
1997	100,806	2170	23415	41024	10700	14147	9350
Growth* (78-97)	9.10	3.42	5.44	9.33	15.59	14.69	19.88
% of total expenditure#	1978	5.94	44.4	39.09	3.54	5.43	1.54
	1997	2.15	23.22	40.70	10.61	14.03	9.27

†Total expenditure calculated by summing individual expenditures for each year. *Annual compound growth rate worked from data given. # Percentage expenditures developed from given data.

Source: Fan and Pardey 1997, Fan 2000 and SSB various years (in Shenggen Fan, Linxiu Zhang, Xiaobo Zhang. 2002. Growth, Inequality, and Poverty in Rural China: The Role of Public Investments. International Food Policy Research Institute Washington, D.C. p. 19).

Table 4.29: Irrigated Area, Consumption of Chemical Fertilisers, Hydropower Stations and Electricity Consumption in Rural Areas

Year	*Irrigated Area (1000 hectares)*	*Consumption of Chemical Fertilizer (10000 tons)*	*Hydropower Station in Rural Areas Number*	*Generating Capacity (10000 kw)*	*Electricity Consumed in Rural Area (100 million kwh)*
1978	44965.0	884.0	82387	228.4	253.1
1980	44888.1	1269.4	80319	304.1	320.8
1985	44035.9	1775.8	55754	380.2	508.9
1989	44917.2	2357.1	50862	416.8	790.5
1990	47403.1	2590.3	52387	428.8	844.5
1991	47822.1	2805.1	49644	456.9	963.2
1992	48590.1	2930.2	48082	478.5	1106.9
1993	48727.9	3151.9	45153	481.9	1244.8
1994	48759.1	3317.9	48722	503.6	1473.9
1995	49281.2	3593.7	40699	519.5	1655.7

(Contd.)

(Contd. Table 4.29)

Year	*Irrigated Area (1000 hectares)*	*Consumption of Chemical Fertilizer (10000 tons)*	*Hydropower Station in Rural Areas Number*	*Generating Capacity (10000 kw)*	*Electricity Consumed in Rural Area (100 million kwh)*
1996	50381.4	3827.9	37743	533.7	1812.7
1997	51238.5	3980.7	36117	562.5	1980.1
1998	52295.6	4083.7	33185	634.8	2042.1
1999	53158.4	4124.3	31678	664.1	2173.4
2000	53820.3	4146.4	29962	698.5	2421.3
2001	54249.4	4253.8	29183	896.6	2610.8
2002	54354.8	4339.4	27633	812.2	2993.4
2003	54014.2	4411.6	26696	862.3	3432.9
2004	54478.4	4636.6	27115	993.8	3933.0
Growth 1978-2004	0.74	6.58	-4.10	5.81	11.12

Table 4.30: Rural Hydropower Construction and Amount of Electric Power Generation

Year Region	*Amount of Investment Completed This Year (10 000 yuan)*	*Capability of Electricity Generation Equipment at the Year-end (kw)*	*Newly Increased Capability of Electricity Generation Equipment*	*Scale of Electric Power Plant under Construction (kw)*	*Scale of Newly Started Electric Power Station This Year*	*Amount of Electric Power Generation (10 000 kwh)*
1990	348848	13978100	791000			4181100
1991	476529	14942700	1009100			4066800
1992	594081	15728195	964769	4170000		4818494
1993	792747	16622781	995124	9600000		5841049
1994	1020937	17566675	1163873	10500000		5771834
1995	1321689	18721073	1207854	10760000		6316247
1996	1442828	20095552	1408342			6496723
1997	1452004	21771773	1780352			7221270
1998	1585787	23390300	1741631			7560916

(Contd.)

(Contd. Table 4.30)

Year Region	*Amount of Investment Completed This Year (10 000 yuan)*	*Capability of Electricity Generation Equipment at the Year-end (kw)*	*Newly Increased Capability of Electricity Generation Equipment*	*Scale of Electric Power Plant under Construction (kw)*	*Scale of Newly Started Electric Power Station This Year*	*Amount of Electric Power Generation (10 000 kwh)*
1999	1833853	25562760	2344285	8717000	386000	7715124
2000	2220993	27487791	2060127	7459500	2384000	8755014
2001	2133741	28787476	1714454	3547500	1462800	9490187
2002	2393195	31044576	1883648	5680800	1419000	10366868
2003	3006249	34157792	2702834	10850143	6385500	10966512
2004	3770733	38655048	4363322	16652425	5362090	11045527
Growth 1978-2004						

in this composition. In 1997 the composition of public expenditure was: R & D, 2.15 per cent; irrigation, 23.22 per cent; education, 40.70 per cent; roads 10.61 per cent; power, 14.03 per cent and; communication, 9.27 per cent. Thus, a decrease occurred in the relative expenditure of R & D and irrigation, while as proportion of expenditure on education, roads, power and communication increased. All these statistics are presented in Table 4.28.

The development of infrastructure can be inferred from statistics presented in Table 4.29. The absolute irrigated area increased at a marginal rate of 0.74 per cent. It increased from 44965 thousand hectares in 1978 to 54478 thousand hectares in 2004. The number of hydropower stations in rural areas decreased from 82387 in 1978 to 27115 in 2004. However, there was an increase in the generating capacity of power from 228.4 ten thousand Kw in 1978 to 993.8 ten thousand Kw in 2004. Thus, while the number of power stations decreased quite significantly, the reverse was true of the generating capacity. At the same time, the consumption of electricity in rural areas increased from 25,300 million Kwh in 1978 to 393,300 million Kwh in 2004. The annual growth rate of the same was 11.12 per cent.

Statistics regarding investment and generation of hydropower in rural China are presented in Table 4.30. Year-wise investment increased from 3488 million yuan in 1990 to 37707 million yuan in 2004. As a consequence the scale of electric power generation increased from 41811 million Kwh in 1990 to 110455 million Kwh in 2004. Other related statistics are also given in the table.

4.12. Challenges to Rural China

Compared to other developing economies, China's rural economy has witnessed much positive changes in the past couple of decades. However, its rural transformation is also confronted with formidable challenges. Among the challenges that the economy faces, two are crucial to the future of rural China. The first is the case of already high and growing inequality of income and other indicators of development. On one hand inter-sectoral, i.e., rural-urban, inequality is high and growing over time. On the other inequality at the rural level is also witnessing an increasing trend.

The other factor that is central to the future development of rural China is land rights. The combination of collective ownership and household use of land has become increasingly incompatible. Both these factors have assumed ugly proportions and produced much of the crisis that the rural society is witnessing. The measures taken by the government have produced some positive effects but are far from sufficient to reverse the trend of inequality of income and incompatibility of collective ownership and individual land-use.

4.12.1. Inequality

Inequality of income is one of the major problems that have significant but adverse economic and social consequences for a nation. It indicates that the growth is disproportionately benefiting or neglecting particular sections of the society. This diminishes the opportunities for poorer sections of the society which may result into social crisis and economic instability of the country as a whole.

(A) Rural-Urban Inequality

Despite the fact that income of rural China increased considerably after the reforms, deep inequality not only persisted but also accentuated in the post-reform period. The rural-urban per capita income ratio in 1978 was 0.39 which decreased to 0.30 in 2004. Net per capita income of rural households in 1978 was 133.6 yuan while as the same in case of the urban household was 343.4 yuan. In 2004, per capita income of rural households had increased to 2936.4 yuan while that of the urban households increased to 9421.6 yuan. Thus, while as in 1978 urban households enjoyed a per capita income more than two and half times that of the rural households. In 2004, this differential had increased to three and a quarter times.

The Table 4.31 presents the official statistics regarding the comparative per capita income and its growth of rural and urban households. Upto 1985 the income differential between the rural and urban households decreased. Therefore, rural-urban income inequality during this period decreased. This was the result of the success of reforms in increasing rural income at a much higher rate than the urban income. Such a momentum was not retained afterwards. After, 1985, urban income increased at a rate which allowed the trend of decreasing inequality to be reversed. Inequality continued to increase though with some fluctuations afterwards.

(B) Intra-Rural Inequality

Not only did rural-urban inequality increase in the post-reform period, but inequality at the rural level also underwent significant increase. One of the often used measures of inequality of income is Gini coefficient, the values of which range between 0 and 1. Higher the value of the Gini coefficient higher is the level of inequality. In 2007 the value of Gini coefficient was 0.37 as compared to its value of 0.21 in 1978. Thus, in last twenty nine years, the level of income inequality in rural China has undergone a substantial increase. It implies that progressively lesser and lesser people are taking disproportionate share in the high growth process of the economy.

Table 4.31: Per Capita Annual Income of Urban and Rural Households

Year	*Per Capita Annual Net Income of Rural Households Value (yuan)*	*Index*	*Per Capita Annual Disposable Income of Urban Households Value (yuan)*	*Index*	*Rural/urban per capita income[#]*
1978	133.6	100.0	343.4	100.0	0.39
1980	191.3	139.0	477.6	127.0	0.40
1985	397.6	268.9	739.1	160.4	0.53
1989	601.5	305.7	1373.9	182.5	0.43
1990	686.3	311.2	1510.2	198.1	0.45
1991	708.6	317.4	1700.6	212.4	0.41
1992	784.0	336.2	2026.6	232.9	0.38
1993	921.6	346.9	2577.4	255.1	0.35
1994	1221.0	364.4	3496.2	276.8	0.35
1995	1577.7	383.7	4283.0	290.3	0.36

(Contd.)

(Contd. Table 4.31)

Year	*Per Capita Annual Net Income of Rural Households Value (yuan)*	*Index*	*Per Capita Annual Disposable Income of Urban Households Value (yuan)*	*Index*	*Rural/urban per capita income*#
1996	1926.1	418.2	4838.9	301.6	0.39
1997	2090.1	437.4	5160.3	311.9	0.40
1998	2162.0	456.2	5425.1	329.9	0.39
1999	2210.3	473.5	5854.0	360.6	0.37
2000	2253.4	483.5	6280.0	383.7	0.35
2001	2366.4	503.8	6859.6	416.3	0.34
2002	2475.6	528.0	7702.8	472.1	0.32
2003	2622.2	550.7	8472.2	514.6	0.30
2004	2936.4	588.1	9421.6	554.2	0.31

Calculated from column two and four.

Source: Developed from data by China Statistical Census, 2007. www.allcountries.org/China_statistics.

Table 4.32: Net income and Gini Coefficient

Year	*Net income*	*Gini coefficient*
1978	133.57	0.2124
1980	191.33	0.2407
1985	397.60	0.2264
1990	686.31	0.3099
1995	1577.74	0.3415
2000	2253.42	0.3536
2005	3254.93	0.3751
2007	4140.36	0.3742

Source: China Yearbook 2008: Rural Household Survey. Department of Rural Surveys, National Bureau of Statistics, p. 32.

Table 4.32 provides the trend values of Gini coefficient against rising income in the post-reform period. There has been good correspondence between growth of per capita net income of the rural households and the level of income inequality. Most of this increase in inequality has occurred in the post-1985 phase. This is indicative of the policy ineffectiveness directed at the rural economy of China, as a result of which income growth became less and less equitable. Lately, such a growing trend of inequality has lost its momentum because of the increased government intervention in the rural economy. However, the significant proportion that inequality in the countryside has assumed requires to be reversed to maintain the economic momentum and social cohesion of the country.

The growing rural-urban inequality is also evident in other indicators of development. Table 4.33 presents the comparative statistics of infant mortality rate (IMR) for urban and rural China. During the reform period rural to urban ratio of infant mortality increased from 1.7 to 2.8. In 1981, rural areas had 39.1 IMR (per thousand) against 23.6 IMR in urban China. The same in 2000 was 30.8 in rural areas against 11 in urban areas.

Table 4.33: Rural-Urban Differentials in Infant Mortality

Year	*Rural*	*Urban*	*Rural/Urban*
1981	39.1	23.6	1.7
1990	32.4	19.1	1.7
2000	30.8	11.0	2.8

Source: Zhang and Kanbur (2005), in Tandon, Ajay, and Juzhong Zhuang. 2007. *Inclusiveness of Economic Growth in the People's Republic of China: What Do Population Health Outcomes Tell Us?* Asian Development Bank.

4.12.2. Insecure Property Rights

Land in China does not belong to people. It is still the property of government or collectives of village. After the formation of communes towards late 1950s, land was taken over from the individual households for collective farming. The reforms in late 1970s only gave peasants the right to cultivate land on household basis as against the collective method employed after formation of communes. This was done through leasing the land to individual households for different time periods. Though, the system of land lease programme worked in bringing significant transformation to rural economy of China in the initial phase, its limitations started becoming more pronounced afterwards.

One of the basic limitations of the land-lease programme is that it reduces the incentive for long-term investment for the farmers. After the contract is over, the land may or may not be returned to the earlier farmer. Therefore, the investment plan of the farmers is curtailed short of its expectations by the institution of land-lease. This limits the actual growth and development of the sector to approximate its potential.

Since, land-lease method is implemented by bureaucratic machinery of the state; such an institution provides ample provision of rent seeking. This breeds corruption in the state which hinders the efficient development of the resources. Further, the administrative machinery develops incentive to oppose any change towards more efficient system to replace the existing one. This results in large economic and social loss.

Land is one of the most important assets in the hands of the peasants. This asset can be handy in creating a permanent source of income for the poor and become an assured security for their livelihood and progress. Any impermanence in the land right is an ugly threat to the security and progress of the rural household. The same has actually happened in case of China. This is one of the main reasons of social discontent in rural China. The increase in protests in rural China are mainly related with the land right.

To overcome these limitations, the Chinese government has taken initiatives to make land use rights more prolonged and more permanent, so as to provide security to the peasants. The effectiveness of these measures is quite debatable but their impact has nonetheless been positive for the peasants. Among the series of policies and laws adopted to address this very sensitive issue, four are particularly important.

In 1993, Chinese government for the *first* time adopted a formal policy to provide farmers land-use right for a permanent period of 30 years. The *second* initiative came in 1998, when the 30-year policy was embodied in formal law for the first time as a result of the adoption of the revised Land Management Law. The issuance of land-rights documents was given wide publicity. In 2002, the revised law was followed by the enactment of Rural Land Contracting Law. This clarified the content of land-use right and provided legal remedies for any violation. The fourth initiative followed in 2007 when China adopted a Property Law, which characterises farmers rural land-use rights as property rights or rights *in term* (as opposed to the contractual rights defined by previous laws), providing greater protection for small farmers' rights.[8]

Notwithstanding the implementation of policies and enactment of laws, the loopholes present therein have not allowed any significant change in the basic nature of land-use right or ownership. Peasants are alive to the threat of land readjustment and land taking without commensurate compensation.[9] Most Chinese farmers still lack secure and marketable land rights that would allow them to make long-term investments in land, decisively improve productivity, and accumulate wealth.[10]

References

1. Du Runsheng. 2006. *The Course of China's Rural Reform.* International Food Policy Research Institute, pp.2 -3.
2. Dale Wen. *China Copes with Globalisation:* a mixed review. International Forum on Globalisation (IFG), San Francisco, p. 12.
3. Shenggen Fan, Linxiu Zhang, Xiaobo Zhang. 2002. *Growth, Inequality, and Poverty in Rural China: The Role of Public Investments.* International Food Policy Research Institute Washington, D.C. p. 7.
4. Du Runsheng. 2006. *The Course of China's Rural Reform.* International Food Policy Research Institute, p. 9.
5. Shenggen Fan, Linxiu Zhang, Xiaobo Zhang. 2002. *Growth, Inequality, and Poverty in Rural China: The Role of Public Investments.* International Food Policy Research Institute Washington, D.C. p. 8.
6. Pareto efficient or optimal situation is a situation when perfect competition prevails and factors are employed in the most profitable enterprise due to perfect mobility. Production depends on relative profitability. As production is determined by demand therefore optimal mix of the products, as determined by the intersection of supply and demand in case of each commodity, are produced in an economy. Thus both the factor as well as product markets ensure efficiency in the use of resources in an economy. The drawbacks of the concept does not only arise because of the fact that perfect competition does not prevail, but also whether perfect completion leaves enough room for innovation and investment because perfect competition does not allow extra or supernormal profits, which could be channeled for research and experimentation. Therefore, a trade-off between efficiency and growth in the long rural is unavoidable.
7. Todaro, M.P., Stephen C. Smith. 2003. *Economic Development.* Pearson Education, India, p. 52.

8. Keliang, Zhu, Roy Prosterman. 2007. *Securing Land Rights for Chinese Farmers: A Leap Forward for Stability and Growth*. Center for Global Liberty and Prosperity, Development Policy Analysis, Washington D.C. p. 4.
9. These facts have been well documented in the survey conducted by Rural Development Institute, Seattle, Washington, 2005.
10. Keliang, Zhu, Roy Prosterman. 2007. *op. cit*. p. 4.

5

Relevance of China's Reform Experience to India

5.1 Introduction

Ever since the development planning became common in developing countries, after the World War Second, discussion on alternative development models has been at the centre of policy debate, development economics and other academic fields of political economy. Countries, in terms of planning, have oscillated between extreme forms of command to free market arrangement. Such a spectrum of different possible combinations of market-state arrangement has rendered optimal option on an externally determined rule quite irrelevant. Given all the factors determining the state of development, different economies can have different optimal levels of state-market combination. Even the same combination of market-state spectrum can take diverse forms because same level of state intervention can assume different forms by covering different sectors. Thus successful replication of policies from other countries is highly contingent upon the nature and structure of two economies as well as localisation of a foreign development model. The famous Nobel Laureate, Joseph Stieglitz captioned the latter phenomenon, "scan globally and reinvent locally".

One important international experience that has on the one hand fostered the relevance of the adoption of a successful development strategy experience in any country and at the same time cautioned its unreserved use is the **Marshall Plan**. The finance and capital imported by Europe after the Second World War destruction helped in a speedy recovery and rebuilding of the West European economies. Thus, many development economists were led to believe that accumulation of capital through whatever means was the single most requirement for the development of the underdeveloped countries. However, adoption of this approach, sometimes called **capital fundamentalism,** has failed in promoting either growth or socio-economic development or both. Thus adoption of a strategy in Europe worked while it failed in developing countries.

The reason for this is that economic and social development apart from being complementary are determined by so many varied factors operating in a society that capital's role is relegated to a mere factor from the central determinant of development. The relevance of the adoption of successful development strategies depends on the commonalities of these factors across states which determine the state of development and changes therein.

However, after the success of East Asian countries in achieving stupendous economic progress, countries across globe have sought to learn from their experience. Most of the countries still had no substantial success in doing so, however. The possibilities of such success, in following the successful development model of other economies, depend critically on the relevance of the model to the domestic institutional, political, cultural as well as economic conditions. That is development is a path dependent phenomenon and cannot be achieved by just adjusted exchange rates and introduction of free market arrangement of command planning. Therefore, success of reforms in one economy cannot automatically guarantee their success in other economies.

5.2 Relevance of Comparison between India and China

Despite enormous differences in culture, geography, history, resources, and economic structures, India and China share many commonalities. In many respects these commonalities make China and India much alike than either of these with other countries of the world. Such similarities also provide opportunity for successful economic policies adopted in one country to be relevant for the other.

China and India are the two largest populous countries of the world. Together they constitute approximately forty per cent of the total world population. Both have a vast geographic spread. Both countries attained freedom and became nation states immediately after the Second World War; India in 1947 and China in 1949. Both countries embarked on planning in early 1950s. Currently both countries are in 11th Five Year Plan. While China adopted complete communist system India's arrangement was much flexible but falling in the socialist tradition. Both these economies witnessed moderate economic growth from inception of planning to 1980; 4.2 per cent (Chapter 2) and 3.5 per cent for China and India respectively. After that phase both have been growing pretty fast. However, China grew much faster than India after reforms though lately growth rates of the two economies are converging.

What is significantly different between China and India is the record of achievements in the last thirty years despite so many similarities. Given the set of similarities between the two countries, there is substantial relevance of successful development strategy on part of one country for the other. Therefore, it is highly appropriate to understand the dynamics of change in China because with slight modifications these are likely to be highly effective in India. Commonalities foster compatibilities in policy.

5.3 Country Profiles: India Versus China

Table 5.1 presents some basic geographic indicators of China and India. While China has a surface area of 9.6 million square Kms, India's surface area is 3.2 million square Kms. Thus, China's surface area is three times that of India's. Despite this advantage, China has a disadvantage in having lesser proportion of the arable land area (11 per cent) as compared to India (53.7 per cent) In absolute terms while India has more than one and a half million square Km arable land. China has almost one million square miles only. Both the countries have almost equal proportion of forest land to the total land area, i.e., almost 22 per cent. China's coastline is twice as large as that of India. India's land boundaries are two third that of China.

In Table 5.2, the four main indicators of development of the Chinese and Indian economy are presented. On a comparative analysis of the development indicators, China systematically fairs better than India in most of the indicators by a significant margin. In Purchasing Power Parity (PPP), Gross National Income (GNI) of China in 2007 was $ 7083.5 billions. The same for India was $ 3078.7 billions. Thus, China's national income was 2.3 times larger than that of India. This obviously is a large difference in economic strength of the two countries. Similar difference is also found in case of the per capita income. On PPP basis, in 2007, the per capita income of China was $ 5370 and that of richer than that of India. Thus, on average China's citizens were twice richer than of India. Significant differences are not only found in economic indicators but also in case of social and health indicators. Life expectancy at birth for male in China (2006) was 70 years while in India it was only 63. Similarly, life expectancy at birth for female in China was 74 years while in India it was only 66 years. Thus, life expectancy at birth in China for male was six years and for female eight years higher than India. In case of literacy, China again has a much better.

5.4 Development Policies from 1980s: A Comparison

India and China adopted five year plans to carry forward and achieve the desired results in the socio-economic fields. As discussed in Chapter 2, pre-reform period, China during this phase underwent important

Table 5. 1: Profile of China and India

	Location	*Surface Area (km)*	*Arable land Percentage of land area*	*Forest land Percentage of land area*	*Coastline (kms)*	*Land boundaries (kms)*
	2007	2007	2007	2007	2007	2007
China	35 00 N, 105 00 E	9,598,088	11.1	21.2	14,500	22,117
India	20 00 N, 77 00 E	3,287,260	53.7	22.8	7,000	14,103

Source: World Development Report, 2009 pp. 332-33.

Table 5.2: Key Development Indicators for China and India

Countries	Population (millions) 2007	PPP Gross National Income (GNI) $ billions (2007)	PPP Gross National Income (GNI) $ per capita (2007)	Life expectancy at Birth (2006) Male	Life expectancy at Birth (2006) Female	Adult literacy rate 2005 % aged 15 and older
China	1320	7,083.5	5,370	70	74	91
India	1123	3,078.7	2,740	63	66	61

Source: World Development Report, 2009, p. 352.

institutional changes and towards the end the whole economy was under the control of the government. There was no private sector. However, from 1978 the institutional arrangement provided progressively larger space for private sector. China's reforms, as mentioned in Chapter 4, started in the rural sector with the agricultural sector as the priority area followed by development of the other sectors of the rural economy and spreading progressively to the rest of the economy including notably the foreign sector. This helped the reforms to benefit the rural sector and therefore the record of improvement in the development indicators in China was stronger in comparison to most of the developing or transition economies. Though liberalisation, privatisation, and globalisation occurred in China but this was done in a phased manner so as to avoid costs of abrupt departure from the past institutional arrangement.

In India, some reforms at decreasing the role of the bureaucratic hurdles in the economic development were introduced in the 1980s. However, after the BOP crisis of 1991, there was an implementation of reform programme aimed at opening and liberalisation of most of the sectors of the economy. The emphasis was more on the industrial growth and external balance as well as provision of infrastructure and conducive environment for the services sector of the economy. As the economy moved ahead the external balance with the help of institutional investment and FDI was achieved, services sector grew very fast. However, lately the industrial sector has perfomed much better and is the main source growth. The effectiveness of these development strategies for both the economies is analysed hereunder.

5.5 Policy Effectiveness: A Comparison

The state of development in China and India in early 1980s was almost comparable, rather same. However, after reforms in China in late 1970s, and consequent economic progress, state of development between the two countries started to diverge.

The economic policy of China in this way was substantially more effective than that of India. The effectiveness of economic policy can be gauged from the improvement of different indicators of development. For the sake of brevity as well as to confine the analysis to our subject, we measure this effectiveness in terms of two fundamental indicators of development. The first is growth. From the instrumental perspective, growth is fundamental for increasing the well being of a society as it increases the total output of the economy. The second indicator is the reduction of poverty. From the perspective of outcome, this indicator is one of the most vital to measure the effectiveness of policy in the long run.

Table 5.3: Poverty in China and India

	China				*India*			
	Percentage of pop. living on < $1.08/ day	*Number of people living on < $1.08/day (millions)*	*Percentage pop. living on < $2.15/day*	*Number of people living on < $2.15/day (millions)*	*Percentage pop. living on < $1.08/day*	*Number of people living on < $1.08/ day (millions)*	*Percentage pop. living on < $2.15/ day*	*Number of people living on < $2.15 /day (millions)*
1981	63.8	634	88.1	876	54.3	382	89.6	630
1990	33.0	374	72.2	819	44.3	376	86.4	734
1993	28.4	334	68.1	803	42.1	379	85.5	769
1996	17.4	211	53.3	650	40.6	385	84.5	801
1999	17.8	223	50.1	628	38.8	387	83.2	832
2002	13.8	177	40.9	524	37.5	393	82.1	861
2004	9.9	128	34.9	452	35.8	386	81.1	876
2015 (forecast)	2.6	37	14.1	196	22.1	283	66.8	853

Source: Global Monitoring Report 2007, p. 65.

Table 5.3 below presents the statistics of the income poverty, in both absolute and proportional figures, of China and India from 1981 to 2004. In 1981, almost 64 per cent (634 million) of Chinese population was living below poverty by $ 1.08 a day. Same year India had only 54.3 per cent (382 million) absolutely poor people by $ 1.08 a day standard. Thus in 1981 India was less poor than China. In 1990, only 33 per cent (374 million) of Chinese population was absolutely poor while India had 44.3 per cent (376 million) population in absolute poverty. Thus, within a span of ten years, poverty in China decreased by 30.8 percentage points. While in the same period poverty reduced only by 10 percentage points in India. In 1999, absolute poverty on $ 1.08 basis in China was only 17.8 per cent while as the same in India was 38.8 per cent. Thus, poverty in China decreased in this decade by 15.2 percentage points while in India it decreased only by 5.5 percentage points. From 1999 to 2004, absolute poverty by $ 1.08 a day standard in China reduced by another 4 percentage points to 9.9 per cent. In the same period India's absolute poverty reduced by only 3 percentage points to 35.8 per cent. Thus overall poverty reduction in the entire period from 1981 to 2004 in China was from 63.8 per cent to 9.9 per cent—a reduction of 53.9 percentage points. During the same period, India's poverty in absolute terms reduced from 54.3 per cent to 35.8 per cent—a reduction of 18.5 percentage points. The case of absolute poverty on $ 2.15 per day basis also follows the same comparative trends in two countries.

Table 5.4 reproduces the results of a United Nations study by Hafiz Pasha and T. Palanivel which show differing responses of growth (per capita) to overall economic policy as well as differing poverty reduction rates in China and India. In 1970s, rate of per capita income growth in China was 4.4 per cent while as that of India was only 0.8 per cent. India's growth was substantially lower than that of China. However, poverty reduction in China was quite less than in India in this decade. While China's rate of change in incidence of poverty was - 0.18 per cent that of India was – 2.15 per cent. Therefore, growth elasticity of poverty was - 0.18 per cent in China and -2.15 per cent in India. Development policy on the basis of poverty reduction in India can be said more pro-poor than in China in the decade of 1970s.

In the decade of 1980s, rate of per capita output growth in both the countries increased. Rate of per capita growth in China was 7.8 per cent while in India it was 3.6 per cent. However, rate of poverty reduction in the two countries reversed their earlier trend. In contrast to the India's better poverty reduction performance in 1970, China's profile of poverty reduction improved substantially in this decade. While India's rate of change in incidence in poverty was -2.2 that of China was -9.8. Growth

Table 5.4: Correlation: Income Growth and Poverty Reduction

Country	*1970s*			*1980s*			*1990s*		
	Rate of per capita income growth	*Rate of change in incidence in poverty*	*Growth elasticity of poverty*	*Rate of per capita income growth*	*Rate of change in incidence in poverty*	*Growth elasticity of poverty*	*Rate of per capita income growth*	*Rate of change in incidence in poverty*	*Growth elasticity of poverty*
China	4.4	-0.8	-0.18	7.8	-9.8	-1.26	9.0	-9.8	-1.09
India	0.8	-1.7	-2.15	3.6	-2.2	-0.60	3.6	-2.8	-0.77

Source: Hafiz A. Pasha and T. Palanivel (2004). *Pro-Poor Growth Policies: the Asian Experience*. United Nations Development Programme, pp. 6-7.

Table 5.5: Impact of Growth of GDP Per Capita on Poverty

	GDP/Capita growth	*Initial poverty rate ($1/day)*	*Annual percentage change in poverty rate ($1/day)*	*Elasticity*
India (1994-2005)	4.55	42.1	-1.47	-0.32
China (1999-2004)	8.11	17.8	-11.73	-1.45

Source: Global Monitoring Report, 2007, p. 42.

elasticity of poverty in case of China was -1.26 while that in India it was only -0.6 per cent. Thus, effect of growth on poverty reduction increased significantly in China from 1970s to 1980s. China's economic policy was significantly pro-poor in the decade of 1980s than that of India. For each per cent growth in the per capita income, poverty reduced by 1.26 per cent.

In the decade of 1990s, China improved its growth performance in per capita terms while as India retained its previous decade's position. Rate of per capita income growth in China was 9 per cent. India's growth rate, per capita, was only 3.6 per cent. Rate of change in incidence in poverty in India and China was -9.8 and -2.8 per cent respectively. Growth elasticity of poverty in China was -1.09 per cent while in India it was only -0.77 per cent.

Thus it is clear that not only growth has been lower in India in comparison to China but also growth elasticity of poverty is lower. While low growth reduces the possibility of poverty reduction.

Global Monitoring Report 2007 provides the statistics of per capita GDP growth and poverty reduction for the period 1994-2005 for India and 1999-2004 for China. These are presented in Table 5.5. For their respective periods GDP per capita growth for China was 8.11 per cent while for India it was 4.55 per cent. Initial poverty rate in China was 17.8 per cent while as in India it was 42.1 per cent. Annual change in poverty rate in China was -11.73 per cent while for India it was -1.47 per cent. Growth elasticity of poverty reduction in China was -1.45 while in India it was -0.32 only.

Thus from the time of reforms in the late 1970s, there has been a systematic divergence in improvement of most development indicators between China and India. While progress in China was stupendously fast in India it was painfully slow.

Table 5.6 presents statistics of cereal production and high-value agriculture products in China and India. Though in cereal production, average annual growth from 1990 to 2005 was higher in India (1.4 per cent) than in China (0.0 per cent); per capita production was much higher in case of China (313 kg) than India (219 kg) in 2003-05. Similarly, yield in 2003-05 in China was 5095 kg per hectare while in India it was only 2417 kg per hectare. Annual average growth from 1990 to 2005 in China was lower (1.2 per cent) than India (1.6 per cent).

In high yielding agricultural products, including meat and fruits and vegetable production, substantial differential is observed. Meat production in 2003-05 in China was 58 kg per capita while in India it was only 6 kg per capita. Further growth rate in China was almost double that of India (6.3 per cent in China against 3.2 per cent in India). Fruits and vegetable production in China was 390 kg per capita while in India it was only

Table 5.6: Agricultural Output and Trade

	Cereal Production				*High-Value Agricultural Products*				
	Production		*Yield*		*Meat production*		*Fruits and vegetable production*		*Total food production per capita average annual percentage growth*
	kg/ capita 2003–05	*average annual percentage growth 1990–2005*	*kg/ hectare 2003–05*	*average annual percentage growth 1990–2005*	*kg/ capita 2003–05*	*average annual percentage growth 1990–2005*	*Kg/ capita 2003–05*	*average annual percentage growth 1990–2005*	*1990–2004*
China	313	0.0	5095	1.2	58	6.3	390	9.3	4.4
India	219	1.4	2417	1.6	6	3.2	118	3.8	0.9

Source: World Development Report, 2008, p. 326.

118 kg per capita. Growth rate of the same in China was 9.3 per cent while in India it was only 3.8 per cent from 1990 to 2005. Per capita food production from 1990 to 2004 increased at an annual average growth of 4.4 per cent in China while in India the same was only 0.9 per cent.

5.6 Relevance of Rural Policies of China to India

The experience of China's reform success offers substantial lessons for most of the developing countries. Since India has more similarities with China than most of the other developing countries, this experience is particularly insightful for India. Some of the policy options exercised in China's reforms have been particularly helpful in developing the institutional and technological framework for success. Among the major dimensions of reforms in China that are in particular need of implementation for a successful transformation of the Indian rural sector, and thus of the overall transformation of the economy, are identified below.

Agriculture/Rural Centric

While as the reforms in China started in rural sector, India's reforms in 1990s were more aimed at the secondary and tertiary sector of the economy. From moderate growth in 1990s to high growth in 2000s, the impact of the growth on poverty reduction and rural transformation has been quite meager in India. On the other hand the thrust on the rural sector in China produced output expansion which was automatically distributed in the rural economy and as a consequence poverty reduction and rural transformation was speedy. This experience shows that for a large chunk of developing countries the thrust for poverty reduction should take the route of rural/agricultural sector development. There has to be a renewed emphasis on the rural development in India in its most comprehensive sense. This includes emphasis on proper institutional environment, technical and technological change, and substantial improvement in rural infrastructure.

Decentralisation

The governance system of China is greatly decentralised. Villages and urban areas have their own local governance structures which cater to their local needs. The emergence of township and village enterprises (TVEs) has been a successful phenomenon because of the governance apparatus. So has been the provision of different public goods both in the pre-reform and the post-reform period by the local administrative mechanism. Decentralised governance has, on one hand, provided the incentive for better economic performance as the expanded output was partly shared by the governing body and, on the other hand, the provision of public goods and production activities in the local areas have been efficient because of involvement of local people who are direct beneficiaries of these activities.

In comparison to China, the decentralised governance mechanism in the form of Panchayat raj in rural areas of India has been largely unsuccessful. The provision of local public goods and involvement in other economic activities has been largely an engagement of the state and central governments with little intervention on part of these institutions. This has marred the incentive for the local people in the good performance of these activities. Simultaneously, the level of corruption has been high due to lack of effective intervention by the proposed recipients of the benefits of the schemes. Thus to make the rural sector of the economy vibrant and well performing, decentralisation of governance of economic and other developmental activities is quite necessary as shown by the Chinese experience. However, the political scenario of India offers rather bleak environment for a successful drive for the same.

Human Resource Development

Not only have Chinese efforts at the human resource development been substantially higher in comparison to India but even the way of doing has been quite different. There has been a substantial emphasis on the technical expertise on the areas of economic activities rather than a theoretical focus on subjective issues. Mao's rustication process though stopped after the Cultural Revolution in which the main emphasis was actual contribution to the economy. However, the emphasis on the technological know how for average student has been kept intact.

The performance of the Indian economy has been marred by the absence of an educated and skilled workforce. For the economy to perform well there has to be a special emphasis on the development of the quality of the labour market in terms of the level of education and skill. For that India has to accentuate its efforts at human resource development by a substantial quantum.

5.7 Conclusion

While as India and China share many features, yet their performance has been quite different in the last three decades. The effective lessons that India has to learn from China include substantial emphasis on investment in agriculture sector, decentralisation of governance and human resource development.

6

Summary and Conclusion

The expansion of Chinese economy in the aftermath of the reforms initiated in the late 1970s, with its profound impact on the development indicators, has been one of the most outstanding success stories of any economy in recent times. Much of this changed state of Chinese economy had favourable economic and social consequences for the Chinese people.

At the time of its proclamation, China was a deeply backward country with a very poor socio-economic fabric. Till the reforms in 1978 policy fluctuated quite widely and so were the results on the economic and social aspects of collective life. From the institutional side there was almost a complete transformation of the economy in this period. From the promulgation of the Agrarian Reform Law in 1950, aimed at large-scale ownership change of land, through mutual aid teams, elementary cooperatives, advanced cooperatives and finally the communes, the socialist transformation of the agriculture was essentially completed in 1958. In case of industry, the same formulae of step-wise transformation to sate and collective ownership through direct and indirect means were adopted.

The expansion of the economy at a moderate growth did not have sufficient potential to bring about transformation of the society. Particularly low rate of growth in the agricultural sector left tens of millions into miserable poverty. Most of the people being residents of countryside did not benefit much from the moderate growth of the overall economy, due to almost stagnant agriculture.

Nonetheless even in the pre-reform period the social indicators of development improved measurably. Four features of the planning seem to have played important role in the Chinese case which explains the possibility of low growth and high social development. The first is the *Chinese perspective of human resource development* with a thrust on pragmatism in education to serve the immediate needs of the economy made educated people direct contributors to economy rather than white collar experts. The other three features include: *continuous efforts at infrastructure development, decentralised planning* and *pro-rural policies*.

However, despite many achievements to its credit, the pre-reform period was not successful to bring poverty rate down to a reasonable level. China at the end of this period had enormous poverty particularly in rural areas. Per capita income was very low and other indicators of development like infant mortality, child mortality, literacy, maternal mortality, sanitation, and infrastructure and energy per capita, were considerably unfavourable by the developed country standards.

In the past three decades China was the fastest growing economy of the world. This was the result of a stream of reforms initiated in late 1970s. Towards the concluding phase of the pre-reform period, policy effectiveness had reached its saturation level and economy was undergoing a state of complete stagnation. The introduction of reforms changed the whole scenario, brought significant vitality to the economy which approximated 10 per cent annual growth since then. The reforms started with relaxing the rules of central planning and progressed continuously to affect a more market oriented economy. Performance of the economy not only resulted from the reforms but also lead to further reforms. Thus reforms and economic performance were mutually reinforcing continuum of processes.

Impressive economic performance of the past three decades was largely a result of the institutional changes in the economy juxtaposed with appropriate macroeconomic policies. The former considerably changed the property right regime which furnished the necessary incentives for hard work, efficiency, and investment. In the initial phase this was particularly important for the primary sector. Macroeconomic policies were regularly adjusted to maintain a high growth propensity while taking care of the stability. Variations in the growth performance reveal that the policy was more effective in the former than the latter. Sustained growth over this duration was maintained by constantly enhancing the supply side potential while maintaining a growing demand. The former notably involved building infrastructure and the latter the institutionalisation of the domestic and international market.

The reforms in China had many peculiar characteristics which were not shared by other transition economies and which had a large impact on the outcome of the reforms. The process of liberalisation, privatisation and globalisation played a significant role in bringing vibrancy to the economy. However, China's approach in this regard was quite different from other centrally planned economies, either communist or otherwise, which opted to switch over to market based or capitalist arrangement.

The economic transformation of the rural economy proceeded from an institutional change of far reaching consequences. The first step of the reform replaced the commune-based agricultural production system with a family based production system. On the whole, the reforms occurred in two reasonably distinct phases. The first phase focused on decentralising the system of agricultural production, while the second phase emphasised liberalising factor and output markets.

The economy of rural China was largely agrarian at the inception of the reforms. With the implementation of Household Responsibility System and opening of markets as well as implementation of open door policy, productivity increased substantially. This led to a significant increase in the income of the rural population. As both the demand and supply possibilities changed, rural economy underwent a profound structural change. This was manifested by the emergence and dominance of non-farm activities as well as development of rural industry. Both of these activities changed the employment composition of the rural economy.

The success of the reforms emerged from their peculiar nature. Rural reforms were gradual, partial, and experimental and in many ways deliberately incomplete and vague. At the institutional level, apart from the adoption of market oriented economy, the responsibility system and township village enterprises were the two basic pillars on which the success of the rural transformation centered. Much of the success of the reforms was based on their peculiar way of the opening up to market and changing the institutional arrangement of the economy than simple transition from plan to market as done by other erstwhile centrally planned economies.

The implementation of the reforms opened the way for a profound structural change in the rural economy. Not only was the overall share of the primary sector reduced in the economy but the non-farm activities assumed ever increasing share. There was a significant reduction in the relative importance of farming in the agriculture with a concomitant increase in significance of animal husbandry and fishery.

In 1978 the share of farming in the agriculture output was four-fifth, which decreased to one-half by 2004. Share of animal husbandry increased from almost one-seventh to one-third during the same period. Fishery's share in the agriculture output also increased measurably while as the share of forestry increased marginally.

Similar changes were felt in the employment of the rural China where a structural change away from farm activities towards non-farm and industrial sector took place. The contribution of secondary sector increased from almost negligible level in 1978 to almost one-fifth of total employment while as that of the tertiary sector also increased from negligible level to one-fifth in 2004.

The reforms brought about a profound change in most of the macroeconomic indicators like total output, per capita income, employment, productivity, consumption, asset formation, expenditure, etc. Following the reforms in late 1970s, output of the primary sector experienced three-fold increase. The total gross value output of the primary sector increased at an average compound growth rate twice the pre-reform period. The per capita income in the period experienced a double digit growth rate. This was the main factor in reducing rural poverty. This change in the output was brought possible by increase in the productivity in agriculture—because arable land did not increase by any significant margin—during the same.

In the post-reform period, rural economy witnessed unprecedented growth in the non-farm sector, both from employment and output perspectives. Non-farm output growth played a significant role in the expansion of the total output of the economy following reforms. Furthermore, the share of rural employment to this sector increased more than four fold in this period, from 1978 to 1997. After the reforms, China's agriculture also underwent technological transformation. Use of fertilisers, irrigation and tractor-ploughing as well as other mechanisation process received boost.

On the basis of annual growth rates of total private household expenditure within these three decades, the entire period can be divided into two sub periods. Before 1995, the growth rate of expenditure was quite significant while afterwards it decreased measurably. This trend corresponds to the fact that growth of net income also declined in the post-1995 period for rural households. As the income failed to increase by pre-1995 rates, the rate of poverty reduction in the economy slowed. Therefore, direct methods had to be adopted for poverty reduction.

While as the main items in the consumption basket in 1978 were food, clothing and residence, other items including transport, education, recreation, medicine and health care attained good level of significance during the post-reform period. The rural household living expenditure not only decreased as proportion of the total expenditure but has had a change in its own composition. After the reforms it has diversified and included many items which were altogether absent or marginally present at the inception of the reforms. After the reforms the durable asset basket of rural households showed both quantitative and qualitative improvement.

The impact of the rural reforms and consequent expansion of the rural economy on the countryside was profound and perceptible. Poverty reduced at a pace and with a magnitude unprecedented in the history of humanity. As per the official statistics, more than two hundred thirty million people came out of poverty in a period of three decades.

Though China's literacy record of the pre-reform period was quite impressive, however, at the time of reform almost one-third of the rural population was illiterate which decreased to almost one-twentieth; recording more than twenty percentage points reduction from 1985-2006. Given the sheer size of the population, the record of illiteracy reduction was significant.

Among the challenges that the economy faces, two are crucial to the future of rural China. The first is the case of already high and growing inequality of income and other indicators of development. On one hand inter sectoral, i.e., rural-urban, inequality is high and growing over time and, on the other, inequality at the rural level is also witnessing an increasing trend. The other factor that is central to the future development of rural China is land rights. The combination of collective ownership and household use of land has become increasingly incompatible.

The state of development in China and India in early 1980s was almost comparable, rather same. However, after reforms in China in late 1970s, and consequent economic progress, state of development between the two countries started to diverge. Despite good growth record after the reforms in last decade of the twentieth century, India failed to reduce poverty at a reasonable pace and to bring about a transformation of its rural economy. China's reform experience has important lessons for Indian economy in following three areas: a renewed *thrust on the rural economy* and primary sector, as India with its predominant rural population will benefit more from rural biased economic policies; *decentralised planning* and execution because it will increase the appropriateness and effectiveness of economic incentives and investments; and a much larger *investment on human resource development* with emphasis on health, education and most importantly skill development in the countryside. However, for their effectiveness all of these must evolve from the existing institutional arrangement with significant caution on compatibility with domestic culture.

APPENDIX

(A) MACROECONOMIC VARIABLES

Table 1 : Official Estimates of Chinese GDP by Sector, 1952-77 (million 1987 Yuan)

Year	*GDP in Yuan*	*Agriculture*	*Industry and Construction*	*Transport and Communication Commerce Nonmaterial services*	*GDP in million 1990 GK$*	*PCY dollars*[*]
1952	155 548	112 038	14769	28741	231 550	538
1953	170 834	114 167	20067	36600	254 305	552
1954	174 992	116 072	22809	36111	260 495	557
1955	187 677	125 259	24664	37754	279 378	577
1956	208 252	131 085	33904	43263	310 006	616
1957	216 739	135 118	36127	45494	322 640	636
1958	244 716	135 679	55124	53913	364 287	690
1959	244 603	114 167	68137	62299	364 119	686
1960	232 962	114 167	71672	65833	346 790	662
1961	185 987	96 913	40019	49055	276 862	553
1962	182 305	101 283	36491	44531	271 381	550
1963	201 304	112 711	42101	46492	299 663	590

(Contd.)

(Contd. Table 1)

Year	GDP in Yuan	Agriculture	Industry and Construction	Transport and Communication Commerce Nonmaterial services	GDP in million 1990 GK$	PCY dollars*
1964	234 097	127 276	52877	53944	348 479	645
1965	267 404	139 600	65097	62707	398 061	702
1966	289 399	149 683	79066	60290	430 803	746
1967	281 735	152 484	68255	60996	419 394	707
1968	273 432	150 132	61469	61821	407 034	675
1969	302 941	151 364	81879	69698	450 961	713
1970	347 506	163 016	110140	74350	517 301	778
1971	368 634	166 041	123679	78914	548 753	795
1972	378 675	164 585	131413	82677	563 700	798
1973	408 508	179 374	142039	87095	608 110	838
1974	419 761	186 768	144344	88649	624 861	835
1975	450 772	190 577	167022	93173	671 024	871
1976	444 345	187 216	163391	93738	661 457	853
1977	469 576	183 071	184135	102370	699 016	894

Source: Chinese Economic Performance in the Long Run, second edition, revised and updated: 960-2030. OECD 2007, p. 160.

*Maddison calculations, p. 159.

Table 2: Official Estimates of Chinese GDP by Sector, 1952-2003

Year	*GDP in Yuan*	*GDP in dollars*	*Agriculture*	*Industry and Construction*	*Transport and Communication Commerce Nonmaterial services*	*PCY dollars*
1952	155 548	231 550	112038	14769	28741	538
1957	216 739	322 640	135 118	36127	45494	636
1962	182 305	271 381	101 283	36491	44531	550
1965	267 404	398 061	139 600	65097	62707	702
1970	347 506	517 301	163 016	110140	74350	778
1975	450 772	671 024	190 577	167022	93173	871
1977	469576	699016	183071	184135	102370	894

Source: Chinese Economic Performance in the Long Run, Second Edition, Revised And Updated: 960-2030. OECD 2007, p. 160.

Table 3: Growth Rates

Period	GDP		Agriculture		Industry/Construction		Services	
	average annual compound growth rate	*Total growth in the period (per cent)*	*average annual compound growth rate*	*Total growth in the period (per cent)*	*average annual compound growth rate*	*Total growth in the period (per cent)*	*average annual compound growth rate*	*Total growth in the period (per cent)*
1953-57	06.86	39.33	03.81	20.60	19.59	144.60	09.62	58.28
1958-62	-03.40	-15.88	-05.60	-25.04	00.20	01.57	-00.42	-02.11
1963-65	13.62	46.67	11.28	37.83	21.28	78.39	12.08	40.81
1966-70	05.38	30.00	03.14	16.77	11.09	69.19	03.46	18.56
1971-75	05.34	29.71	03.17	16.90	08.68	51.64	04.61	25.31
1976-77	02.06	04.17	-01.98	-03.93	04.99	10.24	04.81	09.87
1953-77	04.51	201.88	01.98	63.40	10.61	1146.76	05.21	256.18

Source: Calculated by Author from Official Data (Presented by Chinese Economic Performance in the Long Run, Second Edition, Revised and Updated: 960-2030. OECD 2007, p. 160)

Table 4: Gross Domestic Product Sector-wise

Year	*Agriculture*	*Industry and Construction*	*Transport and Communication Commerce Non-material Services*
1952	72.02	09.49	18.47
1957	62.34	16.66	20.99
1962	55.55	20.01	24.42
1965	52.20	24.34	23.45
1970	46.91	31.69	21.39
1975	42.27	37.05	20.66
1977	38.98	39.21	21.80

Source: Calculated by Authors from Official Data (quoted by Chinese Economic Performance in the Long Run, Second Edition, Revised and Updated: 960-2030. OECD 2007, p. 160)

Table 5: Employment by Sector, Old Classification, China 1952–2003

(000s at mid–year)

Year	*Farming Forestry Fishery and Sidelines*	*Industry and Construction*	*"Material" Services*	*"Non–Material" Services*	*Total*
1952	171 070	14 479	11 684	10 023	207 256
1957	189 175	22 795	11 776	13 194	236 940
1962	204 940	24 255	12 860	18 450	260 505
1965	230 750	22 650	12 850	18 780	285 030
1970	274 390	32 355	14 560	19 980	341 285
1975	292 975	48 605	17 170	21 935	380 685
1978	288 060	63 405	20 220	28 965	400 650

Source: 1952–77 end–year estimates from SSB, *China Statistical Yearbook 1993*, pp. 100-101 (quoted by Maddison in *Chinese economic performance in the long run*)

Table 6: Employment by Sector, Old Classification, China 1952–2003

(000s at mid–year)

Year	*Farming Forestry Fishery and Sidelines*	*Industry and Construction*	*"Material" Services/"Non–Material" Services*	*Total*
1952	171 070	14 479	21707	207 256
1957	189 175	22 795	24970	236 940
1962	204 940	24 255	31310	260 505
1965	230 750	22 650	31630	285 030
1970	274 390	32 355	34540	341 285
1975	292 975	48 605	39105	380 685
1977	293460	56325	44300	394085

Source: 1952–77 end–year estimates from SSB, *China Statistical Yearbook 1993*, pp.100-101 (quoted by Maddison in *Chinese Economic Performance in the Long Run*)

Table 7: Employment by Sector, Old Classification, China 1952–2003

(000s at mid–year)

Year	*Farming Forestry Fishery and Sidelines*	*Industry and Construction*	*Transport and Communication Commerce Non-material Services*
1952	82.54	6.98	10.47
1957	79.84	9.62	10.53
1962	78.67	9.31	12.01
1965	80.95	7.94	11.09
1970	80.39	9.48	10.12
1975	76.95	12.76	10.27
1978	71.89	15.82	12.27

Source: Developed from above figures.

Table 8: State Investment in Capital Construction by Sector (Per cent) 1953-89

(from Official Figures)

Period	*Industry*	*Construction*	*Agriculture*	*Transport*	*Commerce*	*Other*
1953-57	42.5	3.7	7.1	15.3	3.6	27.3
1958-62	60.4	1.4	11.3	13.5	1.9	11.5
1963-65	49.9	2.1	17.6	12.7	2.5	15.2
1966-70	55.5	1.8	10.7	15.4	2.2	14.4
1971-75	55.4	1.6	9.8	18.0	2.9	12.3
1976-80	52.9	1.9	10.6	13.0	3.8	17.8
1981-85	45.4	1.8	5.0	13.3	5.9	28.6
1986-89	49.9	1.2	3.5	14.5	3.5	27.9

Source: Simon G Powell. *In China: From Communes to Commodity Economy 1978-1990*. Studies on East Asia, Manchester University Press (1992), p. 51.

INSTITUTIONAL DIMENSIONS

Table 9: Output Shares by Ownership in Chinese Industry, 1953-91

(Official Figures)

Year	*State*	*Collective*	*Individual*	*Other**	*Total*
1953	43.04	3.87	19.26	33.83	100
1957	53.77	19.03	0.83	26.37	100
1958	89.17	10.83			100
1965	90.07	9.93			100
1975	81.09	18.91			100
1979	78.47	21.53			100
1980	75.96	23.54	0.02	0.48	100
1985	64.86	31.08	1.85	1.21	100
1990	54.60	35.62	5.39	4.38	100
1991	51.94	35.70	5.70	5.66	100

*Joint Ventures by State and Collective, State and Individual, Collective and Individual, China and Foreigners/and Enterprises Owned by Overseas Chinese and Foreigners.

Source: Yanrui Wu. *Productive Performance of Chinese Enterprises: An Empirical Study*. Macmillan Press Ltd. (1996) p. 32.

Table 10: Sources of Retail Sale 1952-89

(from official figures)

Year	*State*	*Collective (SMC)*	*Individual*	*Peasant sales to non-agrarian pop.*
1952	34.6	0.00	61.2	4.3
1957	73.9	19.5	3.2	3.3
1965	83.3	12.9	1.9	1.9
1978	90.5	7.4	0.1	1.9
1979	88.3	8.9	0.2	2.6
1980	84.0	12.0	0.7	3.2
1981	80.1	14.5	1.6	3.8
1982	76.6	16.1	2.9	4.3
1983	72.2	16.7	6.5	4.7
1984	45.7	39.7	9.6	8.6
1985	40.5	37.3	15.4	6.8
1986	39.4	36.4	16.3	7.6
1987	38.6	35.7	17.4	7.9
1988	39.5	34.4	17.8	8.0
1989	39.1	33.2	18.6	8.6

Source: Simon G Powell. *In China: From Communes to Commodity Economy 1978-1990*. Studies on East Asia, Manchester University Press (1992), p. 78.

HEALTH

Table 11: Health Indicators of China

Year	*Longevity*	*Infant Mortality*
1949	35.0	117
1955	47.5	100.5
1960	53.0	70
1965	55.5	68
1970	59.5	65
1975	62.5	60
1980	68.0	56

Source: Willy Kraus, pp. 331-332.

Table 12: Life-expectancy, 1947-2000

Year	*Life-expectancy*
1947	35.0
1957	57.0
1981	67.9
1990	68.3
2000	71.4

Source: *China Human Development Report 2005*: Development With Equity. UNDP/China Development Research Foundation, Published by China Translation and Publication Corporation (2005) p. 54.

Table 13: National Health Expenditure between 1949 and 1984

Time-Period	*Total Health Expenditure (million yuan)*	*Health Expenditure As Percent of Total State Expenditure*
1949-52	0.559	1.52
1953-57	1.455	1.08
1958-62	2.345	1.02
1963-65	1.884	1.56
1966-70	3.835	1.52
1971-75	6.562	1.67
1976-80	11.365	2.17

Source: *China Health Yearbook, Beijing*: The Peoples Medical Publishing House, 1985, p. 59 [cited: Chinas Economic Reforms: Costs and Benefits of Incrementalism. Ed. Qimiao Fan and Peter Nolan, Macmillan, p. 205].

Table 14: Per Capita Consumption of Consumer Goods, 1956, 1966, 1976 and 1983

Consumer goods	*1956*	*1966*	*1976*	*1983*
Grain (kg per capita)	204.3	189.6	190.3	232.2
Vegetable Oil (kg per capita)	2.6	1.8	1.6	2.9
Pork (kg per capita)	4.7	7.0	7.4	12.3
Sugar (kg per capita)	1.5	1.8	2.3	4.5
Cloth (meters per capita)	8.6	6.6	7.9	10.3
Coal (kg per capita)	84.1	104.4	95.9	151.9

Source: State Statistical Bureau, *Statistical Yearbook of China*, 1984 p. 447 [Quoted By Robert Michael Field. The Performance of Industry during the Cultural Revolution: Second Thoughts. *The China Quarterly*, No 108 (Dec., 1986), p. 638]

Table 15: Food Production for Selected Years 1957-65

(official figures from China's Agricultural Yearbook 1980)

Year	*Total Food Grain Production (million tones)*	*Per Capita Food Grain Production (kg)*
1957	195.05	302
1960	143.50	217
1961	147.50	222
1962	160.00	238
1965	194.50	268

Source: A. J. Jowett. The Growth of China's Population, 1949-82 (With Special Reference to the Demographic Disaster of 1960-61). *The Geographical Journal,* Vol. 150, No. 2 (Jul., 1984), p. 161.

Table 16: Birth Rates and Death Rates in Rural and Urban China

(Official Figures from State Statistical Bureau, Beijing 1981)

Year	*Birth Rate (per thousand)*			*Death Rate (per thousand)*		
	Total	*Rural*	*Urban*	*Total*	*Rural*	*Urban*
1954	38.0	37.5	42.5	13.2	13.7	8.1
1957	34.0	32.8	44.5	10.8	11.1	8.5
1963	43.6	43.4	45.0	10.1	10.6	7.2
1965	38.1	39.5	27.6	9.6	10.0	5.9
1971	30.7	31.9	21.9	7.3	7.6	5.5
1975	23.1	24.2	15.2	7.3	7.6	5.6
1979	17.9	18.5	13.9	6.2	6.4	5.1

Source: State Statistical Bureau, Beijing, 1981, in A. J. Jowett. The Growth of China's Population: 1949-82 (With Special Reference to the Demographic Disaster Of 1960-61). *The Geographical Journal,* Vol. 150, No. 2 (Jul., 1984), p. 165.

Table 17

Period	*Life expectancy*	*Infant mortality*	*Under five mortality rate*
1970-1975	63.2	85	120
1995-2000	69.8	32	40

Source: Human Development Report 2002: Deepening Democracy in Fragmented World, p.175.

(B) EDUCATION

Table 18: Elementary and Secondary Schools, Total Enrollment, and Rural Enrollment, 1949-77

Year	*Primary*		*Academic Secondary Primary (Junior, Senior High)*	
	Schools (1000s)	*Total enrollment (millions)*	*Schools (1000s)*	*Total enrollment (millions)*
1949	346.8	24.4	4.0	1.0
1952	527.0	51.1	4.3	2.5
1957	547.3	64.3	11.1	6.3
1962	668.3	69.2	19.5	7.5
1965	1,681.9	116.2	18.1	9.3
1970	961.1	105.3	n.a. (93.0, 1972)	26.4
1975	1,093.3	150.9	123.5	44.7
1977	982.3	146.2	201.3	67.8

Ministry of Education, Department of Planning (E.), *Achievement of Education in China: Statistics, 1949-1983* (Beijing: People's Education Press, 1985), pp. 184-85, 197, 213, 220; State Education Commission (ed.), *Achievement of Education in China: Statistics, 1986-1990* (Beijing: People's Education Press, 1991), pp. 59, 66, 74, 76; in Emily Hannum. Political Change and the Urban-Rural Gap in Basic Education in China, 1949-1990. *Comparative Education Review*, Vol. 43, No. 2 (May, 1999), p. 196.

Table 19: Enrollment of School-Age Children in Elementary School, 1952-1987

Year	*Total Number of School-Age Children*	*Number Enrolled in School*	*Enrollment Ratio (Per cent)*
1949			
1952	66,424,000	32,681,000	49.2
1957	80,777,000	49,866,000	61.7
1962	108,360,000	60,820,000	56.1
1965	116,032,000	98,291,000	84.7
1970			
1975	122,619,000	118,685,000	95.0
1977	121,009,000	116,795,000	95.5

Source: China Statistical Yearbook (1988, p. 889).

Note: Number of school-age children prior to 1975 includes all 6-11-year-olds. The number for 1975 and after is for 6-10-year-olds. John N. Hawkins and Regie Stites. *Strengthening the Future's Foundation: Elementary Education Reform in the People's Republic of China.* The Elementary School Journal, Vol. 92, No. 1, Special Issue: International Education (Sep., 1991), pp. 41-60.

Table 20: Participants and Graduates of Anti-Illiteracy Classes in the People's Republic of China, 1949-77

Period	*Adult Graduates (millions)*
1949-52	04.06
1953-57	23.91
1958-62	72.35
1963-65	02.39
1966-70	
1971-75	
1976-77	14.12

Source: China Education Yearbook, 1949-1 ᾽1, Beijing: Education Press, 1984, p. 1037; China Statistics, 1988, p. 892 as quoted by Regie Stites and Ladislaus Semali. *Adult Literacy for Social Equality or Economic Growth? Changing Agendas for Mass Literacy in China and Tanzania.* Comparative Education Review, Vol. 35, No. 1, Feb., 1991 p. 52.

(C) INFRASTRUCTURE

Table 21: Transport infrastructure
Infrastructure in China 1949-77 (Thousand Kilometers) Official Figures

Years	*Railways*	*Highways*	*Waterways*	*Airways (Domestic plus international Routes)*	*Pipelines*
1949	21.8	80.76	73.6	11.39	
1952	22.9	126.6	95.0	13.12	
1957	26.7	254.6	144.1	26.44	
1962	34.6	463.5	161.9	35.30	0.10
1965	36.4	514.5	157.7	39.40	0.40
1970	41.0	636.7	148.4	40.60	1.20
1975	46.0	**783.6**	135.6	**84.20**	**5.30**
1977	47.4	**855.6**	137.4	**132.1**	**6.70**

Source: Claude Comtois. *Transport and Territorial Development in China 1949-1985*. Modern Asian Studies, Vol. 24, No. 4 (Oct., 1990), pp. 786-87.

Table 22: Growth Rate of Infrastructure from 1949-77

(per annum average compound growth rate)

Period	*Railways*		*Highways*		*Waterways*		*Airways (Domestic plus international Routes)*		*Pipelines*	
	average annual compound growth rate	*Total growth in the period (per cent)*	*average annual compound growth rate*	*Total growth in the period (per cent)*	*average annual compound growth rate*	*Total growth in the period (per cent)*	*average annual compound growth rate*	*Total growth in the period (per cent)*	*average annual compound growth rate*	*Total growth in the period (per cent)*
1949-52	1.65	05.04	16.16	56.76	08.88	29.07	04.82	15.18		
1953-57	3.11	16.59	14.99	101.1	08.68	51.68	15.04	101.5		
1958-62	5.32	29.58	12.72	82.05	02.35	12.35	05.95	33.50		
1963-65	1.70	05.20	03.54	11.00	? 0.87	-2.59	03.73	11.61	58.74	300.0
1966-70	2.40	12.63	04.35	23.75	? 1.20	-5.89	00.60	03.04	24.50	200.0
1971-75	2.32	12.19	04.23	23.07	? 1.78	-8.62	15.70	107.3	34.59	341.6
1976-77	1.50	03.04	04.49	09.18	00.66	01.32	25.25	56.88	12.43	26.4

Source: Developed from official data given by Claude Comtois (1990). *Transport and Territorial Development in China 1949-1985*. Modern Asian Studies, Vol. 24, No. 4 (Oct., 1990), pp. 786-87.

Table 23: Irrigation in China 1949-77

(Official Data)

Years	*Irrigated Area (million hectares)*	*Irrigated Area as Per cent of Arable Land*
1949		
1952	22	23.25
1957	27	26.17
1962	31	32.94
1965	33	34.67
1970	38	38.80
1975	43	47.60
1980	45	46.12

Source: Shenggen Fan Linxiu Zhang Xiaobo Zhang. *Growth, Inequality, and Poverty in Rural China*; *the Role of Public Investments*. Research Report 125 International Food Policy Research Institute Washington, D.C. p. 21.

Table 24: ENERGY : Fossil Fuels and Electricity in the PRC 1949-74

Years	*Raw Coal (million metric tones)*	*Crude Oil (million metric tones)*	*Natural Gas (billion cubic meters)*	*Electricity Generation (billion kilowatt-hours)*
1949	32.43	0.12	0.00	4.31
1952	66.49	0.44	0.00	7.26
1957	130.73	1.47	0.33	19.34
1962	180.00	6.00	3.27	30.00
1965	220.00	10.60	11.32	42.00
1970	300.00	26.40	16.00	60.00
1974	390.00	63.60	35.00	108.00

Source: *Energy in China: Achievements and Prospects* by Vaclav Smil. The China Quarterly, No. 65 (Mar., 1976), pp. 62-63. The author has used various sources to develop the appropriate figures.

Table 25: Growth in Fuels and Electricity in PRC 1949-74

Period	Raw Coal		Crude Oil		Natural Gas		Electricity	
	average annual compound growth rate	*Total growth in the period (per cent)*	*average annual compound growth rate*	*Total growth in the period (per cent)*	*average annual compound growth rate*	*Total growth in the period (per cent)*	*average annual compound growth rate*	*Total growth in the period (per cent)*
1949-52	27.03	105.02	54.20	266.6			18.99	68.44
1953-57	14.47	96.61	27.28	234.1			21.65	166.39
1958-62	06.60	37.68	32.49	308.16	58.20	890.90	09.18	55.11
1963-65	06.92	22.22	20.88	76.66	51.28	246.17	11.87	40.00
1966-70	06.40	36.36	20.02	149.05	07.17	41.34	07.40	42.85
1971-74	06.78	30.00	24.58	140.90	21.61	118.75	15.83	80.00

Source: developed by the author from figures presented by Vaclav Smil (1976).

EXTERNAL SECTOR

Table 26: Merchandise Trade of China

(Million US Dollars at Current Exchange Rates)

Years	*Exports*	*Imports*	*Trade Turnover*	*Trade Balance*
1950	550	580	1130	-30
1952	820	1120	1940	-300
1957	1600	1500	3100	100
1962	1490	1170	2660	320
1965	2230	2020	4250	210
1970	2260	2330	4590	-70
1975	7260	7490	14750	-230
1977	7590	7210	14800	380

Source: Extracted from Maddison, *Chinese Economic Performance in the Long Run* (OECD 2007) p. 174.

Table 27: The Yuan-Dollar Exchange Rate, 1952-77

(Official Figures)

Year	*Exchange rate (yuan/$100)*
1952	261.70
1957	246.18
1962	246.18
1965	246.18
1970	246.18
1975	196.63
1977	173.00

Source: Nicholas R. Lardy. Foreign Trade and Economic Reform in China, 1978-1990, Cambridge University Press (1992) p. 149.

Table 28: Share of World Merchandise Exports 1948, 1973 and 2000

(Percentage)

Country	*1948*	*1973*	*2000*
China	0.9	1.0	4.0
Japan	0.4	6.4	7.7

Source: World Economic and Social Survey 2001, p. 155.

(E) Agriculture

Table 29: Indices of Prices Received and Paid by Farmers, 1950-79

(1950=100)

Year	*Purchase Price of Farm and Sideline Products*	*Prices of Industrial Products Sold in Rural Areas*	*Terms of Trade**
1952	121.6	109.7	110.8
1957	146.2	112.1	130.4
1965	187.9	118.4	158.7
1974	204.5	110.0	185.9
1975	208.7	109.6	190.4
1976	209.7	n.a.	n.a.
1977	209.2	n.a.	n.a.
1978	217.4	109.8	198.0
1979	265.5	109.9	241.6

Source: Robert C. Hsu. Agricultural Financial Polices in China, 1949-80. *Asian Survey*, Vol. 22, No. 7 (Jul., 1982) p. 642.

*ratio between purchase prices of farm and sideline products and prices of industrial products sold in rural areas.

Table 30: Agriculture Tax as Percentage of National Agriculture Output, 1949-80

Year	*Percentage*
1949	13.89
1952	13.20
1957	11.51
1961	6.70
1970	6.00
1975	5.00
1980	4.00

Source: Robert C. Hsu. Agricultural Financial Polices in China, 1949-80. *Asian Survey*, Vol. 22, No. 7 (Jul., 1982) p.645.

Table 31: Share of Total State Aid to Agriculture, 1950-80

Year	*Share of Total State Aid To Agriculture in Total State Expenditure*	*Share of State Investment in Agriculture in Total State Capital Investment*
1950	3.1	11.4
1952	5.0	12.0
1957	8.1	14.4(1956)
1963	16.0-18.0	13.0 (1960)
1964	16.0-18.0	n.a.
1978	12.7	4.2
1970s (average)	10.0	

Source: Robert C. Hsu. Agricultural Financial Polices in China, 1949-80. *Asian Survey*, Vol. 22, No. 7 (Jul., 1982) p. 647.

Table 32: Tractor-Plowed Area and Chemical Fertilizer Consumption in China, 1952-84

Year	*Tractor-Plowed Area (In 10,000 Ha)*	*Consumption of Chemical Fertilizers (In 10,000 Tons*
1952	13.6	7.8
1957	263.6	37.3
1962	828.4	63.0
1965	1557.9	194.2
1978	4,067.0	884.0
1979	4,241.9	1,086.3
1980	4,099.0	1,269.4
1981	3,647.7	1,334.9
1982	3,511.5	1,513.4
1983	3,357.2	1,659.8
1984	3,492.2	1,739.8

Source: Editoriai Board of China Agriculture Yearbook, *China Agriculture Yearbook 1985* (Beijing: Agricultural Publishing House, 1985), p. 89. [Cited: Justin Yifu Lin, The Household Responsibility System in China's Agricultural Reform: A Theoretical and Empirical Study. *Economic Development and Cultural Change*, Vol. 36, No. 3, Supplement: Why Does Overcrowded, Resource-Poor East Asia Succeed: Lessons For The LDCs? (Apr., 1988), p. S215]

Table 33: Technological Change in Agriculture

(Official Figures)

Year	*Proportion of Area Irrigated (Per cent)*	*Proportion of Area Machine Ploughed (Per cent)*	*Large And Medium Tractors In Use (In 1000s)*	*Small Tractors in Use (In 1000s)*	*Chemical Fertilizers Used Per Hectare (kg)*
1952	20.0	0.1	1.3	Nil	Neg.
1957	27.3	2.6	14.7	Nil	Neg.
1965	30.5	15.6	72.6	4	19.4
1978	45.0	40.7	557.0	1373	89.0
1979	45.0	42.2	667.0	1671	109.0
1980	44.9	41.0	745.0	1874	127.8
1981	44.6	36.5	792.0	2037	134.5

Source: Keith Griffin (Ed.) *Institutional Reform and Economic Development in the Chinese Countryside*. The Macmillan Press Ltd (1984) p. 269.

Table 34: Gross Value of Agricultural Output by Sector

(Per cent)

Year	*Crop farming*	*Forestry*	*Animal husbandry*	*Subsidiaries*	*Fisheries*
1957	80.6	1.7	12.9	4.3	0.5
1965	75.8	2.0	14.0	6.5	1.7
1970	74.7	2.2	12.9	8.7	1.5
1976	69.3	3.3	13.9	12.0	1.5
1977	67.5	3.2	13.1	14.1	1.5
1978	67.8	3.0	13.2	14.6	1.4

Source: *Jingji Yanjiu Ziliao*, 70 (May 1980) [Quoted By, Greg O'Leary; Andrew Watson. The Role of Peoples Commune in Rural Development in China. *Pacific Affairs,* Vol. 55, No. 4. (Winter, 1982-83), p. 604.

Table 35: Output of Selected Agricultural Commodities 1971-83 (million tones)

(official statistics)

Year	*Grain*	*Cotton*	*Oilseeds (peanuts, rapeseed and sesame seed)*	*Sugarcane*	*Meat*
1971	250.14	2.105	4.113	13.139	n.a.
1972	240.48	1.958	4.118	16.416	n.a.
1973	264.94	2.542	4.186	16.965	n.a.
1974	275.27	2.461	4.414	16.432	n.a.
1975	284.52	2.381	4.521	16.667	7.972
1976	286.31	2.055	4.008	16.631	7.805
1977	282.73	2.049	4.017	17.752	7.800
1978	304.77	2.167	5.218	21.116	8.563
1979	332.12	2.207	6.435	21.508	12.624
1980	320.56	2.707	7.691	22.807	12.054
1981	325.02	2.986	10.205	29.668	12.609
1982	354.50	2.598	11.817	36.882	13.508
1983	387.28	2.637	10.550	31.141	14.021

Source: China Statistical Yearbook 1984 pp. 141-47 and p. 160. (Andrew Watson. Agricultural Reform and China's Foreign Trade. *The Australian Journal of Chinese Affairs, No. 14.* (Jul., 1985), pp. 39-63.

INDUSTRY

Table 36: Relative Rates Growth of Light and Heavy Industries

(Official Figures)

Year/Period	*Light Industry (Annual Average Growth)*	*Heavy Industry (Annual Average Growth)*
1950-52	29.0	48.9
1953-57	12.9	25.4
1958-62	1.1	6.6
1963-65	21.2	14.9
1966-78	8.3	11.8
1952-78	9.1	13.6
1979	9.6	7.7
1980	18.4	1.4
1981	14.1	-4.7

Source: Keith Griffin (Ed.) *Institutional Reform and Economic Development in the Chinese Countryside*. The Macmillan Press Ltd. (1984) p. 297.

Table 37: Industrial Fixed Investment in China, 1952-78

(Billion yuan in current prices)

Period	*Light Industry*		*Heavy Industry*		**Total fixed Investment (billion yuan)*	**Average Annual Investment (billion yuan)*
	Amount (billion yuan)	*Share (Per cent)*	*Amount*	*Share (Per cent)*		
First Five Year Plan (1952-57)	3.75	15.0	21.28	85.0	25.03	5.00
Second Five Year Plan (1958-62)	7.66	10.1	65.17	89.9	72.83	14.56
Adjustment Period (1963-65)	1.65	7.8	19.37	92.2	21.02	7.00
Third Five Year Plan (1966-70)	4.26	7.9	49.89	92.1	54.15	10.38
Fourth Five Year Plan (1971-75)	10.30	10.5	87.49	89.5	97.79	19.55
Fifth Five Year Plan (1976-78)	7.48	10.6	62.45	89.4	69.93	23.31

Source: Lin, Cai and Li (1994: 62) Quoted By Justin Yifu Lin And Yang Yao in *Enterprise Reform in China Ownership, Transition, and Performance*. Ed. Gary H. Jefferson and Inderjit Singh. Oxford University Press/World Bank.

* The two columns are added by the author and are not present in the original table presented by Lin, Cai, and Li.

Table 38: Human Development Expenditure

(million yuan)

Year	*Culture*	*Education*	*Health care*
1950	29	376	72
1952	68	895	297
1957	124	1952	482
1958	134	1983	454
1960	231	3178	814
1965	168	2912	929
1966	202	3443	987
1969		2704	931
1970	206	2756	1047
1975	354	4828	1992
1979	475	7696	3173

Source: *State Statistical Data on Revenue and Expenditure*, May 1982, in China Human Development Report 1999: Transition and the State p. 23 UNDP (1999).

Table 39: The Development of Healthcare, 1952-79

Year	*Health care institutions*	*Hospital beds (1000)*			*Medical technical personnel (1,000)*	
		Total	*County level*	*Per cent country level*	*Total*	*Rural*
1952	38,987	160	39	24.3	690	343
1957	122,954	295	74	25.1	1,039	408
1958	196,829	426	113	26.5	1,329	409
1960	261,195	655	200	30.5	1,505	414
1962	217,985	690	253	36.7	1,414	474
1965	222,266	766	308	40.2	1,532	494
1969	153891	993	538	53.9	1,471	455
1972	135,127	1,337	785	58.7	1,708	453
1975	151,733	1,598	961	60.1	2,058	510
1979	176,793	1,932	1,192	61.7	2,647	[illegible]

Source: Statistical Data on the National Economy. State Statistical Bureau; July 1990; Statistical Yearbook of 1998, in China Human Development Report 1999: Transition and the State UNDP (1999). p. 29.

Table 40: Population Growth, 1950-1979

Year	*Total (mills.)*	*Birth rate (per thousand)*	*Death rate (per thousand)*	*Natural Increase rate (per thousand)*
1950	551.96	37.00	18.00	19.00
1951	563.00	37.80	17.80	20.00
1952	574.82	37.00	17.00	20.00
1953	587.96	37.00	14.00	23.00
1954	602.66	37.97	13.18	24.79
1955	614.65	32.60	12.28	20.32
1956	628.28	31.90	11.40	20.50
1957	646.53	34.03	10.80	23.23
1958	659.94	29.22	11.98	17.24
1959	672.07	24.78	14.59	10.19
1960	662.07	20.86	25.43	-4.57
1961	658.59	18.02	14.24	3.78
1962	672.95	37.01	10.02	26.99
1963	691.72	43.37	10.04	33.33
1964	704.99	39.14	11.50	27.64

(Contd.)

(Contd. Table 40)

Year	*Total (mills.)*	*Birth rate (per thousand)*	*Death rate (per thousand)*	*Natural Increase rate (per thousand)*
1965	725.38	37.88	9.50	28.38
1966	745.42	35.05	8.83	26.22
1967	763.68	33.96	8.43	25.53
1968	785.34	35.59	8.21	27.38
1969	806.71	34.11	8.03	26.08
1970	829.92	33.43	7.60	25.83
1971	852.29	30.65	7.32	23.33
1972	871.77	29.77	7.61	22.16
1973	892.11	27.93	7.04	20.89
1974	908.59	24.82	7.34	17.48
1975	924.20	23.01	7.32	15.69
1976	937.17	19.91	7.25	12.66
1977	949.74	18.93	6.87	12.06
1978	962.59	18.25	6.25	12.00
1979	975.42	17.82	6.21	11.61

Source: Statistical Data on National Economy. State Statistical Bureau. July 1990, in China Human Development Report 1999: Transition and the State p. 25 UNDP (1999).

Table 41: Distribution of Students Over Three Levels of Education

Year	Proportion of Students in Population	Students per 10,000 population		
		University or College	Middle School	Primary School
1949	4.76	2.2	23	450
1952	9.47	3.3	55	889
1957	11.11	6.8	110	994
1962	11.65	12.3	124	1,029
1965	18.09	9.3	197	1,602
1970	15.97	0.6	321	1,276
1975	21.40	5.4	493	1,641
1979	21.41	10.5	621	1,510

Source: Brief Statistical Data on the National Economy (1949-1988), July, 1989, China Human Development Report 1999: Transition and the State UNDP (1999), p. 28.

Table 42: Structure of Energy Consumption

Year	*Total Consumption*	*Share of Total Per cent* *Coal*	*Petroleum*	*Natural Gas*	*Hydropower*
1957	96.4	92.3	4.6	0.1	3.0
1965	189.0	86.5	10.3	0.9	2.7
1970	292.91	80.9	14.7	0.9	3.5
1978	571.44	70.7	22.7	3.2	3.4

Source: Statistical Yearbook of China, 1998; in China Human Development Report 1999: Transition and the State UNDP (1999). p. 34.

Table 43: Education Expenditures, 1950-1979

Year	*Educational funds (millions of yuan)*	*Total govt. expenditure (millions of yuan)*	*Education's share of total expenditure (per cent)*
1950	376	6803	5.53
1957	1952	30,421	6.42
1958	1983	40,940	4.84
1960	3178	65,414	4.86
1961	2678	35,602	7.52
1966	3443	54,156	6.36
1969	2704	52,586	5.14
1972	3854	76,636	5.03
1975	4826	82,088	5.88
1979	7996	127,311	6.28

Source: *State Statistical Data on Revenue and Expenditure*, May 1982, in China Human Development Report 1999: Transition and the State UNDP (1999). p. 29.

Table 44: Unemployment Rate, 1949-79

Year	*Total (millions)*	*Per cent*
1949	4.74	23.6
1950	4.38	13.2
1951	4.01	10.8
1952	3.77	10.5
1953	3.33	10.1
1954	3.21	6.6
1955	3.15	5.9
1956	2.13	5.3
1957	2.00	5.4
1978	5.30	4.9
1979	5.68	3.8

Source: Statistical Data on Labor and Wages in China; 1949-1985, July 1987; in *China Human Development Report 1999: Transition and the State UNDP (1999)*. p. 32.

MACROECONOMIC VARIABLES

Table 1: GDP and its Sectoral Distribution

Year	GDP in Yuan	Agriculture	Industry and Construction	Transport and Communication Commerce Non-material Services	GDP in million 1990 GK$	PCY dollars*
	GDP	Primary Sector	Secondary Sector	Tertiary Sector	GDP in Dollars	
1978	517 055	190 577	210506	115972	769 694	
1979	553 619	202 341	227244	124034	824 123	
1980	591 537	199 316	259211	133010	880 569	
1981	625 645	213 209	264123	148313	931 342	
1982	683 311	237 858	278673	166780	1 017 184	
1983	748 349	247 476	308017	192856	1 114 001	
1984	873 657	290 852	352333	230472	1 300 535	
1985	989 196	296 118	418086	274992	1 472 528	
1986	1 074 231	305 977	461433	306821	1 599 112	
1987	1 196 250	320 430	525160	350660	1 780 751	
1988	1 326 193	328 497	600410	397276	1 974 186	
1989	1 374 762	338 692	621068	415002	2 046 486	

(Contd.)

(Contd. Table 1)

Year	*GDP in Yuan*	*Agriculture*	*Industry and Construction*	*Transport and Communication Commerce Non-material Services*	*GDP in million 1990 GK$*	*PCY dollars**
	GDP	*Primary Sector*	*Secondary Sector*	*Tertiary Sector*	*GDP in Dollars*	
1990	1 426 734	363 453	640461	422820	2 123 852	
1991	1 546 895	372 006	729474	445415	2 302 725	
1992	1 789 559	389 539	883713	516307	2 663 957	
1993	2 045 083	407 835	1059401	577847	3 044 333	
1994	2 319 636	424 224	1254353	641059	3 453 036	
1995	2 576 592	445 378	1428461	702753	3 835 543	
1996	2 837 907	468 057	1601838	768012	4 224 540	
1997	3 103 602	484 447	1770572	848583	4 620 056	
1998	3 348 107	501 408	1928239	918460	4 984 029	
1999	3 603 851	515 511	2085720	1002620	5 364 732	
2000	3 909 685	527 898	2282932	1098855	5 820 000	
2001	4 230 329	542 763	2477395	1210171	6 297 315	
2002	4 616 659	558 391	2722229	1336039	6 872 410	
2003	5 104 266	572 302	3067935	1464029	7 598 267	

Source: SSB and Hitotsubash University Institute of Economic Research. 1997. The Historical National Accounts of the People's Republic of China, 1952-1990, Tokyo. In Maddison, Angus. Chinese Economic Performance in the Long Run. Development Center Studies OECD, 2007, pp. 159-160.

Table 2: GDP: Growth and Change in Composition

Year		*Growth rates*				*Structural change*	
	GDP	*Primary*	*Secondary*	*Tertiary*	*Primary*	*Secondary*	*Tertiary*
92	15.68	4.71	21.14	15.91	21.75	49.40	28.85
93	14.27	4.69	19.88	11.91	19.95	51.80	28.25
94	13.42	4.01	18.40	10.93	18.30	54.07	27.63
95	11.07	4.98	13.88	9.62	17.30	55.43	27.27
96	10.14	5.09	12.13	9.28	16.50	56.44	27.06
97	9.36	3.50	10.53	10.49	15.60	57.05	27.35
98	7.87	3.50	8.90	8.23	14.97	57.60	27.43
99	7.63	2.81	8.16	9.16	14.30	57.88	27.82
2000	8.48	2.39	9.45	9.59	13.50	58.40	28.10
01	8.20	2.81	8.51	10.13	12.84	58.56	28.60
02	9.13	2.87	9.88	10.40	12.10	58.96	28.94
03	10.56	2.49	12.69	9.57	11.21	60.10	28.68
1978-	**9.20**	**4.31**	**10.85**	**10.24**	**36.85**	**40.71**	**22.43**
2003					**11.21**	**60.10**	**28.68**

(Contd.)

(Contd. Table 2)

Year	*Growth rates*				*Structural change*		
	GDP	*Primary*	*Secondary*	*Tertiary*	*Primary*	*Secondary*	*Tertiary*
92	15.68	4.71	21.14	15.91	21.75	49.40	28.85
93	14.27	4.69	19.88	11.91	19.95	51.80	28.25
94	13.42	4.01	18.40	10.93	18.30	54.07	27.63
95	11.07	4.98	13.88	9.62	17.30	55.43	27.27
96	10.14	5.09	12.13	9.28	16.50	56.44	27.06
97	9.36	3.50	10.53	10.49	15.60	57.05	27.35
98	7.87	3.50	8.90	8.23	14.97	57.60	27.43
99	7.63	2.81	8.16	9.16	14.30	57.88	27.82
2000	8.48	2.39	9.45	9.59	13.50	58.40	28.10
01	8.20	2.81	8.51	10.13	12.84	58.56	28.60
02	9.13	2.87	9.88	10.40	12.10	58.96	28.94
03	10.56	2.49	12.69	9.57	11.21	60.10	28.68
1978-	**9.20**	**4.31**	**10.85**	**10.24**	**36.85**	**40.71**	**22.43**
2003					**11.21**	**60.10**	**28.68**

Source: Developed from the official statistics presented in Table 1.

Table 3: Employment

Year	Farming/forestry/ fishery/sidelines Absolute	Industry and construction Absolute	Material and non-material services Absolute	Total Absolute
1978	288060	63405	49185	400650
1979	284760	70795	53335	408890
1980	288780	74605	56545	419930
1981	294495	78550	60385	433430
1982	303180	81745	63175	448100
1983	310050	85125	66475	461650
1984	310095	91345	74715	476155
1985	309990	99870	83490	493350
1986	311920	108000	88850	508770
1987	314585	114710	94030	523325
1988	319560	119390	99655	538605
1989	327370	120640	104630	552640

(Contd.)

(Contd. Table 3)

Year	*Farming/forestry/ fishery/sidelines Absolute*	*Industry and construction Absolute*	*Material and non-material services Absolute*	*Total Absolute*
1990	336710	120490	105805	563005
1991	345365	122755	110035	578155
1992	348755	126540	116670	591965
1993	343805	131980	122490	598275
1994	336760	137395	134065	608220
1995	332020	141385	145650	619055
1996	329640	143305	153210	626155
1997	330025	142790	159730	632545
1998	331635	134310	164205	630150
1999	333625	125615	165030	624270
2000	334240	124745	168361	627346
2001	331645	125385	173125	630155
2002	327305	128245	178610	634160
2003	327421	127417	185444	640282
1978-2003				

Source: SSB and Hitotsubash University Institute of Economic Research. 1997. The Historical National Accounts of the People's Republic of China, 1952-1990, Tokyo. In Maddison, Angus. Chinese Economic Performance in the Long Run. Development Center Studies OECD, 2007, pp. 159-160.

Table 4: Employment: Growth and Change in Composition

Year	Annual Growth Rate				Structural Change Percentage of Total Employment			
	Total	Primary	Secondary	Tertiary	Primary	Secondary	Tertiary	Total
1978					71.90	15.82	12.27	100.00
1979	2.05	-1.14	11.65	8.43	69.64	17.31	13.04	100.00
1980	2.70	1.41	5.38	6.01	68.77	17.76	13.46	100.00
1981	3.21	1.98	5.28	6.97	67.94	18.12	13.93	100.00
1982	3.38	2.94	4.06	4.62	67.65	18.24	14.10	100.00
1983	3.02	2.26	4.13	5.22	67.16	18.43	14.40	100.00
1984	3.14	0.01	7.30	12.40	65.12	19.18	15.70	100.00
1985	3.61	-0.03	9.33	11.74	62.83	20.24	16.92	100.00
1986	3.12	0.62	8.14	6.42	61.31	21.22	17.46	100.00
1987	2.86	0.85	6.21	5.83	60.11	21.91	17.96	100.00
1988	2.91	1.58	4.07	5.98	59.33	22.16	18.50	100.00
1989	2.60	2.44	1.04	5.00	59.23	21.18	18.93	100.00
1990	1.88	2.86	-1.02	1.12	59.80	21.40	18.79	100.00

(Contd.)

(Contd. Table 4)

Year	Annual Growth Rate				Structural Change Percentage of Total Employment			
	Total	Primary	Secondary	Tertiary	Primary	Secondary	Tertiary	Total
1991	2.69	2.55	1.87	4.00	59.73	21.23	19.03	100.00
1992	2.38	0.98	3.08	6.03	58.91	21.37	19.70	100.00
1993	1.06	-1.41	4.30	4.98	57.46	22.06	20.47	100.00
1994	1.61	-2.04	4.10	9.44	55.36	22.59	22.04	100.00
1995	1.78	-1.40	2.90	8.64	53.63	22.83	23.52	100.00
1996	1.14	-0.71	1.35	5.19	52.64	22.88	24.46	100.00
1997	1.02	0.11	-0.35	4.25	52.17	22.57	25.25	100.00
1998	-0.37	0.48	-5.93	2.80	52.62	21.31	26.05	100.00
1999	-0.93	0.60	-6.47	0.50	53.44	20.12	26.43	100.00
2000	0.49	0.18	-0.70	2.01	53.27	19.88	26.83	100.00
2001	0.44	-0.77	0.51	2.83	52.63	19.89	24.47	100.00
2002	0.63	-1.30	2.28	3.16	51.61	20.22	28.16	100.00
2003	0.96	0.03	-0.64	3.82	51.13	19.90	28.96	100.00
1978	1.81	0.49	2.72	5.23	71.90	15.82	12.27	100.00
-								
2003					51.13	19.90	28.96	

Source: Developed from the official statistics presented in Table 3.

Table 5: Growth: GDP and Employment

Year		GDP			Employment			
	GDP	Primary	Secondary	Tertiary	Total	Primary	Secondary	Tertiary
1978								
79	7.07	6.17	7.95	6.95	2.05	-1.14	11.65	8.43
80	6.85	? 1.50	4.06	7.23	2.70	1.41	5.38	6.01
81	5.76	6.97	1.89	11.50	3.21	1.98	5.28	6.97
82	9.21	11.56	5.50	12.45	3.38	2.94	4.06	4.62
83	9.52	4.04	10.52	15.63	3.02	2.26	4.13	5.22
84	16.74	17.52	14.38	19.50	3.14	0.01	7.30	12.40
85	13.22	1.81	18.66	19.31	3.61	-0.03	9.33	11.74
86	8.60	3.32	10.36	11.57	3.12	0.62	8.14	6.42
87	11.36	4.72	13.81	14.28	2.86	0.85	6.21	5.83
88	10.86	2.51	14.32	13.29	2.91	1.58	4.07	5.98
89	3.66	3.10	3.44	4.46	2.60	2.44	1.04	5.00
90	3.78	7.31	3.12	1.88	1.88	2.86	-1.02	1.12

(Contd.)

(Contd. Table 5)

Year		*GDP*				*Employment*		
	GDP	*Primary*	*Secondary*	*Tertiary*	*Total*	*Primary*	*Secondary*	*Tertiary*
91	8.42	2.35	13.89	5.34	2.69	2.55	1.87	4.00
92	15.68	4.71	21.14	15.91	2.38	0.98	3.08	6.03
93	14.27	4.69	19.88	11.91	1.06	-1.41	4.30	4.98
94	13.42	4.01	18.40	10.93	1.61	-2.04	4.10	9.44
95	11.07	4.98	13.88	9.62	1.78	-1.40	2.90	8.64
96	10.14	5.09	12.13	9.28	1.14	-0.71	1.35	5.19
97	9.36	3.50	10.53	10.49	1.02	0.11	-0.35	4.25
98	7.87	3.50	8.90	8.23	-0.37	0.48	-5.93	2.80
99	7.63	2.81	8.16	9.16	-0.93	0.60	-6.47	0.50
2000	8.48	2.39	9.45	9.59	0.49	0.18	-0.70	2.01
01	8.20	2.81	8.51	10.13	0.44	-0.77	0.51	2.83
02	9.13	2.87	9.88	10.40	0.63	-1.30	2.28	3.16
03	10.56	2.49	12.69	9.57	0.96	0.03	-0.64	3.82
1978-2003	**9.20**	**4.31**	**10.85**	**10.24**	1.81	0.49	2.72	5.23

Source: Developed from the official statistics presented in Tables 1 and 3.

Table 6: Output Growth: GDP, Primary, Secondary, Tertiary

Year	GDP	Average Growth of the Sub-Period	Primary	Average Growth of the Sub-Period	Secondary	Average Growth of the Sub-Period	Tertiary	Average Growth of the Sub-Period
1978								
79	7.07	**(1)**	6.17	**(1)**	7.95	**(1)**	6.95	**(1)**
80	6.85		-1.50		4.06		7.23	7.09
81	5.76		6.97		1.89		11.50	**(2)**
82	9.21		11.56		5.50	4.85	12.45	
83	9.52	7.68	4.04		10.52	**(2)**	15.63	
84	16.74	**(2)**	17.52	7.46	14.38		19.50	
85	13.22		1.81	**(2)**	18.66		19.31	
86	8.60		3.32		10.36		11.57	
87	11.36		4.72		13.81		14.28	
88	10.86	12.15	2.51		14.32	13.67	13.29	14.69
89	3.66	**(3)**	3.10		3.44	**(3)**	4.46	**(3)**
90	3.78		7.31		3.12	3.28	1.88	
		5.28		3.59				3.89

(Contd.)

(Contd. Table 6)

Year	*GDP*	*Average Growth of the Sub-Period*	*Primary*	*Average Growth of the Sub-Period*	*Secondary*	*Average Growth of the Sub-Period*	*Tertiary*	*Average Growth of the Sub-Period*
91	8.42		2.35		13.89	**(4)**	5.34	
92	15.68	**(4)**	4.71	**(3)**	21.14		15.91	**(4)**
93	14.27		4.69		19.88		11.91	
94	13.42		4.01		18.40		10.93	12.91
95	11.07		4.98		13.88		9.62	**(5)**
96	10.14	12.90	5.09		12.13		9.28	
97	9.36	**(5)**	3.50		10.53	15.69	10.49	
98	7.87		3.50	4.35	8.90	**(5)**	8.23	
99	7.63		2.81	**(4)**	8.16		9.16	
2000	8.48		2.39		9.45		9.59	
01	8.20		2.81		8.51		10.13	
02	9.13	8.44	2.87		9.88	8.98	10.40	
03	10.56	10.56	2.49	2.67	12.69	12.69	9.57	9.60
1978-2003	**9.20**		**4.31**		**10.85**		**10.24**	

Source: developed from the official statistics presented in Table 1.

Table 7: Employment Growth: Total, Primary, Secondary, Tertiary

Year	Total		Primary		Secondary		Tertiary	
1978								
79	2.05	**(1)**	-1.14		11.65		8.43	**(1)**
80	2.70	2.37	1.41	**(1)**	5.38	**(1)**	6.01	
81	3.21	**(2)**	1.98		5.28		6.97	
82	3.38		2.94		4.06		4.62	
83	3.02		2.26	2.14	4.13	4.71	5.22	6.25
84	3.14		0.01	**(2)**	7.30	**(2)**	12.40	**(2)**
85	3.61		-0.03		9.33		11.74	12.07
86	3.12	3.24	0.62		8.14		6.42	**(3)**
87	2.86	**(3)**	0.85	0.36	6.21		5.83	
88	2.91		1.58	**(3)**	4.07	7.01	5.98	
89	2.60		2.44		1.04	**(3)**	5.00	
90	1.88		2.86		-1.02		1.12	
91	2.69		2.55		1.87	0.63	4.00	
		2.55		2.08				5.57

(Contd.)

(Contd. Table 7)

Year	*Total*		*Primary*		*Secondary*		*Tertiary*	
92	2.38		0.98		3.08	**(4)**	6.03	
93	1.06	**(4)**	-1.41	**(4)**	4.30		4.98	
94	1.61		-2.04		4.10		9.44	
95	1.78		-1.40		2.90		8.64	
96	1.14		-0.71	-1.39	1.35	3.14	5.19	
97	1.02	1.32	0.11	**(5)**	-0.35	**(5)**	4.25	
98	-0.37	**(5)**	0.48		-5.93		2.80	**(4)**
99	-0.93	-0.65	0.60		-6.47		0.50	
2000	0.49	**(6)**	0.18	0.34	-0.70	-3.36	2.01	
01	0.44		-0.77	**(6)**	0.51	**(6)**	2.83	
02	0.63		-1.30		2.28		3.16	
03	0.96	0.63	0.03	-0.68	-0.64	0.71	3.82	2.52
1978-2003	1.81		0.49		2.72		5.23	

Source: Developed from the official statistics presented in Table 3.

Bibliography

Alpermann, Björn. 2001. The Post-Election Administration of Chinese Villages. *The China Journal*, No. 46. pp. 45-67.

Anderson, Kym and Rodney Tyers. 1985. China's Economic Growth, Structural Transformation and Food Trade. *The Australian Journal of Chinese Affairs*, No. 14. pp. 65-83.

Ash, Robert F. 1992. The Agricultural Sector in China: Performance and Policy Dilemmas during the 1990s. *The China Quarterly*, No. 131, Special Issue: The Chinese Economy in the 1990s. pp. 545-576.

Ash, Robert F Richard Louis Edmonds. 1998. China's Land Resources, Environment and Agricultural Production. *The China Quarterly*, No. 156, Special Issue: China's Environment. pp. 836-879.

Ash, Robert F. 1988. The Evolution of Agricultural Policy. *The China Quarterly*, No. 116. pp. 529-555.

Ash, Robert F.; Richard Louis Edmonds. 1998. China's Land Resources, Environment and Agricultural Production *the China Quarterly*, No. 156, Special Issue: China's Environment. pp. 836-879.

Aufrecht, Steven E. and Li Siu Bun. 1995. Reform with Chinese Characteristics: The Context of Chinese Civil Service Reform *Public Administration Review*, Vol. 55, No. 2. pp. 175-182.

Aziz, Sartaj. 1978. *Rural Development: Learning from China*. The Macmillan Press Ltd. London.

Bagchi, Amaresh. 1989. A Decade of Economic Reform in China: A Retrospect. *Economic and Political Weekly*, Vol. 24, No. 25, pp. 1407-1411, 1413-1415.

Bardhan, Pranab K. 1970. *Chinese and Indian Agriculture: A Broad Comparison of Recent Policy and Performance*. The Journal of Asian Studies, Vol. 29, No. 3, pp. 515-537.

Baum, Richard D. 1964. *"Red and Expert": the Political Ideological Foundations of China's Great Leap Forward.* Asian Survey, Vol. 4, No. 9 pp. 1048-1057.

Bhattasali, Deepak, Shantong Li, and Will Martin (Ed.). 2004. *China and the WTO Accession, Policy Reform, and Poverty Reduction Strategies*. World Bank/Oxford University Press.

Borensztein, Eduardo and Jonathan D. Ostry. 1996. Accounting for China's Economic Performance. *The American Economic Review,* Vol. 86, No. 2, pp. 224-228.

Brauw, Alan de et al. 2000. Responsiveness, Flexibility, and Market Liberalization in China's Agriculture. *American Journal of Agricultural Economics*, Vol. 82, No. 5, Proceedings Issue, pp.1133-1139.

Bredo, William. *1959. Rural Industrialisation for Agriculture Development.* Journal of Farm Economics, Vol. 41, No. 5, pp. 1332-1344.

Brodsgaard, Kjeld Erik. 1983. *Pragmatic Change: Readjustment and Reform in the Chinese Economy, 1953-1981, Part 1.* Modern China, Vol. 9, No. 1 pp. 37-83.

Brown George P.1995. Arable Land Loss in Rural China: Policy and Implementation in Jiangsu Province *Asian Survey*, Vol. 35, No. 10. pp. 922-940.

Bruce L. Reynolds. 1978. Two Models of Agricultural Development: A Context for Current Chinese Policy. *The China Quarterly*, No. 76, pp. 842-872.

Byrd, William A. and Lyn Qingsong (ed.). 1990. China's Rural Industry: Structure, Development and Reform. World Bank/Oxford University Press.

Carter, Colin A. 1997. The Urban-Rural Income Gap in China: Implications for Global Food Markets. *American Journal of Agricultural Economics*, Vol. 79, No. 5, Proceedings Issue, pp. 1410-1418.

Chen, Pi-chao. 1972. *Overurbanisation, Rustication of Urban-Educated Youths, and Politics of Rural Transformation: the Case of China.* Comparative Politics, Vol. 4, No. 3. pp. 361-386.

Chen, Shaohua, et. al. 2006. Di Bao: A Guaranteed Minimum Income in Urban China? *Policy Research Working Paper, the World Bank, Development Research Group, Poverty Team.*

Chen, Sheying. 2002. Economic Reform and Social Change in China: Past, Present, and Future of the Economic State. *International Journal of Politics, Culture and Society*, Vol. 15, No. 4, pp. 569-589.

Cheng Enjiang. 1997. Market Reforms and Provision of Credit for Grain Purchases in China. *The China Quarterly*, No. 151, pp. 633-653.

Chinn Dennis L. 1980. Cooperative Farming in North China Author: The Quarterly Journal of Economics, Vol. 94, No. 2, pp. 279-297.

Chow Gregory C. 2007. China's Economic Transformation. Blackwell Publishing, Australia.

Chow, Gregory C. 1987. Development of a More Market-Oriented Economy in China *Science, New Series*, Vol. 235, No. 4786, pp. 295-299.

Clark, Colin. 1965. *Economic Growth in Communist China.* China quarterly, No. 21

Clark, Colin. 1976. *Economic Development in Commur'st China.* The Journal of Political Economy, Vol. 84, No. 2, pp. 239-264.

Cohen Paul A. 1988. The Post-Mao Reforms in Historical Perspective. *The Journal of Asian Studies*, Vol. 47, No. 3. pp. 518-540.

Comtois, Claude. 1990. *Transport and Territorial Development in China 1949-1985.* Modern Asian Studies, Vol. 24, No. 4 (Oct 1990), pp. 777-818.

Cressey, George B. 1934. Agricultural Regions of Asia. Part VI—China. *Economic Geography*, Vol. 10, No. 2. pp. 109-142.

Dahlman, Carl J. and Jean-Eric Aubert. 2001. *China and the Knowledge Economy Seizing the 21st Century.* WBI Development Studies, the World Bank Washington, D.C.

Dale Wen. *China Copes with Globalisation: A Mixed Review.* International Forum on Globalization (IFG), San Francisco, p. 12.

Dalsimer, Marlyn and Laurie Nisonoff. 1987. The Implications of the New Agricultural and One-Child Family Policies for Rural Chinese Women. *Feminist Studies*, Vol. 13, No. 3, pp. 583-607.

Das, Dilip K. 2006. China and India: A Tale of Two Economies. Routledge, Taylor and Francis Group, London and New York.

Datta, K.L. 2004. Central Planning: A Case Study of China. Concept Publishing Company, New Delhi

Deb, Kalipada. 1993. The Chinese Economy: Changes and Challenges in the Post-Mao Era. Sterling Publishing Private Limited.

Deininger, Klaus and Songqing Jin. 2002. The Impact of Property Rights on Household's Investment, Risk Coping, and Policy Preference. *Policy Research Working Paper, the World Bank, Development Research Group, Rural Development.*

Dernberger, Robert F. 1972. *Radical Ideology and Economic Development in China: the Cultural Revolution and its Impact on the Economy.* Asian Survey, Vol. 12, No. 12, pp. 1048-1065.

Dernberger, Robert F. 1980. Agricultural Development: The Key Link in China's Four Modernisations Programme. *American Journal of Agricultural Economics*, Vol. 62, No. 2, pp. 331-338.

Dollar, David. 2007. Poverty, Inequality, and Social Disparities during China's Economic Reform. *Policy Research Working Paper, the World Bank Beijing Office.*

Domes, Jurgen. 1982. *New Policies in the Communes: Notes on Rural Societal Structure in China, 1976-81.* The Journal of Asian Studies, Vol. 41, No. 2, pp. 253-267.

Donnithorne, Audrey. 1966. *State Procurement of Agriculture Policies in China I.* Soviet Studies, Vol. 18, No. 1, pp. 213-224.

Donnithorne, Audrey. 1966. *State Procurement of Agriculture Policies in China II.* Soviet Studies, Vol. 18, No. 2, pp. 38-56.

Donnithorne, Audrey. 1972. *China's Cellular Economy: Some Economic Trends since the Cultural Revolution.* The China Quarterly, No. 52, pp. 605-619.

Du Runsheng. 2006. The Course of China's Rural Reform. *International Food Policy Research Institute.*

Durenberger, Robert F. 1972. *Radical Ideology and Economic Development in China: The Cultural Revolution and its Impact on the Economy.* Asian Survey, Vol. 12 No. 12, *The Cultural Revolution and its Aftermath.*

Eckstein, Alexander. 1973. *Economic Growth and Change in China: A Twenty Years Perspective.* The China Quarterly, No. 54, pp. 211-241.

Economic Policy and Political Power in Communist China. Annals of American Academy of Political and Social Science, Vol. 349, *Communist China and the Soviet Bloc (Sep.).*

Emily Hannum. 1999. Political Change and the Urban-Rural Gap in Basic Education in China, 1949-1990. *Comparative Education Review*, Vol. 43, No. 2.

Fan Shenggen. 1991. Effects of Technological Change and Institutional Reform on Production Growth in Chinese Agriculture. *American Journal of Agricultural Economics*, Vol. 73, No. 2, pp. 266-275.

Fan, Liang-Shing. 1973. *The Economy and Foreign Trade of China.* Law and Contemporary Problems, Vol. 38, No. 2, *Trade with China,* pp. 249-259.

Fan, Shenggen and Zhang, Linxiu and Zhang, Xiaobo. 2002. Growth, Inequality, and Poverty in Rural China; the Role of Public Investments. *Research Report 125 International Food Policy Research Institute Washington, D.C.*

Field, Robert Michael. 1986. *The Performance of Industry during the Cultural Revolution: Second Thoughts.* The China Quarterly, No. 108, pp. 625-642.

Foreign Language Press. 2006. Analysis and Forecast on China's Rural Economy (2004-2005). Rural Development Institute, Chinese Academy of Social Science, Rural Survey Organisation, National Bureau of Statistics of China.

Frolic, B. Michael. 1978. *Reflections on Chinese Development Model.* Social Forces, Vol. 57, No. 2, Special Issue, pp. 384-418.

Fukuda-Parr, Sakiko et. al. 2002. Capacity for Development: New Solutions to Old Problems. United Nations Development Programme.

Fureng, Dong. 1986. China's price reform, *Cambridge Journal of Economics*, 10,291-300.

Gang, Fan. 1994. *Incremental Changes and Dual-Track Transition: Understanding the Case of China*. Economic Policy, Vol. 9, No. 19, pp. 100-122.

Gary H. Jefferson and Inderjit Singh Ed. Enterprise Reform in China Ownership, Transition, and Performance. Oxford University Press/World Bank.

Ghosh, Arun. 1995. *Development Paradigms: China and India since 1949*. Economic and Political Weekly, Vol. 30, No. 7/8, pp. 355, 357-358.

Goldstein, Steven M. 1995. China in Transition: The Political Foundations of Incremental Reform. *The China Quarterly*, No. 144, Special Issue: China's Transitional Economy, pp. 1105-1131.

Griffin, Keith and Ashwani Saith. 1981. Growth and Equality in Rural China. International Labor Organisation.

Griffin, Keith (Ed.) *1984*. Institutional Reform and Economic Development in the Chinese Countryside. The Macmillan Press Ltd.

Guihong, Zhang. 2006. *The Rise of China: India's Perceptions and Responses*. South Asian Survey. *13: 1* pp. 93-102.

Hannan, Kate. 1998. Industrial Change in China: Economic Restructuring and Conflicting Interests. Routledge, New York.

Hannum, Emily. 1999. *Political Change and the Rural-Urban Gap in Education in China, 1949-90*. Comparative Education Review, Vol. 43, No. 2 (May, 1999), 193-211.

Harding, Harry. 1972. *Political Trends in China since Cultural Revolution*. Annals of the American Academy of Political and Social Science, Vol. 402, China in the World Today (Jul.).

Harrold Peter. 1992. China's Reform Experience to Date. World Bank Discussion Papers, China and Mongolia Department.

Hawkins, John N. 1976. *Family Planning Education and Health Care Delivery in the Peoples Republic of China: Implications for Educational Alternatives*. Comparative Educational Review, Vol. 20, No. 2, pp. 151-164.

Hawkins, John N. and Regie Stites. 1991. *Strengthening the Future's Foundation: Elementary Education Reform in the People's Republic of China*. The Elementary School Journal, Vol. 92, No. 1, Special Issue: International Education, pp 41-60.

Henderson, J Vernon and Chun-Chung Au. 2006. *Are Chinese Cities Too Small?* Review of Economic Studies 73, 549-576.

Hisa, Ronald. 1954. *The Chinese Economy under Communist Planning*. Pacific Affairs, Vol. 27, No. 2, pp. 112-123.

Hisa, Ronald. 1959. *China's Industrial Growth, 1953-57.* Annals of the American Academy of Political and Social Science, Vol. 321, pp. 71-81.

Ho, Peter, et. al. 2004. *Rural Development in Transitional China: the New Agriculture.* Frank Cass Publishers London England.

Ho, Samuel P. S. 1995. Rural Non-Agriculture Development in Post-Reform China: Growth, Development Patterns, and Issues. *Pacific Affairs,* Vol. 68, No. 3, pp. 360-391.

Ho Samuel P. S. and George C. S. Lin. 2003. Emerging Land Markets in Rural and Urban China: Policies and Practices. *The China Quarterly*, No. 175, pp. 681-707.

Ho, Toby. 2000. *Managing Risk: The Suppression of Private Entrepreneurs in China in the 1950s.* Risk Management, Vol. 2, No. 2.

Ho, Peter. 2001. *Who Owns China's Land? Policies, Property Rights and Deliberate Institutional Ambiguity.* The China Quarterly, No. 166, pp. 394-421.

Hollister, William W. 1964. *Capital Formation in Communist China.* The China Quarterly, No. 17 (Jan.-Mar.,).

Hou, Ching-Ming. 1968. *Sources of Agricultural Growth in Communist China.* The Journal of Asian Studies, Vol. 27, No. 4, pp. 721-737.

Hsu Robert C. 1985. Conceptions of the Market in Post-Mao China: An Interpretive Essay. *Modern China*, Vol. 11, No. 4, pp. 436-460.

Hsu, Robert C. 1982. *Agricultural Financial Polices In China, 1949-80.* Asian Survey, Vol. 22, No. 7, pp. 638-658.

Hsu, Robert C. 1979. Agricultural Mechanization in China: Policies, Problems, and Prospects. *Asian Survey*, Vol. 19, No. 5, pp. 436-449.

Hu, Zuliu F. and Mohsin Khan. 1997. Why is China Growing so fast? Staff Papers—International Monetary Fund, Vol. 44, No. 1, pp. 103-131.

United Nations. Human Development Report 2002: Deepening Democracy in Fragmented World. UNDP.

Ishikawa, Shigeru. 1983. *China's Economic Growth Since 1949—An Assessment.* The China Quarterly, No. 94, pp. 242-281.

Jian, Song. 1985. Reforms and Open Policy in China. *Science, New Series*, Vol. 229, No. 4713, pp. 525-527.

Jin, Songqing et. al. 2002. The Creation and Spread of Technology and Total Factor Productivity in China's Agriculture. *American Journal of Agricultural Economics*, Vol. 84, No. 4, pp. 916-930.

John Knight and Lina Song. 1993. The Spatial Contribution to Income Inequality in Rural China. *Cambridge Journal of Economics* 1993,17, 195-213.

Johnson, D. Gale. 2000. Agricultural Adjustment in China: Problems and Prospects *Population and Development Review*, Vol. 26, No. 2, pp. 319-334.

Joseph, William A. 1986. *A Tragedy of Good Intentions: Post-Mao Views of the Great Leap Forward.* Modern China, Vol. 12, No. 4, pp. 419-457.

Joshi, Gopa. 1980. *Youth Employment and Economic Development in China.* Social Scientist, Vol. 9, No. 1, pp. 33-46.

Jowett A. J. 1984. *Growth of Chinas Population, 1949-1982 (with Special Reference to the Demographic Disaster of 1960-61).* The Geographical Journal, Vol. 150, No. 2, pp. 155-170.

K. W. 1966. *China's Third Five-Year Plan.* The China Quarterly, No. 25, pp. 171-175.

Karen Hardee; Zhenming Xie; Baochang Gu. 2004. Family Planning and Women's Lives in Rural China. *International Family Planning Perspectives*, Vol. 30, No. 2, pp. 68-76.

Keidel, Albert. 2007. China's Economic Fluctuations: Implications for its Rural Economy. Final Report. Carnegie Endowment for International Peace. Massachusetts Avenue, NW, Washington, DC.

Keliang, Zhu, Roy Prosterman. 2007. Securing Land Rights for Chinese Farmers: A Leap Forward for Stability and Growth. Center for Global Liberty and Prosperity, Development Policy Analysis, Washington D.C. p. 4.

Kirby, E. Stuart. 1958. *Economic Planning and Policy in Communist China.* International Affairs (Royal Institute of International Affairs 1944), Vol. 34, No. 2, pp. 174-183.

Klatt, Werner. 1981. The Chinese Model. *International Affairs (Royal Institute of International Affairs 1944-)*, Vol. 57, No. 3, pp. 473-476.

Kraus, Willy. 1982. Economic Development and Social Change in the Peoples Republic of China. Springer-Verlag New York Inc.

Kuijs, Louis and Tao Wang. 2005. China's Pattern of Growth: Moving to Sustainability and Reducing Inequality. Policy Research Working Paper, the World Bank, East Asia and Pacific Region, Poverty Reduction and Economic Management Sector Department.

Kuijs, Louis. 2006. How will China's Saving-Investment Balance Evolve? *Policy Research Working Paper. The World Bank, East Asia and Pacific Region, Poverty Reduction and Economic Management Sector Department.*

Kuo-Chun Chao. 1959. *Leadership in the Chinese Communist Party.* Annals of The American Academy of Political and Social Science, Vol. 321, pp. 40-50.

Kuo-Chün, Chao. 1958. Organised Leadership and Agricultural Technology in Modern China Agricultural History, Vol. 32, No. 1, pp. 25-31.

Lardy, Nicholas R. 1986. Prospects and Some Policy Problems of Agricultural Development in China. *American Journal of Agricultural Economics*, Vol. 68, No. 2, pp. 451-457.

Lardy, Nicholas R. 1992. *Foreign Trade and Economic Reforms in China, 1978-1990*. Cambridge University Press.

Lardy, Nicholas R. 1998. *China's Unfinished Economic Revolution*. Brookings Institute Press, Washington D.C.

Li, Choh-Ming. 1964. *Chinas Industrial Development, 1958-63*. The China Quarterly, No. 17.

Liang, Zai. 2001. The Age of Migration in China. *Population and Development Review*, Vol. 27, No. 3, pp. 499-524.

Lin, Justin Yifu. 1987. *The Household Responsibility System Reform in China: A Peasant's Institutional Choice*. The American Journal of Agriculture Economics, Vol. 69, No. 2, pp. 410-415.

Lin, Justin Yifu. 1988. *The Household Responsibility System Reform in China: A Theoretical and Empirical Study*. Economic Development and Cultural Change, Vol. 36, No. 3, pp. S199-S224.

Lin, Justin Yifu. 1990. *Collectivization and China's Agricultural Crisis In 1959-1961*. The Journal of Political Economy, Vol. 98, No. 6, pp. 1228-1252.

Lin, Justin Yifu. 2004. *Development Strategies for Inclusive Growth in Developing Asia*. Asian Development Review, Vol. 21, no. 2, pp. 1-27.

Lin, Justin Yufi, et al. 1994. China's China's Economic Reforms: Pointers for Other economies in Transition The World Bank Agriculture and Natural Resources Department Agricultural Polices Division June 1994.

Lindert Peter H. 1999. The Bad Earth? China's Soils and Agricultural Development since the 1930s. *Economic Development and Cultural Change*, Vol. 47, No. 4, pp. 701-736.

Lippit, Victor D. 1975. *The Great Leap Forward Reconsidered*. Modern China, Vol. 1, pp. 92-115.

Lloyd, G Reynolds. 1975. *China as a Less Developed Economy*, The American Economic Review, Vol. 65, No. 3.

Maddison, Angus. 2007. Chinese Economic Performance In The Long Run. Development Center Studies OECD.

Maddison, Angus. The World Economy: A Millennial Perspective. OECD/Academic Foundation 2006.

Malenbaum, Wilfred. 1982. *Modern Economic Growth in India and China: The Comparison Revisited (1950-1980)*. Economic Development and Cultural Change, Vol. 31, No. 1, pp. 45-84.

McMillan, John; John Whalley; Lijing Zhu. 1989. The Impact of China's Economic Reforms on Agricultural Productivity Growth. *The Journal of Political Economy*, Vol. 97, No. 4, pp. 781-807.

McMillan, John; John Whalley; Lijing Zhu. 1989. The Impact of China's Economic Reforms on Agricultural Productivity Growth. *The Journal of Political Economy*, Vol. 97, No. 4, pp. 781-807.

Meier, Gerald M. 1984. Emerging From Poverty: The Economics that Really Matters. Oxford University Press, New York.

Mohapatra, Sandeep, et. al. 2006. *Climbing the Development Ladder: Economic Development and the Evolution of Occupations in Rural China.* Journal of Development Studies, Vol. 42, No. 6, 1023-1055,

Moorsteen, Richard. 1959. *Economic Prospects for Communist China.* World Politics, Vol. 11, No. 2, pp. 192-220.

National Bureau of Statistics. 2008. China Yearbook 2008: Rural Household Survey. *Department of Rural Surveys.*

Naughton, Barry. 1995. Growing Out of Plan: Chinese Economic Reform, *1978-1993.* Cambridge University Press.

Ness, Peter Van (Ed.). *1989.* Market Reforms in Socialist Societies: Comparing China and Hungary. Lynne Rienner Publishers London.

Nickum, James E. 1978. Labour accumulation in rural China and its role since the Cultural Revolution, *Cambridge Journal of Economics,* 2, 273-286.

Niu, Ruofeng and Peter H. Calkins 1986. Towards an Agricultural Economy for China in a New Age: Progress, Problems, Response, and Prospects. *American Journal of Agricultural Economics*, Vol. 68, No. 2, pp. 445-450.

Nolan, Peter and Robert F. Ash. 1995. *China's Economy on the Eve of Reform.* The China Quarterly, No. 144, Special Issue: China's Transition Economy, pp. 980-998.

Nolan, Peter. 1983. De-Collectivization of Agriculture in China, 1979-82: A Long-Term Perspective. *Economic and Political Weekly*, Vol. 18, No. 32, pp. 1395-1406.

Nolan, Peter. 1993. Economic Reform, Poverty and Migration in China Economic and Political Weekly, Vol. 28, No. 26, pp. 1369-1377.

O'Leary, Greg and Andrew Watson. 1983. *The Role of the Peoples Communes in Rural Development in China.* Pacific Affairs, Vol. 55, No. 4, pp. 593-612.

Ody, Anthony J. 1992. *Rural Enterprise Development in China, 1988-90.* World Bank Discussion Papers. China and Mongolia Department Series.

Oi Jean C. 1986. Peasant Households between Plan and Market: Cadre Control over Agricultural Inputs. *Modern China*, Vol. 12, No. 2, pp. 230-251.

Oi Jean C. 1999. Two Decades of Rural Reform in China: An Overview and Assessment. *The China Quarterly*, No. 159, Special Issue: The People's Republic of China after 50 Years, pp. 616-628.

Orleans, Leo A. 1961. *Problems of Manpower Absorption in Rural China.* The China Quarterly, No. 7, pp. 57-68.

Patnaik, Utsa. 1996. Some Considerations on Rural Investment, Employment, and Consumption in the Post-Reform Period of China. *Social Scientist*, Vol. 24, No. 11/12, pp. 50-61.

Pei, Xiaolin. 2002. The Contribution of Collective Landownership to China's Economic Transition and Rural Industrialization: A Resource Allocation Model. *Modern China*, Vol. 28, No. 3, pp. 279-314.

Peng, Yusheng. 1992. Wage Determination in Rural and Urban China: A Comparison of Public and Private Industrial Sectors. *American Sociological Review*, Vol. 57, No. 2, pp. 198-213.

Peng, Yusheng. 1999. Agricultural and Nonagricultural Growth and Inter-county Inequality in China, 1985-1991. *Modern China*, Vol. 25, No. 3, pp. 235-263.

Perkins, Dwight H. 1964. *Centralization and Decentralization in Mainland China's Agriculture, 1949-62.* The Quarterly Journal of Economics, Vol. 78. No. 2, pp. 208-237.

Perkins, Dwight H. 1964. *Price Stability and Development in Mainland China (1951-63).* The Journal of Political Economy, Vol. 72, No. 4, pp. 360-375.

Perkins, Dwight H. 1971-72. *Is there a China Market?* Foreign Policy, No. 5, pp. 88-106.

Perkins, Dwight H. 1973. *Plans and their Implementation in the People's Republic of China.* The American Economic Review, Vol. 63, No. 2, pp. 224-231.

Perry, Elizabeth J. 1984. *Collective Violence in China.* Theory and Society, Vol. 13, No. 3, pp. 427-454.

Powell, Simon G. 1992. In China: From Communes to Commodity Economy 1978-1990. Studies on East Asia. Manchester University Press.

Prime, Penelope B and Kishore G. Kulkarni (Ed.). 2007. Economic Development in India and China: New Perspectives on Progress and Change. Serials Publications, New Delhi.

Pritchard, Earl H. 1951. *The Political Ferment in China 1911-1951,* Annals of the American Academy of Political and Social Science, Vol. 227, Report on China, pp. 1-12.

Putterman Louis. 1992. Institutional Boundaries, Structural Change, and Economic Reform in China: An Introduction. *Modern China*, Vol. 18, No. 1, pp. 3-13.

Putterman, Louis. 1987. *The Incentive Problem and the Demise of Team Farming in China.* Journal of Development Economics, 26, 103-127, North-Holland.

Putterman, Louis. 1995. The Role of Ownership and Property Rights in China's Economic Transition. *The China Quarterly*, No. 144, Special Issue: China's Transitional Economy, pp. 1047-1064.

Putterman, Louis. 1992. Dualism and Reform in China. *Economic Development and Cultural Change*, Vol. 40, No. 3, pp. 467-493.

Putterman, Louis and Xiao-Yuan Dong. 2000. *China's State-Owned Enterprises: Their Role, Job Creation, Efficiency in Long-Term Perspective.* Modern China, Vol. 26, No. 4, pp. 403-447.

Pye, Lucian W. 1986. *Reassessing the Cultural Revolution.* The China Quarterly, No. 108, pp. 597-612.

Pye, Lucian W. 1999. *An Overview of 50 Years of the People's Republic of China: Some Progress, But Big Problems.* The China Quarterly, No. 159, Special Issue: the Peoples Republic of China after 50 Years, pp. 569-579.

Quanhe Yang; Fei Guo. 1996. Occupational Attainments of Rural to Urban Temporary Economic Migrants in China, 1985-1990. *International Migration Review*, Vol. 30, No. 3, pp. 771-787.

Radhakrishna, R. (ed.) 2008. India Development Report 2008. *I*ndra Gandhi Institute of Development Research.

Rawski, Thomas G. 1975. *Problems of Technology Absorption in Chinese Industry.* The American Economic Review, Vol. 65, No. 2, pp. 383-388.

Reynolds, Bruce L. 1988. Chinese Economic Reforms: How Far, How Fast? Academic Press, Inc.

Reynolds, Lloyd G. 1975. *China as a Less Developed Economy.* The American Economic Review, Vol. 65, No. 3, pp. 418-428.

Riskin, Carl. 1978. *China's Rural Industries: Self-Reliant System or Independent Kingdoms?* The China Quarterly, No. 73, pp. 77-98.

Rosse, Robert M. 1954. *The Working of Communist China's Five Year Plan.* Pacific Affairs, Vol. 27, No. 1, pp. 16-26.

Rozelle Scott and Richard N. Boisvert. 1993. Grain Policy in Chinese Villages: Yield Response to Pricing, Procurement, and Loan Policies. *American Journal of Agricultural Economics*, Vol. 75, No. 2, pp. 339-349.

Rozelle, Scott. 1996. Stagnation without Equity: Patterns of Growth and Inequality in China's Rural Economy. *The China Journal*, No. 35, pp. 63-92.

Runsheng, Du. 1989. Many People, Little Land: China's Rural Economic Reform. Foreign Language Press, Beijing.

Schram, Stuart R. 1994. *Mao Zedong a Hundred Years on: the Legacy of a Ruler.* The China Quarterly, No. 137, pp. 125-143.

Schurmann, Franz. 1963. *Economic Policy and Political Power in Communist China.* Annals of The American Academy of Political and Social Science, Vol. 349, pp. 49-69.

Schwartz, Benjamin. 1973. *China's Development Experience 1949-72.* Proceedings of the Academy of Political Science, Vol. 31, No. 1, China's Development Experience, pp. 17-26.

Seybolt, J. 1974. *Higher Education in China.* Higher Education, Vol. 3, No. 3, pp. 265-283.

Shabad, Theodore. 1955. *Communist China's Five Year Plan.* Far Eastern Survey, Vol. 24, No. 12, pp. 189-191.

Shenggen Fan, Linxiu Zhang, Xiaobo Zhang. 2002. Growth, Inequality, and Poverty in Rural China: the Role of Public Investments. Research Report 125 International Food Policy Research Institute Washington, D.C.

Shi, Anqing. 2006. Migration in Towns in China, a Tale of Three Provinces: Evidence from Preliminary Tabulations of 2000 Census. Policy Research Working Paper, the World Bank, Development Research Group, Growth and Investment Team.

Shih, Joseph Anderson. 1972. *Science and Technology in China.* Asian Survey, Vol. 12, No. 8, pp. 662-675.

Sicular Terry. 1995. Redefining State, Plan and Market: China's Reforms in Agricultural Commerce. *The China Quarterly*, No. 144, Special Issue: China's Transitional Economy, pp. 1020-1046.

Sicular, Terry. 1988. Plan and Market in China's Agricultural Commerce. *The Journal of Political Economy*, Vol. 96, No. 2, pp. 283-307.

Sigurdson, Jon. 1973. Rural Economic Planning. Proceedings of the American Academy of Political Science, Vol. 31, No. 1, China Development Experience, pp. 68-79.

Sigurdson, Jon. 1976. *Development of Rural Areas in India and China.* Ambio, Vol. 5, No. 3, pp. 98-107.

Singh, Ajit Kumar. 1985. Economic Development and Inequalities in Communist China 1949-1975, Himalaya Publishing House Bombay.

Smil, Vaclav. 1976. *Energy in China: Achievements and Prospects.* The China Quarterly, No. 65.

Smil, Vaclav. 1999. China's Agricultural Land. *The China Quarterly*, No. 158, pp. 414-429.

So, Alvin Y. 2003. *China's Development Miracle: Origins, Transformations, and Challenges*. M. E. Sharpe, Armonk, New York.

Stavis Benedict. 1976. China's Rural Local Institutions in Comparative Perspective. *Asian Survey*, Vol. 16, No. 4, pp. 381-396.

Stavis, Benedict. 1991. Market Reforms and Changes in Crop Productivity: Insights from China. *Pacific Affairs*, Vol. 64, No. 3, pp. 373-383.

Stites, Regie and Semali, Ladislaus. 1991. *Adult Literacy for Social Equality or Economic Growth? Changing Agendas for Mass Literacy in China and Tanzania.* Comparative Education Review, Vol. 35, No. 1, Feb.

Stone, Bruce. 1985. The Basis for Chinese Agricultural Growth in the 1980s and 1990s: A Comment on Document No. 1, 1984. *The China Quarterly*, No. 101, pp. 114-121.

Swamy, Subramanian. 1973. *Economic Growth in China and India, 1952-1970: A Comparative Appraisal.* Economic Development and Cultural Change, Vol. 21, No. 4, Part 2, pp. 1-84.

Tam, On-Kit. 1988. Rural Finance in China. *The China Quarterly*, No. 113, pp. 60-76.

Tandon, Ajay, and Juzhong Zhuang. 2007. Inclusiveness of Economic Growth in the People's Republic of China: What Do Population Health Outcomes Tell Us? Asian Development Bank.

Tao, Ran and Zhigang Xu. 2007. *Urbanization, Rural Land System and Social Security for Migrants in China.* Journal of Development Studies, Vol. 43, No. 7, 1301-1320.

Taylor, Jeffrey R. 1988. Rural Employment Trends and the Legacy of Surplus Labour, 1978-86. *The China Quarterly*, No. 116, pp. 736-766.

Teiwes, Frederick C. 1974. *Before and After the Cultural Revolution.* The China Quarterly, No. 58.

Tenev, Stoyan and Chunlin Zhang. 2002. *Corporate Governance and Enterprise Reform in China. Building the Institutions of Modern Markets.* World Bank and the International Finance Corporation Washington, D.C.

Thomas S. B. 1956. *Communist Chinas Agricultural Policy, 1954-56.* Pacific Affairs, Vol. 29, No. 2, pp. 141-160.

Thornton, John L. 2006. China's Leadership Gap. Foreign Affairs November/ December 2006. pp. 133-140. Washington.

Todaro, M. P., Stephen C. Smith. 2003. Economic Development. Pearson Education, India.

Tseng, Wanda and David Cowen. 2005. India's and China's Recent Experience with Reform and Growth. International Monetary Fund/ Palgrave Macmillan.

UNDP/China Development Research Foundation. 2005. China Human Development Report 2005: Development with Equity. China Translation and Publication Corporation.

UNDP/China Development Research Foundation. 2008. China Human Development Report 2007/08. Access for All: Basic Public Services for 1.3 Billion People. China Translation and Publishing Corporation, 2008.

UNICEF. 2007. The State of the World Children 2008: Child Survival. United Nations.

United Nations. 1959. World Economic Report 1958. United Nations Department of Economic Affairs New York, 1959.

United Nations. 1962. World Economic Report 1961. United Nations Department of Economic Affairs New York, 1962.

United Nations. 1951. World Economic Report 1949-50. United Nations Department of Economic Affairs, New York.

United Nations. 1952. World Economic Report, 1950-51. United Nations Department of Economic Affairs New York, April.

United Nations. 1953. World Economic Report 1951-52. United Nations Department of Economic Affairs New York.

United Nations. 1954. World Economic Report 1952-53. United Nations Department of Economic Affairs, New York.

United Nations. 1955. World Economic Report, 1953-54. United Nations Department of Economic Affairs, New York.

United Nations. 1956. World Economic Report, 1955. United Nations Department of Economic Affairs, New York.

United Nations. 1957. World Economic Report 1956. United Nations Department of Economic Affairs, New York.

United Nations. 1958. World Economic Report, 1957. United Nations Department of Economic Affairs, New York.

United Nations. 1959. World Economic Report 1958. United Nations Department of Economic Affairs, New York.

United Nations. 1961. World Economic Report, 1960. United Nations Department of Economic Affairs, New York.

United Nations. 1962. World Economic Report, 1961. United Nations Department of Economic Affairs, New York.

United Nations. 1963. World Economic Report, 1961: Current Economic Developments. United Nations Department of Economic Affairs New York

United Nations. 1999. World Economic and Social Survey 1999: Trends and Policies in the World Economy. United Nations New York,

United Nations. 2002. Human Development Report 2002: Deepening Democracy in Fragmented World. United Nations Development Programme.

United Nations. World Economic and Social Survey: Trends and Policies in the World Economy. United Nations New York,

United Nations/ Ministry of Foreign Affairs, China. 2008. *China's Progress towards the Millennium Development Goals*, 2008 Report.

United Nations. 2003. Updated Common Country Assessment. United Nations Resident Coordinator System in China, Beijing.

UNDP. 1997. China Human Development Report 1997: Human Development and Poverty Alleviation. United Nations Development Programme, UN.

UNDP. 2002. China Human Development Report 2002: Making Green Development a Choice. United Nations Development Programme/ Stockholm Environment Institute/ Oxford University Press.

UNDP. 2005. China Human Development Report 2005: Development with Equity. United Nations Development Programme China/China Development Research Foundation.

UNDP. 2008. China Human Development Report 1999: Transition and the State. United Nations Development Programme China/China Financial and Economic Publishing House.

UNDP. 2008. China Human Development Report 2007/08, Access for all: Basic Public Services for 1.3 Billion People. United Nations Development Programme China/China Institute for Reform and Development.

UNDP/World Bank. 2001. China: Overcoming Rural Poverty. *Rural Development and Natural Resources East Asia and Pacific Region.*

Urwin, Tim. 2007. *No End to Poverty.* Journal of Development Studies, Vol. 43, No. 5, 929-953.

Veeck, Gregory, Wang Shaohua. 2000. Challenges to Family Farming in China. *Geographical Review*, Vol. 90, No. 1, pp. 57-82.

Vermeer, E. B. 1982. Rural Economic Change and the Role of the State in China, 1962-78 *Asian Survey*, Vol. 22, No. 9, pp. 823-842.

Vermeer, E. B. 1982. *Rural Economic Change and the Role of the State in China, 1962-78.* Asian Survey, Vol. 22, No. 9, pp. 823-842.

Wagstaff, Adam, et. al. 2007. Extending Health Insurance to Rural Population: an Impact Evaluation of China's New Cooperative Medical Scheme. Policy Research Working Paper, The World Bank, Development Research Group Public, Public Service Team and East Asia and Pacific Region, Human Sector Department.

Wagstaff, Adam, et. al. 2009. *Reforming China's Rural Health System.* The World Bank.

Walder, Andrew G. 1989. Social Change in Post-Revolution China. *Annual Review of Sociology*, Vol. 15, pp. 405-424.

Wang Jinxia et al. 2008. *How China's Farmers Adapt to Climate Change*. The World Bank Development Research Group Sustainable Rural and Urban Development Team October 2008.

Wang, Jirong; Eric J. Wailes; Gail L. Cramer. 1996. A Shadow-Price Frontier Measurement of Profit Efficiency in Chinese Agriculture *American Journal of Agricultural Economics*, Vol. 78, No. 1, pp. 146-156.

Wang, Robert S. 1975. *Educational Reforms and the Cultural Revolution: The Chinese Evaluation Process.* Asian Survey, Vol. 15, No. 9.

Wang, Virginia Li. 1976. *Food Distribution as a Guarantee for Nutrition and Health: China's Experience.* The Milbank Memorial Fund Quarterly. Health and Society, Vol. 54, No. 2, pp. 145-165.

Waters, Harry J. 1997. China's Economic Development Strategies for the 21st Century. Quorum Books, London.

Watson, Andrew. 1985. *Agricultural Reform and China's Foreign Trade.* The Australian Journal of Chinese Affairs, No. 14, pp. 39-63.

Weisskopf, Thomas E. 1975. *China and India: Contrasting Experience in Economic Development.* The American Economic Review, Vol. 65, No. 2, Papers and Proceedings of the Eighty-Seventh Annual Meeting of the American Economic Association, pp. 356-364.

Wen, Chi-Pang and Charles W. Hays. 1976. *Health Care Financing in China.* Medical Care, Vol. 14, No. 14, 3, pp. 241-254.

Wenhua, Li, Min Qingwen. 1999. Integrated Farming Systems an Important Approach toward Sustainable Agriculture in China. *Ambio*, Vol. 28, No. 8, Ecosystem Research and Management in China, pp. 655-662.

White, Gordon. 1991. *The Chinese State in the Era of Reform: The Road to Crisis*. M. E. Sharpe, Inc. Armonk, New York.

Wiemer Calla. 1992. Price Reform and Structural Change: Distributional Impediments to Allocative Gains. *Modern China*, Vol. 18, No. 2, pp. 171-196.

Wiens Thomas B.1976. Peasant Risk Aversion and Allocative Behavior: A Quadratic Programming Experiment. *American Journal of Agricultural Economics*, Vol. 58, No. 4, Part 1, pp. 629-635.

Wiens, Thomas B. 1978. *Chinese Agriculture: Continued Self-reliance.* American Journal of Agriculture Economics, Vol. 60, No. 5, pp. 872-877.

Wiens, Thomas B. 1987. *Issues in the Structural Reform of Chinese Agriculture.* Journal of Comparative Economics, 11, 372-384.

Winters, L. Alan and Shahid Yusuf (Ed.). 2007. Dancing with Giants: China, India, and the Global Economy. World Bank/Institute of Policy Studies, Singapore.

Wolf, Martin. 2005. *Why is China Growing So Slowly? For All Its Success China is still not Living Up to Its Potential.* Foreign Policy, No. 146, pp. 50-51.

Womack, Brantley. 1986. *Where Mao went wrong: Epistemology and Ideology in Mao's Leftist Politics.* The Australian Journal of Chinese Affairs, No. 16, pp. 23-40.

Wong, Christine P. W. 1986. The Economics of Shortage and Problems of Reform in Chinese Industry. *Journal of Comparative Economics*, 10, 363-387.

Wong Linda and Huen Wai-Po. 1998. Reforming the Household Registration System: A Preliminary Glimpse of the Blue Chop Household Registration System in Shanghai and Shenzhen. *International Migration Review*, Vol. 32, No. 4, pp. 974-994.

Woo, Wing Thye and Bao, Shuming. 2003. China: Case Study on Human Development Progress towards the Millennium Development Goals at the Sub-National Level. Background Paper for Human Development Report UNDP

World Bank. 1980. World Development Report 1980. The World Bank/Oxford University Press, Washington D.C. U.S.A.

World Bank. 1996. World Development Report 1996: From Plan to Market. *The World Bank/ Oxford University Press, Oxford University Press,* Washington D.C. U.S.A.

World Bank. 1997. World Development Report 1997: The State in a Changing World. The World Bank Washington D.C. U.S.A.

World Bank. 2000. World Development Report 1999/2000: Entering the Twenty First Century. *The World Bank/Oxford University Press,* Washington D.C. U.S.A.

World Bank. 2001. *World Development Report 2000/2001: Attacking Poverty.* The World Bank/Oxford University Press, Washington D.C. U.S.A.

World Bank. 2001. *China: Overcoming Rural Poverty*. The World Bank Washington DC.

World Bank. 2003. *China Promoting Growth with Equity*. Country Economic Memorandum. Report No. 24169-CHA. Poverty Reduction and Economic Management Unit East Asia and Pacific Region.

World Bank. 2005. *East Asia Decentralises Making Local Government Work.* The World Bank Washington, D.C.

World Bank. 2006. *China Governance, Investment Climate, and Harmonious Society: Competitiveness Enhancements for 120 Cities in China*. Poverty Reduction and Economic Management, Financial and Private Sector Development Unit East Asia and Pacific Region.

World Bank. 2007. *China: Public Services for Building the New Socialist Countryside*. Rural Development, Natural Resource and Environmental Sustainable Development Department, East Asia and Pacific Region.

World Bank/ UNDP. 2001. *China Overcoming Rural Poverty*. Rural Development and Natural Resources Unit East Asia and Pacific Region.

Wu, Jinglian. 2005. Understanding and Interpreting Chinese Economic Reform. Thomson South-Western, Singapore.

Wu, Yanrui. 1996. Productive Performance of Chinese Enterprises: An Empirical Study. Macmillan Press Ltd

Wu, Yuan-Li. 1968. *Economics, Ideology and the Cultural Revolution.* Asian Survey, Vol. 8, No. 3, pp. 223-235.

Wu, Yuan-Li. 1968. *Ideology and Cultural Revolution.* Asian Survey, Vol. 8, No. 3.

Xiao-qiang, Wang. 1998. *China's Price and Enterprise Reform.* Macmillan Press Limited.

Yao, Shujie. *Economic Growth, Income Distribution and Poverty Reduction in Contemporary China.* Routledge Curzon, Taylor and Francis Group, London and New York.

Yao, Shujie and Xiaming Liu. 2003. *Sustaining China's Economic Growth in the Twenty-First Century*. Routledge Curzon Taylor and Francis Group, London and New York.

Yaohui Zhao. 1999. Labour Migration and Earnings Differences: The Case of Rural China *Economic Development and Cultural Change*, Vol. 47, No. 4, pp. 767-782.

Yep, Ray. 2001. The Evolution of Shareholding Enterprise Reform in Rural China: A Manager Empowerment Thesis. *Pacific Affairs*, Vol. 74, No. 1, pp. 53-73.

Yiling Fu.1980. Capitalism in Chinese Agriculture: On the Laws Governing Its Development. *Modern China*, Vol. 6, No. 3, pp. 311-316.

Yusuf, Shahid and Kaoru Nabeshima. 2006. Two Decades of Reform: the Changing Organisation Dynamics of Chinese Industrial Firms. *Policy Research Working Papers, World Bank Development Research Group.*

Zai, Liang; Zhongdong Ma. 2004. China's Floating Population: New Evidence from the 2000 Census. *Population and Development Review*, Vol. 30, No. 3, pp. 467-488.

Zeng, Douglas Zhihua. 2005. *China's Employment Challenges and Strategies after the WTO Accession*. World Bank Policy Research Working Paper 3522

Zhao, Zhongwei. 2006. *Income inequality, Unequal Health Care Access, and Mortality in China.* Population and Development Review, Vol. 32, No. 3, pp. 461-483.

Zhou, Zhang-Yue. 1988. Grain Marketing Systems in China and India: A Comparative Perspective. *Modern Asian Studies*, Vol. 32, No. 2, pp. 459-512.

Zweig, David. 1986. Prosperity and Conflict in Post-Mao Rural China. *The China Quarterly*, No. 105, pp. 1-18.

Index

A

Absolute poverty, 25, 63, 122, 189, 224
Adjustment period, 53
Adjustment-cost, 25
Adult literacy rate, 129
Advanced cooperatives, 38, 41
Agencies for special diseases, 126
Agrarian Reform Law, 32, 66, 231
Agricultural
  revolution, 16, 41
  sector, 16-18, 35, 40-42, 45, 50, 60, 148, 195, 222, 231
Agricultural tax, 40, 47, 57, 61
Agriculture, 31, 33, 35-38, 40, 41, 44, 45, 60, 64, 67, 86, 106, 137, 139, 140, 146, 148, 149, 153, 162, 184, 195, 227, 233, 234
Agriculture
  Bank of China, 38
  output, 148, 233
  transformation, 139
Airways, 34, 43, 51, 54, 58, 62, 65 68
Alan de Brauw, 25
Animal husbandry, 22, 40, 53, 57, 64, 140, 143, 146, 195, 197, 233
Arable land, 59, 62, 219, 234
Asian Development Bank, 92
Assar Lindbeck, 22
Average life expectancy, 62, 126

B

Banking, 20, 90
Basic sectors of the economy, 96
Biomass and waste, 131
Bond issues, 90
Bottom-up approach, 85
Bottom-up strategy, 85

C

Capital goods, 13, 42, 49
Central
  Bank, 90, 91
  fixed revenue, 89
Chaing Kai-shek, 28
Child
  care centers, 126
  mortality, 67, 69, 232
Chinas merchandise trade, 43
Chinese
  Communist strategy of developing agriculture, 41
  Economic Reform, 24
  People's Bank, 38
  Rural Industrialisation, 19
Civil war, 28, 29, 37
Coastal open cities, 92

Collective
  farm, 38, 46, 48
  ownership, 19, 66, 209, 231, 235
Collectivisation, 20, 35, 36, 38, 63
Commercialisation, 139, 148, 154, 158, 174
Commune, 46, 47, 88, 137, 214, 231
  system, 47, 52, 138
Communist Party of China (CPC), 28
Communist theory of industrialisation, 35
Comparative advantage theory, 19
Consumer-goods industry, 35
Contract
  purchasing, 138
  responsibility system, 89, 90
Crop production, 148
Crude oil production, 34, 43, 51, 55, 59, 62
Cultural Revolution, 30, 55-59, 61, 63, 68, 104, 138, 230

D

Death rate, 34, 42, 50, 54, 58, 62, 65, 67
Decentralised economy, 22
Delivery quota, 88
Demand and supply factors, 148
Demand
  constraint, 158
  side, 67, 139, 148, 154, 174, 189
Demographic differential, 16
Developing
  countries, 11, 13-15, 129, 136, 146, 217, 218, 229
  economies, 11, 13, 16, 209
Development Economics, 13, 23, 217
Development policy, 16, 224
Development strategies, 17, 218, 222
Dual-Track Price Reform, 87

E

East Asian economies, 14
Economic Responsibility System in, 88
Economic transformation, 18, 66, 96, 137, 166, 189, 233
Ectoral Composition of Employment, 101
Egalitarianism, 35, 38
Elasticity of employment, 158
Electricity generation, 34, 55, 59
Elementary cooperatives, 38, 41, 66, 231
Employment, 85, 91, 100, 101, 108, 112
  elasticity, 100, 101, 142, 195
  elasticity of GDP growth, 100
Employment growth, 100, 101, 108, 115, 195
Energy consumption, 131
Energy deficit of China, 131
Enterprise Reform in China, 18, 19
Expanding enterprise autonomy, 88

F

Farm Sector, 158
Farming, 40, 52, 53, 57, 61, 64, 88, 140, 233
Fengyang County, 137
First Five Year Plan, 35, 36, 39, 43, 49
First Plan, 30, 35-37, 39, 41, 42, 44, 47
Fiscal Policy, 89
Fiscal reforms, 90
Food grains, 44, 153
  production per agricultural labourer, 153
  security, 42, 148
  supply, 153

Foreign Trade, 20, 49, 92, 259
Forestry, 40, 53, 57, 64, 140, 143, 146, 195, 233

G

Gang of Four, 63
Gender composition, 129
Global pollution, 131
Government failure, 14
Gradualism, 85
  approach, 38, 85
Great Leap disaster, 65, 66, 67
Great Leap failure, 26
Gross Domestic Product, 29, 93
Growth rate of employment, 100, 101, 108, 115
Growth rate of primary sector, 106
Guangdong, 89, 91, 92
Gustav Ranis, 18

H

Health Expenditure, 42, 124
Health indicators, 124, 126, 219
Health Infrastructure, 126
Heavy and capital-goods industry, 35
Heavy industrial products, 33, 36
Heavy industry, 33, 35, 37, 41, 46, 49, 54, 57, 61, 67
Household Registration System, 23, 304
Household Responsibility System, 86, 137, 233
Hubei and Liaoning provinces, 23
Human development, 153
Human Development Index, 16
Hydro-electricity, 131
Hyper-inflation, 37

I

Ideological education, 58
Industrial revolution, 16
Industry, 16, 19-21, 31, 33, 41, 49, 54, 96, 233
Infant mortality, 30, 62, 69, 124, 213
Inflation, 30, 36, 143
Institutional change, 21, 30, 32, 37,, 46, 52, 56, 60, 64, 84, 85, 137, 189, 232, 233
Institutional transformation, 31, 39
International Monetary Fund, 14
Irrigated area, 40, 43, 47, 51, 59, 62, 68, 162, 209
Irrigation, 22, 40, 41, 46, 48, 49, 51, 59, 67, 68, 139, 162, 202, 209

J

Japanese invasion of China, 28
John C. H. Fei, 18
Joint State-Private Industrial Enterprises, 38
Jose Antonio, 14
Justin Yifu Lin, 19

K

Kalipada Deb, 21

L

Labour market reform, 91
Land reform programme, 32, 38
  reforms, 17
  reform campaign, 31
Level of autarky, 22
Life expectancy at birth, 30, 34, 42, 67, 126, 219
Light industry, 33, 35, 37, 41, 46, 49, 54, 61, 65
Literacy in the pre-reform period, 129
Liu Shaoqi, 52, 55, 56
Living expenditure, 175, 178, 179, 234
Living standard, 166, 169

Local revenue, 89, 90
Local tax bureaus, 90

M

Macroeconomic Indicators, 12, 17, 31, 37, 52, 234
Macroeconomic Variables, 45, 56, 60, 93
Manchuria, 33, 36, 41
Mao Zedong, 28, 52, 58
Market economy, 20, 87, 88, 91
  failure, 13, 14, 17
  forces, 93, 153
  mechanism, 13, 85, 148, 192
  purchases, 138
  oriented reforms, 20
Mechanisation process, 162, 234
Merchandise exports, 44
  trade, 43, 51, 55, 59, 62
Methodology, 26
Migration, 16, 18, 24, 195
Mixed economy, 20
Monopolistic power, 13

N

National People's Congress, 91
National tax bureau, 90
Nationalist Party, 28
Natural gas production, 55, 59, 62
Non-farm activities, 140, 233
Non-farm Activity, 23
Non-farm sector, 137, 158, 234
Non-personal expenditure, 124
Nuclear sectors, 131
Number of health workers, 129

O

Opium War, 28
Output-quota contracting, 24
Overtaking hypothesis, 18
Ownership Transition, 18, 19

P

Pareto-inferior allocation of resources, 20
Peoples' Bank of China, 90
Per capita income, 14, 26, 31, 45, 85, 166, 169, 210, 219, 224, 227, 234
  capita output, 36, 148, 224
Perfect competition, 149
Pipelines, 51, 54, 58, 62, 65, 68
Post Revolution Period, 30, 63
Post-Mao Era, 21, 291
Post-reform period, 17, 26, 84, 86 100, 104, 106, 108, 112, 115, 118, 122, 124, 126, 129, 130, 136, 140, 142, 149, 158, 162, 175, 179, 188, 192, 199, 210, 229, 234
Poverty reduction, 22, 23, 85, 86, 122, 184, 189, 224, 227, 229, 234
Pre-reform communist China, 20
Pre-reform period, 20, 21, 26, 27, 28, 60, 65, 67
Preobrazhenski, 35
Primary
  schools, 29, 33, 50, 61, 130
  sector, 22, 31, 37, 45, 52, 56, 232, 233, 234, 235
  sector contribution to GDP, 96
  sector employment, 108, 142
Primary sector transformation, 139
Private
  plots, 46, 52, 138
  universities, 42
Privatisation, 85, 86, 89, 174, 222, 232
Product-mix, 149, 158
Production brigade, 47, 66
Production responsibility system, 138
Production system, 15, 137, 162, 202, 233

Production team, 24, 46, 52
Productivity, 15, 16, 18, 19, 22, 26, 96, 138, 139, 142, 148, 149, 188, 233, 234
Profitability, 90, 143, 148, 158
Property rights, 19, 21, 23, 92, 139, 166, 215

Q

Quota requirements, 86, 137

R

Rationalisation, 118
Raw coal production, 43, 51, 59, 62
Readjustment period, 52, 53, 54, 55, 57, 65
Real wages, 36, 158, 162
Red Guard units, 55
Red Guards, 56
Rehabilitation period, 32, 34, 68
Rehabilitation Phase, 30, 33, 35
Resolution on Unified Enterprise Basic Pension, 91
Responsibility contracting, 24
Ross Garnaut, 20
Rural
  economy, 136, 137, 148, 158, 172, 174, 175, 192, 202, 209, 214, 222, 233, 234, 235
  Employment, 158, 162, 192, 195, 234
Rural households, 154, 169
Rural Income Inequality, 23
Rural industry in China, 19
Rural markets, 46, 138
Rural population, 32, 86, 140, 148, 179, 199, 233, 235
Rural poverty, 136, 166, 188, 189, 234
Rural reforms, 24, 25, 233, 234
Rural sector, 11, 15, 16, 26, 86, 136, 137, 172, 222, 229, 230
Rural Township and Village Enterprises, 89
Rural transformation, 15, 17, 20, 136, 229, 233

S

Second Five Year Plan: Great Leap Forward, 30, 44
Secondary schools, 29, 34, 42, 50, 54, 61, 65
Secondary sector, 32, 37, 45, 56, 96, 100, 101, 108, 112, 115, 118, 142, 174, 233
Self-sufficiency, 36
Services sector output, 118
Shandong, 89
Shanghai complex, 36
Shanghai Stock Exchange, 90
Shock-therapy approach, 85
Shujie Yao, 22
Sichuan Province, 88
Sino-Soviet split, 44
Social capital, 19
Social Disparities, 23
Social safety net, 23
Socialist democracy, 91
Socio-economic, 21, 23, 26
Socio-economic hegemony, 38
Southwest China, 43
Soviet
  development strategy, 35
  Model, 30, 35, 48
  Union, 35, 36, 42, 44
Special economic zones, 92
Special policies, 92
Stalinist model, 35
State capitalism, 38
State Enterprise Employees, 91
State Enterprises, 18
State enterprises, 87, 89, 90

Structural change, 17, 18, 21, 26, 96 101, 146, 172, 192, 233
Structural Change in GDP, 96
Structural transformation, 129, 142
Subsistence, 18, 46, 136, 189
sector, 18
Swap markets, 93

T

Taiwan, 28, 92
Telecommunication services, 43
Terry Sicular, 20
Tertiary sector, 32, 37, 56, 60, 64, 96, 101, 118, 139, 140, 142, 174
The leap years, 44, 45
Third Five Year Plan, 30, 55, 58
Tian Men, 63
Total employment growth, 122, 192
Township health centers, 126
Trade balance, 51
Trade balance, 59
Transition economies 25, 84, 85, 86, 222, 232
Trickle-down effect, 17
Two-tiered exchange rate system, 93

U

Under-five mortality rate 62, 124
Unemployment Insurance, 91
Union of Soviet Socialist Republics, 41
United Nations, 92, 224
United States, 92
Unlimited Supplies of Labour, 17
Urban areas, 16
Urban biased policies, 16, 22

W

Waterways, 30, 34, 43, 51, 54, 62, 68
Welfare state, 13, 136
Western Europe, 44
William Arthur Lewis, 17
Workforce, 129, 192, 230
World Bank, 14, 19, 22, 23, 26, 92
World Development Report 2008, 15, 86
World Trade Organisation (WTO), 14, 92
World War Second, 11, 13, 217
Wuhan complex, 36

Y

Yongjia County, 137

Z

Zhang Chunqiao, 63
Zhou Enlai, 63
Zhu De, 63
Zhu Rongji, 90